BEHOLD THE KINGDOM

By: Curry R. Blake

General Overseer of

John G. Lake Ministries

and

Dominion Life

International Apostolic Church

Copyright 2013 by Curry R. Blake
All Rights Reserved

Published by
CHRISTIAN REALITY BOOKS
P.O. Box 742947
Dallas TX 75374
1-888-293-6591

Cover Design by John E. Blake.

Unless otherwise noted, all Scripture quotations are taken from the King James Bible.

This book or parts thereof may not be reproduced in any form without written permission of the publisher.

Printed in the United States of America.

This document was taken from Sunday Sermons, 2-03-2013 through 3-10-2013, presented by Curry R. Blake.

TABLE OF CONTENTS

Kingdom Agenda	1
Understanding the Kingdoms	57
Keys of the Kingdom	113
The Government of God	177
Kingdom Administrators – Part 1	227
Kingdom Administrators – Part 2	285
All That Jesus Began Both To Do And Teach	343

© 2013 Curry R. Blake – John G. Lake Ministries

© 2013 Curry R. Blake – John G. Lake Ministries

KINGDOM AGENDA

Sermon given by Curry R. Blake

God's highest priority is to restore the kingdom of heaven, establishing His Kingdom on this earth.

We are going to start in Matthew, chapter 6. Before we go there, I want to bring up a few things, and then we will get right into Matthew chapter 6. I want you to think in line with these things.

The greatest tragedy in life is not death—it's a life without purpose. If you have life without purpose, you're dead before you ever die. You just walk around dead. You need a life with purpose. Jesus came to give us a purpose. He came to give us life, but He came to give us a life with purpose.

The name of the ministry has been John G. Lake Ministries, and we've shortened that to JGLM. I'm ex-military so everything is in acronyms. Everything goes down to initials which makes it easier. We have so many initials you wouldn't believe it. We have the DHT, we have SWAT, we have IAC, and we have DLIAC, which is the church. We've got all of these initials for everything, and you really need a program to keep up with them.

Years ago, when I looked at the letters "JGLM" I saw just the letters, and it was like I didn't see "John G. Lake Ministries." I saw "JGLM," but what I saw afterward was JGLM: "Jesus Gives Life Meaning." I've used that a lot of times, and that is the way I think of JGLM.

JGLM is just the vehicle. It is not important in and of itself; it's just the vehicle. What is important is that "Jesus Gives Life Meaning." It is important that He gives life a mission, and if you ever get a grasp of His mission, you'll get a mission. As I said, "The greatest tragedy in life is not death; it is a life without purpose."

The greatest challenge in life is to know what to do. What shall I do? What do I devote my life to? Many people just devote their lives to themselves, and then, at the end of their lives, they find out that they've wasted their lives.

The greatest mistake in life is being busy but not effective. Many times you can tell if a person doesn't have peace. They'll try to keep their mind busy so that they don't think about the peace that they wish they had.

The greatest failure in life is to be extremely successful in the wrong thing. Think about that. You can be extremely successful in the wrong assignment for your life, and you can devote yourself to something that is wrong. However, you will be so good at it that you excel. When you excel, it is very hard to back out of it.

To align yourself with Gods purposes, you must first die to self.

The single greatest success in life comes from the correct use of time. Time is the most valuable thing we have; it is not unending. The correct use of time comes from correct priorities, so if you are going to use time correctly, you have to have the right priorities. Otherwise, you will waste time. Correct priorities always come from aligning yourself with Gods purposes.

I am big on reverse engineering. It's like I see the overall picture first, and then I see how to get there, step by step. I'm just taking you there step by step.

What we do at JGLM is try to help people in their own individual lives, but at the same time, we try to help them by getting them in line with God's purpose. Once you find God's purpose, everything starts to come into alignment.

Jesus said in the original Greek, "If you will lay down your lower life with its goals, ambitions, and objectives, then I will give you My higher life with its goals, objectives and ambitions." This is found in Matthew 10:39 of the Amplified Bible. It is quite different from the way it says it in the King James.

That's one thing I mention when I talk with people, especially unsaved people, people who aren't walking with God. It's amazing how they think, because when you start talking about walking with God, they automatically think of rules. They think, "Well, if I do that I'll have to stop doing this," or "I'll have to stop doing that." They think, "They are just rules: 'don't do this' and 'don't do that.'"

I try to tell them, "If you really love God, and if you really get hold of His heart, you don't think about dos and don'ts; you just love." You just love people, and you love God; you love people because you love God. If you don't love God, it's hard to love people. If you love God, it gets easier to love people.

Now, one of the keys to loving people is to be dead; die to self. If you don't die to self, people are always going to hurt you. People are always going to offend you, or they're always going to do something, but once you make that commitment and say, "I'm dead; it's no longer I that live but Christ who lives in me," people really don't bother you anymore.

Dead men never get bothered by people. You can walk up to a casket at a funeral, look in there and say, "Well, you're just as ugly now as you ever were," and that dead person isn't going to say a word to you. You're not going to offend them; they're not going to get mad; you can't hurt them. It's good to live dead. I think a lot of people just never get there.

Christianity has basically come to a point now where it's all about band-aids and fixing people. They say, "Make me a better person." Jesus didn't come to make you a better person. He came so that you could die, and you could have His life.

If you look at how He did things and how He talked to people sometimes, He wasn't all about just being polite and politically correct. It's not polite to call a person a dog, and that is what He did at one point. He called the Pharisees, the religious leaders, vipers. That wouldn't go over very well if you tried it. Try that at your next ministerial alliance meeting in your city, and see how it goes. You won't get invited to another one.

God is trying to establish His Kingdom in the hearts of mankind.

We have to get our priorities right. God's purposes are clear. God's whole focus is establishing His Kingdom on this earth, making it on earth as it is in heaven. That's what He's really pushing for, and He is trying to get every person into His Kingdom, which means that they live by Kingdom principles, and they start living out these principles. If people would do that, it would be so amazing what would be taken care of and how things would happen.

The key that we're talking about is that He is trying to establish His Kingdom first in the hearts of mankind. Once He gets the Kingdom in their hearts, it will play out in the rest of their lives. If it doesn't play out in the rest of their lives, it's not in their hearts yet.

The earth should look like heaven.

Matthew 6:9-10,

> 9 After this manner therefore pray ye: Our Father which art in heaven, Hallowed be thy name.
>
> 10 Thy kingdom come. Thy will be done in earth, as *it is* in heaven.

If you want to know what God's will is, there it is. It is plain and simple. Whatever you see on earth that doesn't look like it would in heaven is supposed to be fixed until it looks like heaven. Isn't that simple?

Theologians have complicated the things of God to where people don't even know if they are walking in God's will. People say, "Are you in God's will?" "Well, I think so; I'd like to think so."

I remember the first time I ever met Dr. Sumrall. He was over 70 at that time, and he said, "I've walked with God for 56 years, and I've never been out of the will of God." I was shocked; I'd never heard anybody say something like that. Almost everything I'd heard was that people are mostly out of the will of God, and every now and then their life crosses the will of God and something good happens. Then they're right back out of the will of God again. That's the way most people act; it's the way they think about it.

He said, "All these years I've never been out of the will of God." Everybody asked him, "How can you say that," and he said, "Simple. I saw what He said to do, and I aimed my life in that direction. I've never looked back." He went around the world multiple times, saw all kinds of things, and always kept his life in the will of God, because he was always loving God and loving people. If you have ever listened to him, you might not be so sure that he was loving people. I don't know if you've heard much about him or not.

One time they were in a revival meeting in a school house, and one little girl was sitting there. All of her friends were getting saved, and they asked, "Would you talk to our friend here?" He walked back to her. He was about 18 or 19 years old at that time, and he said, "Don't you want to go to heaven?" She said, "Not really." He said, "Well, then. Go to hell." She passed out. Boom! She fell over. That is not something you usually hear from a preacher.

When she came to, she got saved. They asked, "Well, what happened? Why did you pass out?" "I have never had a preacher tell me to go to hell before." He said, "Well, there are only two places; heaven or hell. You didn't want to go to heaven. Guess what? You're going to hell." "Yeah, but I never thought of it like that." He said, "Well I'm not responsible for that." He said, "All I am responsible for is telling you the truth." Now, that's not what we think of as a loving person, but sometimes you have to love people enough to shoot straight with them. You have to tell them what they don't want to hear, because they need to hear it.

He said in verse 10,

> 10 Thy kingdom come. Thy will be done in earth, as *it is* in heaven.

God's highest priority is to restore the kingdom of heaven, establishing His Kingdom on this earth. Then it will be "on earth as it is in heaven." He really wants earth to be the Garden of Eden, again. We know that, because that's what He set up, and when He set it all up, He said, "It is good." Then He told man to keep it, take care of it, reestablish it, make sure it was taken care of, and to subdue it.

We have this idea that what's going on out there is somehow all messed up according to His will, even though His whole effort has been to get things back to the Garden of Eden. Even Jesus is called the last Adam. Why? He is called that, because He came to restore the Kingdom.

In the Garden there was no altar, there was no temple, there was no church service; there wasn't any of that. It was just man walking with God. We've muddied the waters a lot of the time. I say "we," and I'm talking about "we," as preachers. We have made it so hard to know if we are walking with God. It's not that hard, really, when you get down to it, and look at it.

"Seek ye first the Kingdom of God and His righteousness."

Look at Matthew 6:33. Everybody knows the Scripture. Again, this was Jesus speaking and He said,

> 33 But seek ye first the kingdom of God, and his righteousness; and all these things shall be added unto you.

Seek ye first the Kingdom. You're going to see that everything Jesus ever taught was the Kingdom; that's all He taught over and over again: Kingdom, Kingdom, Kingdom. He said, "Seek ye first the Kingdom…," not last, not when you get time, but first. "Seek ye first the Kingdom of God and His righteousness, and all these things shall be added unto you." What things? To know that, you have to go back and read verse 24. Jesus said,

> 24 No man can serve two masters: for either he will hate the one, and love the other; or else he will hold to the one, and despise the other. Ye cannot serve God and mammon.

No man can serve two masters.

Now think about that—no man can serve two masters. Do you realize that's where most of our problems come from? Most of our problems come from us trying to hold God's hand with one hand and the world with the other. That's where your struggle is, because when heaven and earth collide, there is always going to be a battle.

When you try to straddle the fence, when you try to hold heaven with one hand and the earth with the other, you become the battleground where those two Kingdoms hit. You will serve one or the other. When those hit, there will be a struggle going on, there will be turmoil, there will be turbulence, and all of these things will go on inside of you.

Almost all of the struggles that people go through are because they're standing in the middle between the world and heaven.

That's what the Prophet Elijah said. "Choose; make a choice." Even Joshua said, "Choose you this day whom you will serve. As for me and my house, we will serve the Lord." Make a choice.

One of the worst things I see, more than anything else in the world today, is that people can't make choices. "Should we do it this way?" "Well, I'm not sure." "Well, let's do it that way." "What about this?" "I don't know, because we do this, and we do that."

I'm definitely not going to get political on this aspect, but honestly, the Bible says to pray for our leaders, whether you agree with them or not, or whether you voted for them or not. You pray for them, regardless. They are in a position of power and the Bible is clear that when the righteous are in power, when they rule, then the people are in peace, but whenever the wicked rule, then the people moan, and they groan because of their burdens.

We should be praying that our leaders have godly influence, that they hear the voice of God, and that they have an encounter with God so that they can actually know what God wants and will follow that path.

It's really easy to second guess and say, "Well, you just make this deal and you do that," but when you're there, you find out, "If we do this, this will happen, so we'd better not do that. If we don't do that, then this will happen." It is not always as clear cut as just making that choice. Now, it is always clear cut to make a righteous decision.

Let's read Matthew 6:24 again:

> 24 No man can serve two masters: for either he will hate the one, and love the other; or else he will hold to the one, and despise the other. Ye cannot serve God and mammon.

"*Mammon*" usually refers to *currency*, not just money, but *any currency that has anything to do with this world's system*. It's saying, "You can't love both. You're either going to love God or you're going to love the world." The Apostle John told us, "If you love the world, the love of the Father is not in you." You can't love two masters.

> 25 Therefore I say unto you, Take no thought for your life, what ye shall eat, or what ye shall drink; nor yet for your body, what ye shall put on. Is not the life more than meat, and the body than raiment?

"Therefore I say unto you, Take no thought for your life." What does that mean? You have to die. It's really simple. That's the only way you won't take thought for your life.

> 26 Behold the fowls of the air: for they sow not, neither do they reap, nor gather into barns; yet your heavenly Father feedeth them. Are ye not much better than they?

We talked about this during the DHT, about sowing and reaping. They don't store up, they don't prepare, and yet your Heavenly Father takes care of them. He feeds them.

Man was the crowning glory of God.

Man was the crowning glory of God, so of course, if He takes care of the birds, He's going to take care of us. You can only have one provider, and if you're going to be that provider, guess what? You're going to have a rough life. That's just the way it is. However, if you take God as your provider, and you trust Him as your Heavenly Father, He will take care of you, and your life will get simpler and easier.

27 Which of you by taking thought can add one cubit unto his stature?

28 And why take ye thought for raiment? Consider the lilies of the field, how they grow; they toil not, neither do they spin:

29 And yet I say unto you, That even Solomon in all his glory was not arrayed like one of these.

30 Wherefore, if God so clothe the grass of the field, which to day is, and to morrow is cast into the oven, *shall he* not much more *clothe* you, O ye of little faith?

Jesus was saying that if all you think about is taking care of your needs, then you are going to be a person of little faith. Why? That's because the affairs of this world are going to come in, they are going to entangle you, and they are going to choke out the Word that's in you.

> 31 Therefore take no thought, saying, What shall we eat? or, What shall we drink? or, Wherewithal shall we be clothed?

"Therefore take no thought." This was the second time He said this.

> 32 (For after all these things do the Gentiles seek:) for your heavenly Father knoweth that ye have need of all these things.
>
> 33 But seek first the kingdom of God and his righteousness, and all these things will be added to you.

"For after all these things do the Gentiles seek…" These are the things that people who don't have a God go after. Why? They don't have a God; they have to take care of themselves.

He said, "For your heavenly Father knows that you have need of all these things." Then He said, "If you seek first His Kingdom and His righteousness, all these things will be added to you." The "things" He was talking about were clothing and food. He was talking about you being taken care of as a good father takes care of his child.

Over and over again, I keep trying to bring this across to people: you can trust God; He's trustworthy. Many times we just don't want to take that chance, and we try to do it ourselves, but you can't serve two masters. You're either going to have to serve God or yourself. One of you is going to be the master of your life, and you have to decide who it is going to be. You can't serve both.

You can't serve your own end and serve God's end. There has to be a point where you say, "You are my Lord. I will serve You; I will put Your priorities first." Then you think, "Well, I don't know how I could do that." Believe me, He'll show you. The things that seemed important in your eyes will start falling way.

All of a sudden, you'll start seeing that what counts is literally spending time with God, loving people, taking care of people, and helping people who can't help themselves.

John the Baptist preached: "The kingdom of heaven is at hand."

Go to Matthew chapter 3. We're going to back to when John the Baptist preached.

> 1 In those days came John the Baptist, preaching in the wilderness of Judaea,
>
> 2 And saying, Repent ye: for the kingdom of heaven is at hand.

"Repent ye," turn around or change your mind, "for the kingdom of heaven is at hand."

> 3 For this is he that was spoken of by the prophet Esaias saying, The voice of one crying in the wilderness, Prepare ye the way of the Lord, make his paths straight.

> 4 And the same John had his raiment of camel's hair, and a leathern girdle about his loins; and his meat was locusts and wild honey.

"And the same John had his raiment of camel's hair." Apparently he wasn't thinking about his raiment.

I've heard different stories on this, but actually what they called locusts here was actually a type of plant; it wasn't a cricket or a grasshopper. Everybody always pictures him with crazy hair, camel's hair clothing, and a grasshopper leg sticking out of his mouth. That wasn't necessarily the case. Even if it had been, it wouldn't have mattered, because a locust (the insect), is actually very healthy and has a lot of protein. You can actually survive off of it, not that you would want to, but you could.

> 5 Then went out to him Jerusalem, and all Judaea, and all the region round about Jordan,

"Then went out to him Jerusalem…" Do you hear that? Jerusalem went out to Him, so He had a crowd out in the wilderness. When you get a message from God, you can hide anywhere you want, and people will find you. You don't have to do big advertising campaigns and get a Fifth Avenue or Madison Avenue marketing firm to come in and tell you how to advertise and how to position yourself. You don't have to do that.

People ask me all the time: "How do I get started in the ministry?" I don't know. If you're talking about all that JGLM does, I don't know, because I didn't do this. I just got hold of a message that I was looking for when I needed it; that was when my first daughter died. I just kept searching until I got it, and when I found it, I knew I couldn't keep it to myself.

I had to share it, and I had to start using it to pray for people. I had to minister to people and get them some help. From there it just grew. I've never asked for a place to preach. I've never done any of that, and it just keeps growing.

You can hide, but if you get a message from God, God will make your light shine. He will cause your light to shine, so don't concern yourself with trying to position yourself so you can get into ministry. Just love God and love people, and when you love enough people around you, you'll start loving people farther away. Soon you will be on a mission field somewhere, because you will go, you will help, and you will pray. Just start loving people. That's the best way to work it.

Confessing sins and being baptized was the beginning of the Gospel.

6 And were baptized of him in Jordan, confessing their sins.

Notice, they were "confessing their sins." That's plural. They were talking about what they had done wrong. There is always a lot of controversy over whether we should confess our sins. All of this was the beginning of the Gospel.

7 But when he saw many of the Pharisees and Sadducees come to his baptism, he said unto them, O generation of vipers, who hath warned you to flee from the wrath to come?

John told them,

8 Bring forth therefore fruits meet for repentance:

Your fruit should show that you have repented, not just continue living and say, "Well, God's grace is amazing."

9 And think not to say within yourselves, We have Abraham to *our* father: for I say unto you, that God is able of these stones to raise up children unto Abraham.

10 And now also the axe is laid unto the root of the trees: therefore every tree which bringeth not forth good fruit is hewn down, and cast into the fire.

**John was speaking of Jesus when he said,
"He will baptize you with the Holy Ghost and with fire."**

11 I indeed baptize you with water unto repentance: but he that cometh after me is mightier than I, whose shoes I am not worthy to bear: he shall baptize you with the Holy Ghost, and *with* fire:

12 Whose fan *is* in his hand, and he will throughly purge his floor, and gather his wheat into the garner; but he will burn up the chaff with unquenchable fire.

John said, "He will baptize you with the Holy Ghost and with fire," and "He will burn up the chaff with unquenchable fire."

We take that fire as zeal, and there is a zeal that comes with the Holy Ghost, there's no doubt about it, but part of that fire we call "the baptism by fire." A baptism by fire is not always a good thing. That means you're in the heat of the battle, right then.

Later on, in 1 Corinthians 3:13-15, Paul even talks about that, and he says that you will pass through the fire, and whatever makes it through the fire is what you actually get credit for.

John said of Jesus that He was going to gather the wheat, but all of the straw and chaff were all going to be burned up. We need to realize that although part of the Baptism in the Holy Ghost is purity, there is also fire, which is not always pleasant. There is an aspect of the fire that is zeal, but there is also an aspect of the fire that is purging. Get all the dross, as they would say, all of the chaff in your life burned out so that you can run faster.

So many times, even Paul himself said, "Let us lay aside the sin and the weight." That weight is straw, and it needs to get burned up by the Holy Ghost. It needs to get burned out of your life so that you can run without these bales of hay on your back. You need to get these things out of the way so you can run the race.

Have you ever watched runners? They strip down to the bare minimum; they don't want any extra weight. The bicyclists wear this clothing that is aerodynamic, and it's meant to have this effect where there is no wind resistance on them.

We need to think the same way about our race and get rid of everything we don't need. Everything that doesn't help us win is a hindrance. We're not here to gather. We're not here to store up. We're here to run a race. We're here to advance the Gospel of the Kingdom of God. It is not just my own purpose in life, but it is every Christian's purpose in life to advance the Kingdom; that's the whole point.

Jesus preached the same message that John the Baptist preached.

13 Then cometh Jesus from Galilee to Jordan unto John, to be baptized of him.

14 But John forbad him, saying, I have need to be baptized of thee, and comest thou to me?

15 And Jesus answering said unto him, Suffer *it to be so* now: for thus it becometh us to fulfil all righteousness. Then he suffered him.

16 And Jesus, when he was baptized, went up straightway out of the water: and, lo, the heavens were opened unto him, and he saw the Spirit of God descending like a dove, and lighting upon him:

One of the main points I wanted to hit on was what John said in verse 2, saying, "Repent ye, for the kingdom of heaven is at hand." John preached the kingdom.

I know we are working backward, but look at Matthew 4:17.

> 17 From that time Jesus began to preach, and to say, Repent: for the kingdom of heaven is at hand.

Jesus was saying the same thing that John said. He was preaching the kingdom of heaven.

Jesus said to His disciples, "Follow Me."

> 18 And Jesus, walking by the sea of Galilee, saw two brethren, Simon called Peter, and Andrew his brother, casting a net into the sea: for they were fishers.
>
> 19 And he saith unto them, Follow me, and I will make you fishers of men.
>
> 20 And they straightway left *their* nets, and followed him.

That's amazing in itself. These were businessmen. It said at one point, that they actually had partners in other boats, so they had a fishing company. It wasn't just the disciples out there in a boat. They had a company of other partners, who were also fishing.

Jesus said, "Drop your nets on the other side of the boat," and they said, "We've done this the whole time, and we've got nothing." However, since it was Jesus who said, "Drop it on the other side," Peter said, "Okay, it's Your word; we'll do it." I can imagine Peter saying, "You're a preacher, and I'm a fisherman. I know the fish aren't biting. Being a preacher, you don't know anything about fishing, but we'll do it."

The Scripture said that when they dumped the fish, there were so many that the fish were causing the boats, plural, to sink. Why? Jesus sought first the Kingdom and His righteousness, and all these things were added. Well, fish were currency. If you got enough fish, you had whatever else you needed. Why? That's because you could sell it.

It says that He called them and said, "I will make you fishers of men." They left their nets and followed Him,

21 And going on from thence, he saw other two brethren, James *the son* of Zebedee, and John his brother, in a ship with Zebedee their father, mending their nets; and he called them.

22 And they immediately left the ship and their father, and followed him.

It doesn't give you a lot of details, but you've got to notice this: Jesus called, and they left everything. That was a drastic move. In many ways, for a fisherman to quit fishing is dying. Death would be preferable to some fishermen, but here it was a clean break. Even Matthew the tax collector closed down his shop when Jesus said, "Follow Me."

Now, in verse 22,

> 22 And they immediately left the ship and their father, and followed him.

Jesus preached the Gospel of the Kingdom, and the Good News of God's reign and supremacy over everything.

> 23 And Jesus went about all Galilee, teaching in their synagogues, and preaching the gospel of the kingdom, and healing all manner of sickness and all manner of disease among the people.

What was Jesus preaching? He was preaching the Gospel of the Kingdom. What is the Gospel of the Kingdom? The *"Gospel"* means *Good News*; it means *it is the good news of God's reign and supremacy.*

The Greek word there for *"kingdom"* is *basileia* and it just means *a place where a king has dominion.* That's why it is called, *"king-dom;"* it is the king's dominion.

Jesus was preaching the good news that God has dominion and that God is stronger than anything you'll face, including whatever has you in bondage. God is strong enough to set you free. There is nothing that can have you in so much bondage that God cannot set you free.

There is nothing that has stronger power than God Himself.

The church has to learn that there is nothing that has stronger power than God Himself. We have to be able to display that to the world, because for the most part, people think of the church as a crutch for weak people who need to believe in a "higher power." In one aspect that is exactly true—we have to find that we do need God. You cannot live on your own; you cannot do your own thing.

Jesus demonstrated the Kingdom by healing and setting the captives free.

> 23 And Jesus went about all Galilee, teaching in their synagogues, and preaching the gospel of the kingdom, and healing all manner of sickness and all manner of disease among the people.

Notice: Jesus preached the Gospel of the Kingdom, and then He said, "Now, let me demonstrate it to you. Let me show you what I am talking about." Why? That's because in the Kingdom, there is no sickness, no disease, no pain, and no tears. If there are tears, they're tears of joy and not tears of pain. That's what the kingdom of heaven should be like.

> 24 And his fame went throughout all Syria: and they brought unto him all sick people that were taken with divers diseases and torments, and those which were possessed with devils, and those which were lunatic, and those that had the palsy; and he healed them.

Notice: those that were lunatic and those that were possessed with devils are listed under two different categories there, so there can be mental issues that are not necessarily a devil.

"And they brought unto Him…those that had the palsy; and He healed them." Why? He was demonstrating the Kingdom. He said, "I am the King of this Kingdom, and I'll show you what it is like to live under My rule. If you live under My rule, you'll have peace. If you live under My rule, you'll have health."

If we really lived under Kingdom principles, we wouldn't need any other health care system. There would only be "Kingdom-care," and it would be better, because it would be instant.

However, there is an aspect to this that we need to realize, because where we are, it's always hard. You don't need to bail water out of a sinking ship until you plug the hole. If you just keep bailing water, and the water keeps pouring back in, you're really not doing anything. Now, you may be able to keep it afloat, but you're still taking on water.

That's the way it is in the world, even right now. There is an aspect of the Kingdom that we can demonstrate to the people by getting them healed.

While we do that, it has to literally be a two pronged effort. We cannot just say, "When you get sick, come and get healed." Even that is advancement for a lot of people, even in the church. If they get sick they can actually come and get healed.

We are ambassadors of the Kingdom; we operate under Kingdom authority.

I don't even say, "Come and get prayed for," because we don't pray for you. We actually command the thing to leave you. Why? A kingdom has authority or it's not a kingdom. What we operate in is under Kingdom authority, so we command. We don't beg, and we don't ask; we don't even talk to God about it. We're His representatives; we are already under Kingdom authority.

Ambassadors know the policies of the nation or the kingdom they represent. That's part of their training; they have to know. When they go in to meet with somebody, they have to know the parameters. In other words, they can't ask, "How much can we negotiate, what can we give up, what can we not give up, what are the limits?"

They have to know the limits before they get there. Otherwise, it does no good for them to go, because every time somebody says to them, "Well, we'll give you this for that," they say, "Well, hang on. Let me check with Washington." That doesn't do any good. They have to be able to make the decision, and say, "Yes, we can do that." Why? That's because it is within their parameters and within the realm of their authority to agree to that.

You have to realize that it is within the realm of your authority, as a Kingdom representative, to declare the enemy to leave, to set people free, and to heal their bodies. That is within your realm of authority, not just in my realm of authority. That's you, as a believer. You are the soldier with the boots on the ground. You're the one that gets to knock on the door and say, "Excuse me, are you being held hostage? Are you being held as a prisoner of war? If that's true, I can set you free, right now. I'm here to help." That is your Kingdom authority.

However, it is not enough. Yes, we can do this for the rest of our lives. We can minister healing and have people come in and get healed, and they go out and get sick again and come back in at a later time. You could do that for the rest of your life. The bad part is that it is where a lot of people want to be.

A lot of ministers want it to be that way, because it ensures they will always have a job. Job security is making sure that people are dependent on one person. It really just shows selfishness, because someday, they're not going to be there. That doesn't matter, because they're trying to make sure that they're valuable and not expendable.

Live under the Kingdom principle of living in divine health; live free of sickness and disease.

The idea is that we cannot just get people healed, but we have to actually plug the hole. We have to start teaching the Kingdom principle of living in divine health and living free of sickness or disease.

If you're going to lay hands on the sick, you've got to believe that you can be protected from sickness or disease, because otherwise, you're going to be a little hesitant to lay hands on people. You have to know that you have the right to do this thing.

We have to start teaching it in our Sunday school for the kids and in our children's ministry. We've got to start teaching them that they can live free of sickness and disease and that they can walk strong and healthy all the days of their lives. Why? They need to know that God walks with them.

That's what I mean by plugging the hole. If we start teaching them now, and they start getting hold of this, then as they grow up and start coming into this meeting, they will be prepared. When you are sitting there saying, "I need to go down to the front and get prayed for because I've got this problem going on, and I need to get healed," they'll look at you and say, "Why are you sick? Here, let me lay hands on you."

I remember being in a meeting one time. I had been training the people. After we finished the training, we were holding our healing service at the end. All of these people were coming up, and this little girl came to me and she was standing there, literally crying. I called her over, and I said, "What's the matter?" She said, "Well, nobody wants me to pray for them." This little girl was 10 or 12, very young. Now, for me personally, I would have preferred to have her pray for me.

I told everybody, "Alright, who still needs prayer? If you need prayer, come and line up." They all lined up, because they thought, "Oh, we're going to get Curry Blake to pray for us." They all lined up, and as soon as they all lined up, I said to the young girl, "Come here. Pray." I just stepped back. I just stood there and watched, and they were looking like, "Really? Her?"

When the people came up there, this little girl was standing there, and she asked, "What do you need?" It was like they wanted to say, "I don't want to have to tell you." You could see it on their faces like, "I am an adult." It was awesome to watch, because she said, "Okay, I'll pray for you." (At that time I was still laying hands on the person's head. I had not yet learned to take them by the hands. Everyone else I had taught did, also). This little girl would reach up to put her hands on their heads, and the people standing there had to bend down to let her.

This little girl started laying hands on people, and she came alive. She said, "Be healed in Jesus' name! You're free in Jesus' name!" Somebody said, "Well, the pain is still there." She said, "Jesus isn't a liar! You're healed!" I was like, "Whoa! Yeah!" Then she had them move around a bit, and she said, "Now, do what you couldn't do!" She said, "Isn't that right, Brother Curry?" I said, "That's right, that's right." It was amazing! People were getting healed right and left. It was awesome!

The Beatitudes are the attitudes that you need to embrace to live in the Kingdom of God.

Matthew chapter 5, starting with verse 1,

> 1 And seeing the multitudes, he went up into a mountain: and when he was set, his disciples came unto him:
>
> 2 And he opened his mouth, and taught them, saying,
>
> 3 Blessed *are* the poor in spirit: for theirs is the kingdom of heaven.

Notice the first thing Jesus said, "Blessed *are* the poor in spirit: for theirs is the kingdom of heaven." "*Blessed*," means *spiritually prosperous*. The kingdom of heaven was the first thing He started preaching.

> 4 Blessed *are* they that mourn: for they shall be comforted.
>
> 5 Blessed *are* the meek: for they shall inherit the earth.
>
> 6 Blessed *are* they which do hunger and thirst after righteousness: for they shall be filled.
>
> 7 Blessed *are* the merciful: for they shall obtain mercy.
>
> 8 Blessed *are* the pure in heart: for they shall see God.
>
> 9 Blessed *are* the peacemakers: for they shall be called the children of God.

"Blessed are the peacemakers." Notice here it says peacemakers, not peacekeepers. It doesn't say blessed are the peacekeepers. Let me just say it this way: Ronald Reagan was a peacemaker; Bill Clinton was a peacekeeper. Now, I'm not talking about parties; I'm talking about personality. Ronald Regan said, "We're building this defense so that you don't mess with us. We have peace through superior firepower." You want to make it to where people do not want to take the chance to attack you. Now, that's from a natural viewpoint. He also said, "Trust, but verify."

Now, when you talk about these things, you automatically say, "Oh, he's getting into politics." Well, yes, we're talking Kingdom; that's politics. We're talking the Kingdom of God. There are politics that go along with the Kingdom of God. I'm not talking about parties and that kind of thing. Your view of the world dictates your politics. Your view of the Kingdom dictates your earthly politics. We cannot stand by and watch people die. It is a responsibility; we are our brother's keeper.

Someone gave a movie to me a while back, and it is called, "Beyond the Gates." I don't know if you've heard of it or not, but it is a Christian movie, basically. It is about the Rwanda genocide in 1994 and how these UN peacekeepers stood by and watched while people were murdered. That is the role of a peacekeeper. They had guns, and they had ways to help the people. They had areas that they could have taken those people to, but they didn't do it, because that was beyond what they were sent to do.

That's what the church has done. "Well, we're just spiritual. People who are hungry, we'll bless, but beyond that, it becomes more physical." You can, however, also get to where you're socially minded, to the point where you just feed them and don't get people saved. You just clothe them and don't heal their bodies. You can get that socially minded.

God will take care of your. He will make sure your bellies are full. He will make sure you've got clothes to wear. That's part of the Kingdom of God, but it is also because we seek first His Kingdom, His rule, His supremacy, and His righteousness.

We can't just sit around and be spiritually minded people, only thinking on spiritual things. We can't do that. We've got to touch every aspect. The natural mind, the carnal man, doesn't get it spiritually, so to reach him, you've got to reach him the first time physically. You've got to fill his belly. You've got to put clothes on his back. You've got to show him, "You are valuable to God; you are valuable to me, because you are valuable to God." You've got to show them their worth. They are worth Jesus, because God sent Jesus to die for them.

Whatever you pay for something, that's what that thing is worth. Now other people may look at it and say, "That is not worth that," but whatever you pay for it, that's what it's worth. God paid Jesus for every person on this earth. Every person on this earth is valuable to God.

When you look at these people, you can't just say, "Well, I am thankful that God takes care of me and I'm not like that." That's not what God thinks when He looks at them. Again, we don't want this to be just physical and about food and clothing either, but that's a big part.

Man is made up of three parts—spirit, soul and body. There are the down and outers, and then there are the up and outers. There are people behind fences and brick home walls who are every bit as down and out spiritually as somebody that lives on the street. We have to be able to touch their lives, spirit, soul and body.

When a person lives under those down and out conditions for a long time, even if it's physical, then in their soul they start to think less of themselves. We've got to get to the place where we lift them.

That's what I loved about T. L. Osborne, and I still love about the way he ministers. He always said, "God lifts people; He loves people."

Dr. Sumrall used to say, "The devil always tries to make man lose his dignity, but God always brings man's dignity back." I started thinking about that and looking at these things.

> 9 Blessed *are* the peacemakers: for they shall be called the children of God.
>
> 10 Blessed *are* they which are persecuted for righteousness' sake: for theirs is the kingdom of heaven.

> 11 Blessed are ye, when *men* shall revile you, and persecute *you,* and shall say all manner of evil against you falsely, for my sake.
>
> 12 Rejoice, and be exceeding glad: for great *is* your reward in heaven: for so persecuted they the prophets which were before you.

We know these verses as the Beatitudes. What that means is that these are the attitudes that we need to have. The Beatitudes are the attitudes that you need to embrace. This is what it is like to live in the Kingdom of God, which is what Jesus preached.

Luke 4:16 was talking about Jesus.

> 16 And he came to Nazareth, where he had been brought up: and, as his custom was, he went into the synagogue on the sabbath day, and stood up for to read.
>
> 17 And there was delivered unto him the book of the prophet Esaias. And when he had opened the book, he found the place where it was written,

Then He started to preach, and He said,

> 18 The Spirit of the Lord *is* upon me, because he hath anointed me to preach the gospel to the poor; he hath sent me to heal the brokenhearted, to preach deliverance to the captives, and recovering of sight to the blind, to set at liberty them that are bruised,

19 To preach the acceptable year of the Lord.

The Spirit of the Lord is upon me, because He hath anointed me to: (a) preach the Gospel to the poor; (b) heal the brokenhearted, (c) preach (proclaim) deliverance to the captives, (d) recover sight to the blind, (e) set at liberty them that are bruised, and (f) preach the acceptable year of the Lord.

The reason I brought up the political parties earlier was to say that political parties have what they call platforms. That platform is basically their basis, or the reason for being, or as we would say, "It's their agenda." It is what they are shooting for, and it's what they stand for. It encapsulates how they think and what they are working toward.

What I just read to you is what Jesus said was His agenda; this was His platform. He was saying, "I am here to proclaim the kingdom, and the reason I am here is because God has anointed me to do these things. This is what I am here to do," and He gave a list.

This agenda is the agenda of the Kingdom of God, because Jesus' will was the Father's will. Jesus was the one who taught His disciples to pray this way, "Thy Kingdom come, thy will be done on earth as it is in heaven."

This agenda is also the agenda of any church that is in God's program, meaning in line with God's program. If you are going to be in line with God's will, and if you are going to be in line with His plan, then this platform here, this agenda, is going to be your agenda. That's why He said, "You cannot be my disciple except you lay your life down and you take up My cross."

It would be great to come in here and say, "It's all wonderful, it's all good. God has the ultimate social welfare program. Here's your program. Just take it and run." There is some truth to that—that God does help and that He is interested in every aspect of your life—but Jesus had some requirements. He wasn't trying to make it hard just to make it difficult. He had some requirements, because He said, "This is the way you do it."

I could ask, "Who in here wants to take part in the Olympics? Who wants to run the 880 in the Olympics?" Someone might say, "What have I got to do?" "Oh, just sign up." "Okay, well what kind of training program?" "Oh, don't worry about a training program, just show up and run on the day of the Olympics."

How many of you know that if I could get you into the Olympics, you could maybe show up and run. How many of you know that you aren't going to win? Winning requires training. People say, "What! I've got to train? You killjoy! That just isn't fair. I shouldn't have to train."

"Strait *is* the gate, and narrow *is* the way, which leadeth unto life, and few there be that find it."

Often you hear, "Oh, it's all done. Don't worry about sin; it's been taken care of. It's all good." They don't tell you the things that Jesus, Himself, the King over this Kingdom, said in Matthew 7:21,

> 21 Not every one that saith unto me, Lord, Lord, shall enter into the kingdom of heaven; but he that doeth the will of my Father which is in heaven.

He said that not everyone was going to make it.

Luke 13:24 says,

> 24 Strive to enter in at the strait gate: for many, I say unto you, will seek to enter in, and shall not be able.

Matthew 7:13-14 says,

> 13 Enter ye in at the strait gate: for wide *is* the gate, and broad *is* the way, that leadeth to destruction, and many there be which go in thereat:
>
> 14 Because strait *is* the gate, and narrow *is* the way, which leadeth unto life, and few there be that find it.

Jesus said, "Many seek to find the way in but few find it, because the way in is narrow, but the way that leads to destruction is broad." The path that leads to destruction is out there, where people are living and doing anything they want, but the way to life is narrow.

It's not that God said, "Okay, I'm going to make it narrow, because I only want a few." He said, "Look, this is how to live; if you live outside of that, you die." It wasn't that He was trying to make it hard.

It's just that there is a difference between life and death. All God did was tell us the truth about what it takes to live.

It wasn't that He set the parameters and said, "Do it this way," or "Oh, no, you're one speck over, so there you go; you're gone." It wasn't that He was trying to do that. He said, "The wages of sin is death," so don't sin; stay out of sin. Why? That's because it will kill you. He wasn't trying to say, "Oh, what do you like to do?" "Oh, I like to do this." "No, you can't do that anymore." "Why?" "Because I don't like you having fun, so I'm just going to make that a sin." That wasn't it. He was saying, "These things will kill you."

The best place to play stick-ball is in the street, but what do parents say? "Don't play in the street." "Why? Don't you want us to have fun?" "Yes, and I want you to live a long life, so stay out of the street, because if you play in the street, sooner or later, you'll get hit." Are they just trying to be mean, or are they trying to keep you alive?

That's what Jesus was trying to tell us. He was saying, "This is the way of life. I'm it. You know Me, and you know your Father. You see how I live, you take on My ambitions, and you change your life."

When you lay down your life and take up His life, you make the Kingdom of God your priority.

I'm amazed at the people who claim to be saved, and yet as they are going through their lives, they've got their plans. God saves them, and their lives stay the same. Their plans stay the same; everything stays the same. I don't know how that could happen. That didn't happen with anybody Jesus called. They had plans, they had their goals, they all had businesses, and they walked away from them.

Your life has to change. When you lay down your life and you take up His life, and you make the Kingdom of God your priority, that's what you have to do. You've got to make it your priority to live and your priority to proclaim.

I don't care if you say you are a preacher or not a preacher; I don't care if you say you're in ministry or not in ministry. None of that matters. If you're a citizen of the kingdom of heaven, you have a responsibility to expand that kingdom. You need to be trained to be a disciple so that you will know how to expand it. You need to be taught and shown how to heal the sick, raise the dead, and cast out devils.

Healing the sick, raising the dead, and casting out devils should be your agenda.

The Spirit of the Lord is upon you because He has anointed you to preach the Gospel to the poor. He has sent you to heal the broken hearted, He has sent you to preach, and He has sent you to proclaim deliverance to the captives.

Proclaiming deliverance to the captives is not saying, "God wants to heal you, but until you get that out of your life, until you straighten up, He's not going to." No, proclaiming liberty to the captives and deliverance to the captives is easy. You say, "Captives, you're free;

walk out. Stay free. Here's how you stay free: don't keep doing what you did before. Jesus has set you free, and whom the Son sets free is free indeed. That thing does not have power over you anymore. The things that have power over you now are your desires, so you have to decide that you're going to go after the Kingdom of God."

There is an agenda that the church has to have, and we are getting in line with that; we're putting these things into place.

Matthew 9:35 says,

> 35 And Jesus went about all the cities and villages, teaching in their synagogues, and preaching the gospel of the kingdom, and healing every sickness and every disease among the people.

"And Jesus went about all the cities and villages, teaching in their synagogues, and preaching," proclaiming, "the Gospel of the Kingdom," the Good News of God's supremacy, "and healing," demonstrating God's supremacy by healing, "every sickness and every disease among the people."

A kingdom has to have authority to back up its policies or it's not a kingdom. Our Kingdom, the Kingdom of our God, has the authority to back up its policies. Its policies are that oppression has been judged by God as not conducive to Kingdom life, so you should be free. You shouldn't be oppressed, and you shouldn't be held captive. You shouldn't be sick. You ought to have prosperity.

**God wants you to have enough
so that you can bless any person who needs help.**

I'm not one of these ultra, hyper-prosperity preachers. People in religion say that you should gather, and you should be rich, just to be rich. When they first started, they said it was a "millionaire mentality" and that God was going to birth millionaires. After a while, people got tired of hearing that, so they had to take it a step farther. Now they say, "We're going to have billionaires in the churches."

The bad part is that every time God tries to bring a message into the church, man gets hold of it and twists it to his own good. We have to get away from that and realize this is about the Kingdom of God.

It's not about having things piled up. God wants you to have enough so that you can bless any person who needs help. You ought to be able to help anybody or feed anybody. We should be able to take a family that needs help and put them into a place, and say, "Here's a house. You can live here. We'll help you find a job, and you can live here until you get on your feet and get into a position where you can get your own place." We ought to be able to do that. That would be Kingdom. We ought to have our own place so that when visitors come here, we can put them up.

My goal that I've talked about for years is that I would have a place, such as a hotel or motel, where people could come in and stay in rooms. The televisions in there would be hooked up and no matter what channel they turned it to, someone would be preaching, 24 hours a day. It would be where our Bible School students could actually come in and live.

There may be a family that needs help. Maybe they lost their jobs, or maybe their house burned, or something. If we have a place, then we can put them in there, and say, "Don't worry about it. We've got a cafeteria here, we'll feed you. You work, you save up your money, and when you get enough to go somewhere and move into something else, we'll help you get in there, and then you can make it on your own."

We want to be able to do these things. Why? That's what I would want done for me if I were in that place. That's the essence of it—that we do to others as we would have done to us. That's all I'm trying to do here.

Kingdom isn't about you piling up money so you have the nicest cars, the fanciest houses, and two of everything. It's not about that at all.

The Bible says, "Let him that stole, steal no more, but let him work with his hands so that he has to give to those that have need." The reason you work and the reason you have things is so you have something to give to those who have a need. Imagine that. Suppose a person has been stealing, and then they show a change of heart. Now, instead of stealing, they are giving. It shows a change of heart first, but it works throughout their whole life. Isn't that amazing?

Stay healed; stay well.

We're talking Kingdom here; we're talking about a whole different type of system, and yet Jesus said, "This is how you could live." In this system we've got the perfect health care; we have instant divine health. If you get sick—you get healed. Better yet, stay healed; stay well. You don't have to keep getting sick and getting healed.

I have actually been to a couple of churches where there were no sick, because they got hold of the message, they started preaching it, and then they grew from there. They put everybody who came in through classes, and they learned these teachings, and then they were healthy. They said, "We were going to do a healing service, but glory, we don't need to. We can just preach, or better yet, we can go out on the streets and take it to somebody else." That's what this is about.

Matthew 9:36,

> 36 But when he saw the multitudes, he was moved with compassion on them, because they fainted, and were scattered abroad, as sheep having no shepherd.
>
> 37 Then saith he unto his disciples, The harvest truly *is* plenteous, but the labourers *are* few;
>
> 38 Pray ye therefore the Lord of the harvest, that he will send forth labourers into his harvest.

The words, *"send forth,"* are from the Greek word *ekballo*. *Ekballo* means *send forth; cast out.* It is the same word used for *casting out devils*. He was saying, *"Send forth* (or *cast out*) laborers."

Jesus gave His disciples *"power," (authority)* against unclean spirits.

Matthew 10:1,

> 1 And when he had called unto *him* his twelve disciples, he gave them power *against* unclean spirits, to cast them out, and to heal all manner of sickness and all manner of disease.

Notice that they weren't given names of people. He didn't say, "Go find this person because their lottery number came up. Find them and heal them." He was telling them, in other words, "You have power; you're like a policeman. You have power to arrest any spirit, any sickness, or any disease you see oppressing the people."

Demonstrate the Kingdom's authority with the power to set people free.

We're talking about Kingdom authority here, not individual, delegated authority in the sense of, "Okay, I can do it when God tells me I can but not until then." That's not what Jesus was talking about. He was saying, "You go, and if you find somebody sick, set them free. Freely you have received, freely give."

He had called them together and had given them, *"power (authority)"* against unclean spirits, to cast them out, and to heal all manner of sickness and all manner of disease.

In verse 1, the Greek word used for *"power"* was *exousia* (*authority*) and not *dunamis* (*power*). The KJV translated it *"power"* here, but *authority* would have been better.

Go down to verse 7. He said,

> 7 And as ye go, preach, saying, The kingdom of heaven is at hand.

"As you go, preach, saying, 'The kingdom of heaven is at hand.'" In other words, "The kingdom of heaven is right here."

> 8 Heal the sick, cleanse the lepers, raise the dead, cast out devils: freely ye have received, freely give.

"Heal the sick." Notice, every time you see the kingdom of heaven mentioned you usually see healing in the next sentence. Why? That's because it does no good to preach a kingdom if you cannot demonstrate the kingdom's authority with the power to set people free. The Kingdom of God is not in word only but in demonstration of the Spirit and power. It has to be together.

When we preach about the Kingdom, the people have to know that this Kingdom has the authority to set them free. That's why people should want to push into this Kingdom. They should say, "I want in on this. I want to be in this Kingdom." Why? "Because this King is better than the king I've been serving."

Jesus said, "Heal the sick, cleanse the lepers, raise the dead, and cast out devils." Deal with anything that bothers people. Cast it out, fix it, change it; set people free. We get so religious sometimes in how we see these things. He was just saying to go and help people, and set them free. Find out the problem they have and meet that need.

He said, "Freely you have received, freely give." He wasn't talking about money, He wasn't taking up an offering, but that's usually where we hear that. He was talking about power. He said, "I'm giving you power to give away freely."

Show the people the goodness of God.

Don't pick and choose. You can't tell one person, "You deserve it," and tell another person, "You don't." It is not, "Is there any sin in your life? Yes? Oh, you sinner. God's not going to do anything for you."

We go out into the streets and people get saved by some miracle of God. We talk to them and say, "Well, you need to get saved." They say, "I would like to, but I've got to get my life cleaned up first." No! It hurts us when we hear that. We say, "No, you can't get your life cleaned up. Coming to God is getting your life cleaned up. You can't get cleaned up to come to God, because you can't get clean enough for God. You come to God—He cleans you, He takes care of you. Just come to Him." By some miracle they say, "Okay." They get saved, and we rejoice.

Then we bring that person into the church, and somebody comes in and says, "Who here needs healing?" Then that person we brought in goes forward and says, "Yes, I've got an issue I'm dealing with here. I have some problems, some pain, and sickness." The first thing you hear them get asked is, "Is there any sin in your life?" They say, "Well, I've just been saved two days, so yes, I'm sure there is some sin in there that's working out." They get told, "Well, go back and sit down. God is not going to do anything for you until you get your life clean."

Isn't that amazing? On the street we tell them it's all by grace. We get them in the church and tell them that it's all by works. It's just the opposite of what we tell them on the street.

Instead, show them the goodness of God. Set them free and say, "This is the kind of God that we are talking about; this is the kind of kingdom you're in now."

Set the people free, and then make disciples of them.

We find out what the problem is, why they tend to go toward that, and fix that thing. We tell them, "The reason you're doing this is because you're trying to fill this need with that thing."

You need to be able to say, "Here's what you need: you need to understand what is in the Kingdom for you. You're not fulfilling your purpose. Your purpose is not to be on the street; that's not God's purpose for you. Your purpose is not to live in fornication, or to live by stealing, or to live on drugs; that's not your purpose. You're better than that. Jesus died for you."

Jesus has a better plan than that, and He came to die for you. That means that He has seen potential in you that probably nobody else sees. You can be something in the Kingdom of God. On this earth and this earthly kingdom, people look at you and think you are nothing, and they write you off. God looks at you and says, 'I've got a plan for you.'"

God loves to take the worst and fix them. Why? It shows how good He is at fixing us.

Anybody can train a natural athlete to be a world champion. However, if someone can train a person who is not a natural athlete, one who has no motor skills and who is clumsy, and trips over his own feet to be a world class athlete, what are people going to say? "That person is something, but that trainer is really something!" It was a trainer who took that unskilled person and made them into something.

Our trainer is God. It doesn't matter where you come from, and it doesn't matter what you've done; none of that matters. God can turn you around.

God's goal is for you to "grow up into Him (Jesus) in all things."

Ephesians 4:15,

> 15 But speaking the truth in love, may grow up into him in all things, which is the head, even Christ:

God's goal is that you "grow up into Him (Jesus) in all things." I don't care where you are today, and I don't care where you've been. God can take you all the way to Jesus, because He is that good of a trainer. It has nothing to do with your qualities; He can give you whatever qualities you need.

That's the key: it has nothing to do with you. All you have to do is say, "Here I am. I'm just a stack of clay here. Mold me, fix me, and turn me into what You want me to be," and He will turn you into something. He knows the potential you have in you, because He put it there. He can take the worst and "grow them up into Jesus."

"Freely you have received, freely give." God will take care of you.

Matthew 10:8,

> 8 Heal the sick, cleanse the lepers, raise the dead, cast out devils: freely ye have received, freely give.

Here Jesus was saying, "As you go, preach and do these things; cast these things out, and heal the sick. Freely you have received, freely give."

> 9 Provide neither gold, nor silver, nor brass in your purses,

Why did He say that? He was telling them, "I'm going to show you that I'll take care of you. You don't have to worry about those things. I'll take care of you."

Matthew 6:33,

> 33 But seek ye first the kingdom of God, and his righteousness; and all these things shall be added unto you.

He was saying, "You're seeking first the Kingdom, so don't worry about it; I'll take care of you."

Matthew 10:10,

> 10 Nor scrip for *your* journey, neither two coats, neither shoes, nor yet staves: for the workman is worthy of his meat.

Get busy; God will take care of you.

Take the kingdom of heaven by violence; take it energetically and aggressively.

Matthew 11:12,

> 12 And from the days of John the Baptist until now the kingdom of heaven suffereth violence, and the violent take it by force.

People always look at this verse, and they say, "Violence? What does that mean? I didn't think Jesus was violent." Yes, He got very violent. He turned over tables and ran people out of the temple. He made a whip, and everybody ran out of the temple. People don't run just because you make a whip; people run because they think you are going to use the whip on them. Obviously, He had them convinced.

If you look at the word *"violent"* in the Greek, it is the word *biastēs* and it means *a forcer*. It means literally, *energetic, aggressive*. We think violence means hurting something, but it just means to be energetic, or to be aggressive; it means you go after it. In other words, it means not to be passive. The passive don't inherit the Kingdom of God. The meek do, but the meek aren't passive.

Moses was the meekest of all men, but he wasn't passive. He went into a kingdom and brought a nation out of it. He led an insurrection. He stood up against the mightiest army of the day and won. Why? God was covering his back. He was energetic, he was violent, and he was aggressive. Let's go back to verse 12 in Matthew chapter 11.

Matthew 11:12,

> 12 And from the days of John the Baptist until now the kingdom of heaven suffereth violence, and the violent take it by force.

"The kingdom of heaven suffers violence, and the violent take it by *force*." The word *"force"* there is the Greek word *harpazō* which means *to sieze; take (by force)*.

In 1 Thessalonians 4:17, it says,

> 17 Then we which are alive and remain shall be <u>caught up</u> together with them in the clouds, to meet the Lord in the air: and so shall we ever be with the Lord.

"Then we which are alive and remain shall be caught up together with them in the clouds, to meet the Lord in the air." The words *"caught up"* are from the same word, *harpazō*.

Harpazō here literally means *to be snatched violently out of something*. What it is saying is, "We which are alive and remain shall be *caught up*; we will be *snatched out by force*, *violently*, to be together with Him."

After it said, "From the days of John the Baptist until now the kingdom of heaven suffereth violence," then it said, "and the violent take it by force." In other words, "The *violent*, the *energetic* and the *aggressive*, take the kingdom of heaven suddenly by snatching and grabbing it to themselves."

Now, think about that. Not only do we press in violently, energetically, and aggressively, but we grab hold and we say, "We're hanging on and nothing is taking it from us."

You start thinking, "What does that mean? How does that apply?" He had just told them, "Preach the kingdom; say, 'The kingdom is at hand.'" What do you do? You heal the sick. We have to realize that health is something, and we have to grab hold of the Kingdom of God, and say, "Health is mine. Devil, you can't touch this body!" That's the violent taking the kingdom of heaven by force, because sickness isn't in heaven; health is in heaven.

If we're going to take heaven by force, that's not against God. God says that's what is going to happen, and that's what He wants to happen.

Jesus said, "I want you to be energetic. I want you to be aggressive. I want you to grab hold of the kingdom of heaven, take it to yourself, take it by force, be energetic, be aggressive, and hold onto it. Don't be afraid; be bold." He was saying, "There is health in the kingdom of heaven, so grab health and bring it to you. Grab hold of it. Snatch it suddenly and aggressively."

He said to cleanse the lepers. It is the same thing. What are you doing? You're taking the kingdom of heaven to these people, and you are doing it violently. Now, you're not grabbing them and shaking them, or punching them or hurting them, but you take that leprosy and you look at it, and you say, "Leprosy, you're leaving here now! You get out of this person! Don't you ever come back! I set this person free! Now, go!" Be forceful with it.

It doesn't say beg, it doesn't say cry, it doesn't say weep, it doesn't say intercede; it doesn't say any of that. It says to take the kingdom of heaven by violence; take it aggressively. We have to take it, we have to bring it here and say, "This is the kingdom of heaven; it is at hand.

Do you want to see it? Watch this," and then you set the captives free. That's what it means.

> 12 And from the days of John the Baptist until now the kingdom of heaven suffereth violence, and the violent take it by force.

The energetic take it suddenly. Don't think you're going to ease into this thing; you're not. You're not going to be like Nicodemus, who went to Jesus by night, to talk to Him. There will come a point where you're going to have to stand up boldly.

You have to make a stand.
Jesus said, "If you're not with Me, you're against Me."

Any time there is a revolution, any time there is a change in government, or anything else, there is this quick kind of chaotic type situation. In a situation like that, there are people that you have to tell right away. You will be going from door to door, telling people, "You're either in or you're out. Are you with us or are you against us?" Isn't that what Jesus said? "If you're not with Me, you're against Me." He said, "You've got to realize that you've got to take a stand; you're going to have to take a stand somewhere." The kingdom of heaven requires you to take a stand and say, "This is where I stand: I will stand for health, I will stand for life, I will stand for peace, and I will stand for prosperity in the lives of the people, so we can bless them and help them."

That's part of the Kingdom of God. We are saying, "Thy Kingdom come, Thy will be done on earth as it is in heaven." You look at that sick body, you look at that person in the gutter passed out because of drugs or alcohol and you say, "No, no, no. The kingdom of heaven comes now to this person, and right now, in the name of Jesus, this stops. It's not going to be like this in the kingdom of heaven."

> 21 Neither shall they say, Lo here! or, lo there! for, behold, the Kingdom of God is within you.

The kingdom of heaven is wherever you are, because the Kingdom of God is within you. It lives within you. We are to start to take the kingdom of heaven by force and decide that this is the way it will be. You have got to get violent and aggressive, and you have to decide to take a stand.

Demonstrate Kingdom with spirit, soul, and body.

Jesus said, "I'd rather you be cold or hot, but not lukewarm." Don't straddle the fence. Get on one side or the other. Be a friend of God or an enemy of God, but don't think you're in the middle. There is no middle ground. There is no lukewarm. He said, "If you are lukewarm, I'll spew you out of my mouth." You say, "Well, why would He want us cold?" That's because cold people know they are cold.

It's the lukewarm people who fool themselves, and they think they are okay. Lukewarm people hang around lukewarm people and tell each other they're all hot and on fire. You should always be looking for people that are hotter and more on fire than you are. Let them pull you up. Better yet, you be on fire and pull others up.

Everything Jesus preached was about the Kingdom. Kingdom has authority. There is authority in the Kingdom of God.

We want you to understand the following topics that we covered in this sermon: (a) Kingdom authority, (b) kingdom violence (kingdom of heaven), (c) taking the kingdom with aggression and energy (kingdom of heaven), and (d) moving forward in the things of the Kingdom.

Take the kingdom of heaven by force; be aggressive, be energetic. Move forward in the things of the Kingdom. We're here to demonstrate Kingdom, with spirit, soul and body. Amen.

UNDERSTANDING THE KINGDOMS

Sermon given by Curry R. Blake

The two kingdoms:
The Kingdom of God and the kingdom of heaven.

Turn to Matthew chapter 4. Last week we were talking about what we call Kingdom Agenda and what the Kingdom is about. We started recognizing that there is a lot of controversy, and there are a lot of questions about Kingdom/kingdom. This week we are going to talk about understanding the kingdoms.

We always know that there are two kingdoms at war with one another; the Kingdom of God and His dear Son, and the kingdom of darkness. We're not talking about those two kingdoms today. We're going to be talking about the Kingdom of God, the kingdom of heaven, and what the Bible says about them. You're going to have to follow along closely.

It's not overly complicated, but at the same time you have to pay attention. Follow along as we go through these verses; read them for yourself.

We are going to start in Matthew chapter 4. I'm going to talk about understanding the kingdoms. These are some verses you've heard before. It says in verse 23,

> 23 And Jesus went about all Galilee, teaching in their synagogues, and preaching the gospel of the kingdom, and healing all manner of sickness and all manner of disease among the people.

As we showed last week, and many times before, Jesus taught the Gospel of the Kingdom, and then He demonstrated the Gospel of the Kingdom. He taught the Good News of the Kingdom or the Good News of God's supremacy over everything.

The way Jesus demonstrated it was by healing and setting the captives free. You can't preach a kingdom and say that it's supreme without setting people free. The idea is that whenever that kingdom is preached, there has to be a demonstration. We are going to look at some of that today.

Matthew 9 will be the next chapter. We're going to do what some would call parenthetical teaching. In other words, I'm going to make some statements, and we're going to go to another place, and then we're going to go back to where we were.

Matthew 9:35,

> 35 And Jesus went about all the cities and villages, teaching in their synagogues, and preaching the gospel of the kingdom, and healing every sickness and every disease among the people.

You will notice that the Greek word here for *"preaching"* literally means *to proclaim with an authority, a solemnity, and a gravity that must be listened to and obeyed.* That's a far cry from what many people call preaching. In other words, when Jesus proclaimed the Gospel of the Kingdom it had such a force behind it that it made people say, "I've got to change, and I've got to go this way."

In Matthew 4:23 and Matthew 9:35, it said that He preached the Gospel of the Kingdom. It really doesn't say anything more than that about the Kingdom or what He was preaching about the Kingdom, but we know that He did demonstrate by healing the sick.

Mark 1:14,

> 14 Now after that John was put in prison, Jesus came into Galilee, preaching the gospel of the kingdom of God,

The kingdom of heaven and the Kingdom of God are two different realms, yet the Kingdom of God includes the other.

We're going to be talking about two different terminologies today. We're going to talk about the Gospel of the kingdom of heaven and the Gospel of the Kingdom of God. Most people see those as synonymous, but they are in actuality very different, and we're going to point that out to you today. I'll give you some of the Scriptures and things that show this.

The key here is this: Matthew emphasizes the mission of Jesus to the Jews and to the people of Israel. Every time the term, "the kingdom of heaven," is used, it is in Matthew. It's never used in any other book. The Kingdom of God is mentioned in all of the other Gospels, and it's even included in Matthew and talked about in Matthew. However, the term "the kingdom of heaven" is only mentioned in Matthew.

You will see that in some places in different Gospels, there are parallel passages of the same incident or story being told. In one of the Gospels, for example in Matthew, it will say, "the kingdom of heaven," and maybe in John, Mark, or even Luke, it will say, "The Kingdom of God," yet it will be the same situation. One author brought out "the Kingdom of God," and the other brought out "the kingdom of heaven." You say, "Well, if they're both used in parallel passages, then they have to be the same thing." That's not true.

There are places where the two terms, kingdom of heaven and Kingdom of God, are used in parallel passages in Scripture. That's similar to saying that all New Yorkers are Americans, but not all Americans are New Yorkers. That's basically what it comes down to. The kingdom of heaven and the Kingdom of God are two different realms, yet one includes the other.

All in the Kingdom of God are in the kingdom of heaven, but not all in the kingdom of heaven are in the Kingdom of God.

I know you are thinking, "What? What are you talking about?" Now, that may be shocking, but we will prove it. We're going to look at that, right now.

UNDERSTANDING THE KINGDOMS

Go with me to 1 Corinthians chapter 15. This is where we are going to start getting into the parenthetical teaching. I will bring some points out, and then we will go to another place, and then we will come back and finish this up.

In 1 Corinthians 15:22, it says,

> 22 For as in Adam all die, even so in Christ shall all be made alive.
>
> 23 But every man in his own order: Christ the firstfruits; afterward they that are Christ's at his coming.

**Jesus is going to reign as King
over this kingdom until all enemies are put under His feet.**

> 24 Then *cometh* the end, when he shall have delivered up the kingdom to God, even the Father; when he shall have put down all rule and all authority and power.
>
> 25 For he must reign, till he hath put all enemies under his feet.

Verse 23 says, "But every man in his own order," is talking about all of those that are in Christ. They will be made alive, but there is going to be an order to it: "Christ the firstfruits." We know that is true. Then it says, "Afterward they that are Christ's at His coming," are the others that will be made alive. Then in verse 24, it says, "Then cometh the end." This is the main point I wanted to get to.

Let me go back and start over. "For as in Adam all die, even so in Christ shall all be made alive. But every man in his own order: Christ the firstfruits; afterward they that are Christ's at his coming. Then cometh the end." It talks about Christ's coming, then it says, "Then the end will come." When does the end come? It says, "When He (Christ) shall have delivered up the kingdom to God."

Christ is going to deliver up the kingdom which He is Lord over; He is going to present that to God. Notice when this is going to take place: "…when He shall have put down all rule, all authority, and power."

It says in verse 25, "For He (Christ) must reign, till he hath put all enemies under his feet." He's going to reign as King over this kingdom until all enemies are put under His feet.

I'm going to give you several individual Scriptures in the Gospels that will help you to study it out.

The writings in the Gospels support each other.

In Matthew 18:16, it says, "In the mouth of two or three witnesses a thing shall be established," so I'm going to give you some other Scriptures.

Matthew 22:44 says,

> 44 The LORD said unto my Lord, Sit thou on my right hand, till I make thine enemies thy footstool?

Mark 12:36,

> 36 For David himself said by the Holy Ghost, The LORD said to my Lord, Sit thou on my right hand, till I make thine enemies thy footstool.

This verse in Mark 12:36 says the same thing it says in Matthew 22:44. Let's go to another.

Luke 20:42-43,

> 42 And David himself saith in the book of Psalms, The LORD said unto my Lord, Sit thou on my right hand,
>
> 43 Till I make thine enemies thy footstool.

It says the exact same thing. Those were all in the Gospels.

Go to Acts 2:34 and 35. It says,

> 34 For David is not ascended into the heavens: but he saith himself, The LORD said unto my Lord, Sit thou on my right hand,
>
> 35 Until I make thy foes thy footstool.

Here it is again. God was speaking to Jesus saying, "Sit at my right hand until your enemies be made your footstool."

Now, let's go to Hebrews chapter one. I know we're going all over, but that's because I really want to show you that this is not just some teaching in a corner. This is throughout the entire New Testament. By the time we get finished, you will have a clearer picture of the Kingdom of God and the kingdom of heaven. It's amazing!

Hebrews 1:13,

> 13 But to which of the angels said he at any time, Sit on my right hand, until I make thine enemies thy footstool?

In other words, "Did He ever say this to an angel? Which angel did He ever say this to, 'Sit on my right hand, until I make thine enemies thy footstool?'"

> 14 Are they not all ministering spirits, sent forth to minister for them who shall be heirs of salvation?

He never elevated any angel to that position. First of all, this is the Bible. This is not commentary. This is a direct refuting of the current Jehovah's Witness doctrine. It is a direct refuting, because He never said to any angel, "Sit on my right hand," but He did say that to Jesus.

Hebrews 10:11,

> 11 And every priest standeth daily ministering and offering oftentimes the same sacrifices, which can never take away sins:
>
> 12 But this man, after he had offered one sacrifice for sins for ever, sat down on the right hand of God;

> 13 From henceforth expecting till his enemies be made his footstool.

"And every priest standeth daily ministering and offering oftentimes the same sacrifices, which can never take away sins: But this man (Christ Jesus), after he had offered one sacrifice for sins forever, sat down on the right hand of God." Now, watch this: "From henceforth (from then on), expecting till his enemies be made his footstool."

All three of these Scriptures go on to say that Jesus ascended to heaven and then sat down. He's still seated there, and He is waiting there until all of His enemies are made His footstool. Isn't that what you just read? It says it very plainly.

We are going to go back to 1 Corinthians 15. I just want to put that Scripture in the middle of it.

In 1 Corinthians 15:24, it says,

> 24 Then *cometh* the end, when he shall have delivered up the kingdom to God, even the Father; when he shall have put down all rule and all authority and power.

"Then cometh the end, when He (Jesus) shall have delivered up the kingdom to God." Jesus is going to turn the kingdom over to God. Now, if you turn a kingdom over to someone, it means that, up to that point, they have not received it. We know that Jesus was proclaiming the Kingdom of God, and we know He was proclaiming what was called the kingdom of heaven.

**The kingdom of heaven was offered, and it was rejected.
It was the ultimate rejection.**

We have to realize that here Jesus was proclaiming the kingdom of heaven; it was offered, and it was rejected. At the point that it was rejected, He was crucified. That was the ultimate rejection at that point.

Then, of course, He was raised and resurrected, and then it said that He went to the Father. He said, "I have to go to the Father; if I don't go, I can't send the Spirit back." He went to the Father and then, when He sent the Spirit back, it said that He sat down on the right hand of Majesty.

Every Scripture about Him sitting down has to do with Him sitting down and waiting until His enemies are made His footstool. Technically, He Himself is not making His enemies His footstool. Apparently, from all indications so far, He has turned that job over to somebody else and is waiting until His enemies are made His footstool.

Jesus must reign until He has put all enemies under His feet.

In Ephesians chapter 4:11-13 it tells us about how He has given us the Five-Fold Ministry so that we "grow up into Him in all things." If you read that along with 1 John 3:2, it tells us, "Now we are sons of God, and it does not yet appear what we shall be, but we know that when He appears we shall be like Him." He talks about how all of what was going on in His body was geared toward establishing this kingdom.

We just read in Hebrews 10. Then we went to 1 Corinthians 15, so we're going to pick back up there.

In 1 Corinthians 15:25, it says,

> 25 For he must reign, till he hath put all enemies under his feet.

"For He must reign," notice He is reigning, "till he hath put all enemies under his feet," so Jesus is reigning, but He is seated. Then it says that He will basically hand the kingdom to the Father after He has put down all rebellion. Let's look at this in 1 Corinthians 15:26,

> 26 The last enemy *that* shall be destroyed *is* death.

Death is the last enemy.

> 27 For he hath put all things under his feet. But when he saith all things are put under *him, it is* manifest that he is excepted, which did put all things under him.
>
> 28 And when all things shall be subdued unto him, then shall the Son also himself be subject unto him that put all things under him, that God may be all in all.

"For He hath put all things under his feet. But when He saith all things are put under Him, it is manifest," or obvious, "that He," Jesus, "is excepted, which did put all things under Him. And when all things shall be subdued unto Him…" Did you hear that? "…then shall the

Son also Himself be subject unto Him that put all things under Him, that God may be all in all"

This is where a lot of error comes in, and it's where a lot of people get really confused. They don't see the difference between the two terms: the positional and the experiential. We would even say it like this, "I was saved, and now I'm being saved, and I shall be saved."

When I say, "I was saved," I don't mean that I'm not saved anymore. I'm just saying there was a point in time where I was saved, but then, from the time I got saved until now, I'm being saved. I'm still in the process. At the end, I shall have been saved. In other words, I will have reached the culmination of it; there is a point coming. This is one of the reasons why He says we must endure to the end. Part of that process of being saved is the enduring.

Let's look at verse 28 again:

> 28 And when all things shall be subdued unto him, then shall the Son also himself be subject unto him that put all things under him, that God may be all in all.

"And when all things shall be subdued unto Him, then…" Do you hear that? "Then…" That means not before then.

Verse 27 says that He has put all things under Him. Notice that He is seated, and He is waiting until His enemies become His footstool.

Then in verse 28 it says, "When all things shall be subdued unto Him…" That's when His enemies become His footstool. "Then," at that point, "shall the Son also Himself be subject unto Him that put all things under Him."

Jesus is reigning, seated at the right hand of the Father. He is reigning, and He reigns through us.

Jesus is King of kings and Lord of lords. He's King there, and we're kings here. He is Lord there, and we're lords here. He is working through us, He lives through us, and He is reigning through us. Now, He has won the war, so to speak. There are still some battles we have to fight to put down all of these rebellious things that are going on in this world against Him.

This is where people get to the point where they're ask, "Well, if all of this is going on and God is God, why doesn't He just do something about it?" You don't understand. First and foremost, God is just. He is just, and He does things right. There is an order to things. He is God, and He put Jesus as King over this earth, in that sense.

Jesus sent the Holy Spirit back to work through people.

God gave Adam lordship, and Adam gave lordship over to Satan, the god of this world. Then Jesus came and said, "No, that's not good; that's rebellion. I'm going to re-establish My kingdom." The people He wanted to reestablish it through said, "No, we don't want it." Jesus was crucified, and He left, but He sent His Spirit back to work through people. Then, His Spirit was mainly transferred toward the Gentiles.

If you go back in and look at Daniel 2 and 7, you will see that the kingdom of heaven was prophesied for a future time. It started when they began to preach or proclaim that the kingdom of heaven was at hand. It started at that point on the earth. In Daniel 9, there is the prophecy of the 70 weeks that takes place.

Daniel 9:24,

> 24 Seventy weeks are determined upon thy people and upon thy holy city, to finish the transgression, and to make an end of sins, and to make reconciliation for iniquity, and to bring in everlasting righteousness, and to seal up the vision and prophecy, and to anoint the most Holy.

After the seventy weeks then things will pick back up. There will be a point where Israel will be flooding in. There is this whole process going on.

When Jesus was ascended upon high, after He led captivity captive, He sat down at the right hand of the Father. When He sat down at the right hand of the Father, He sat down as a King saying, "I am here, I'm sitting, and I'm waiting until My army makes My enemies My footstool." That's us. We are the army, not the enemy; just remember that. When you look at these things, you have to understand what is going on.

People say, "Well, God is in control." Not technically. Understand that it is like a country. There is a government that is over that country, but then there are insurrections and rebellion. That country owns that property, but there is a rebellion, so they are not in control of that property. They will say, "We don't have control of this city; we've lost control of this city."

Not too long ago, in Libya, they had that kind of thing going on. They've got the same thing going on in Syria, even now, where the government is supposed to be in control. They say, "We've lost control of this city," or, "We've lost control of the airport." Do you see what I am saying? The country owns it, but the rebels have control of things. Those that are rebelling against the lawful order, you might say, are in rebellion against the lawful king.

God said, "I have a world that is in rebellion, and I want you to go and put down that rebellion." The way Jesus did that was to come and die, and then go back and sit down and say, "Alright, we have won, we have conquered, and it's good. Now, I have an army there that's going to finally be putting down all insurrection and all rebellion."

Jesus said, "Father, I'm just waiting so that when that happens, they will bring it to Me, and I will turn around and hand it to You, and once again, You will be the ultimate, supreme, uncontested God of the universe."

Let's read verse 28 again,

28 And when all things shall be subdued unto him, then shall the Son also himself be subject unto him that put all things under him, that God may be all in all.

There's that transfer. At that point, God gave Jesus the right to rule as a King and to do what needed to be done. Jesus, as God's deputized authority, is doing that. He has deputized us to continue that work until it's all done. Then He's going to be able to turn around and say, "My army has done this, and here it is. Now, I give you back a world that is under Your dominion." Essentially, that's what it comes down to.

Everything that Jesus taught was the Kingdom.

Go to Matthew 13. We're going to start in verse 1. I just want to point some things out. We're going to be looking at these over the next few weeks as a series. I am going to tie this all together so that you can really see a picture of it, because most people just don't see it.

It answers so many questions, and it will help you. The one thing that we have to realize is that everything Jesus taught was the Kingdom; that's what He taught. I don't know how churches get away without teaching it, since that was His message.

At one time He even said, "This Gospel of the Kingdom shall be preached unto all nations as a witness; then the end shall come." This Gospel was not just any gospel. When He said, "This Gospel," He was referring to the Gospel He preached. We have to preach the same

Gospel He preached, and that Gospel is going to be preached unto all the world as a witness, and until that happens, the end can't come.

Jesus used parables, fictitious narratives, to try to give a better understanding of the spiritual truths He was teaching.

Here in Matthew 13:1, it says,

> 1 The same day went Jesus out of the house, and sat by the sea side.
>
> 2 And great multitudes were gathered together unto him, so that he went into a ship, and sat; and the whole multitude stood on the shore.
>
> 3 And he spake many things unto them in parables, saying, Behold, a sower went forth to sow;

The word *"parable"* is the Greek word *parabolay*. It means symbolically, *a fictitious narrative; a similitude*. *Para* means *alongside*. It means *to throw down something alongside something else so that you can better explain it*. It is simply *an illustration; a comparison*. Jesus used natural things to try to give a better understanding of the spiritual truth He was teaching.

If you read parables, you have to realize that not every detail of a parable is supposed to be interpreted to a specific doctrine. It's a story; it's a parable used to give a truth. The key is to find the truth in what

He was trying to say. Don't try to make every detail some special hidden knowledge. If you do that, you will get so confused.

Every time Jesus taught a parable, He told what the parable meant so that we don't have to guess. It's amazing how many people spend time in the parable where He's teaching it, and they don't go down a few verses and read where He said, "This is what this means." Usually, what they come up with is far different from what He meant. Just keep reading.

The following parable is also out of Mark 4, but we are going to read it out of Matthew 13.

Matthew 13 starting with verse 3,

> 3 And he spake many things unto them in parables, saying, Behold, a sower went forth to sow;
>
> 4 And when he sowed, some *seeds* fell by the way side, and the fowls came and devoured them up:
>
> 5 Some fell upon stony places, where they had not much earth: and forthwith they sprung up, because they had no deepness of earth:
>
> 6 And when the sun was up, they were scorched; and because they had no root, they withered away.

> 7 And some fell among thorns; and the thorns sprung up, and choked them:
>
> 8 But other fell into good ground, and brought forth fruit, some an hundredfold, some sixtyfold, some thirtyfold.
>
> 9 Who hath ears to hear, let him hear.
>
> 10 And the disciples came, and said unto him, Why speakest thou unto them in parables?

The disciples asked, "Why are you talking to people in parables? Why don't you just tell them?" Why didn't He? He only explained the parables to the disciples because they were the ones He had chosen to follow Him.

This goes along with 1 Corinthians 2 and 3 where it actually says that the carnal mind doesn't understand the things of the Spirit. The spiritual mind gets it and the spiritual man understands these things, but a carnal mind, a carnal man, does not get them, and to him they are foolishness.

> 11 He answered and said unto them, Because it is given unto you to know the mysteries of the kingdom of heaven, but to them it is not given.

Here Jesus was saying, "The reason they're given to you is because you have decided to follow Me, but the people out there that have not yet made that decision don't need to know the details of these things." If you want to know the secrets of the Kingdom, you've got to connect with Jesus. Otherwise, you will just sit there and wonder.

> 12 For whosoever hath, to him shall be given, and he shall have more abundance: but whosoever hath not, from him shall be taken away even that he hath.
>
> 13 Therefore speak I to them in parables: because they seeing see not; and hearing they hear not, neither do they understand.

The people were listening, and they were seeing all of this, but they still didn't understand it.

> 14 And in them is fulfilled the prophecy of Esaias, which saith, By hearing ye shall hear, and shall not understand; and seeing ye shall see, and shall not perceive:

The "Prophecy of Esaias" was talking about Isaiah the prophet. He was saying, "This prophecy is being fulfilled in the people."

> 15 For this people's heart is waxed gross, and *their* ears are dull of hearing, and their eyes they have closed; lest at any time they should see with *their* eyes, and hear with *their* ears, and should understand with *their* heart, and should be converted, and I should heal them.

"Their eyes they have closed." Even when Jesus was speaking about healing here, He wasn't talking about physical healing. He had healed a lot of people who didn't have a clue about what He was doing.

He was talking about reconnecting them with God, with understanding, and having that connection with God. He was saying that He would heal that ruptured relationship, so to speak.

> 16 But blessed *are* your eyes, for they see: and your ears, for they hear.

Remember: any time you see the word *"blessed,"* you can put *"spiritually prosperous"* in there. *Blessed* literally means: *to be spiritually prosperous*.

> 17 For verily I say unto you, That many prophets and righteous *men* have desired to see *those things* which ye see, and have not seen *them;* and to hear *those things* which ye hear, and have not heard *them.*

> 18 Hear ye therefore the parable of the sower.

Jesus had just told the parable to the people. Then, when He was by Himself with His disciples, He explained it to them.

> 19 When any one heareth the word of the kingdom, and understandeth *it* not, then cometh the wicked *one,* and catcheth away that which was sown in his heart. This is he which received seed by the way side.

When He said, "When any one hears the Word of the Kingdom," He was saying that the parable of the sower, and what is sown, is the Word of the Kingdom. He said, "Now when any one hears the Word of the

Kingdom and understands it not, then cometh the wicked one, and catcheth away that which was sown in his heart." If you don't understand it, then what you don't understand, you don't get to keep. You have to understand it, or it will be stolen.

People say, "Well, the thief comes to steal, kill, and destroy." Yes, and let's say you hear healing preached. Guess how he tries to come and steal it? He usually tries to make you or one of your loved ones sick. He's trying to steal that Word in your heart by getting you refocused on the natural, which keeps you from moving into the spiritual.

Notice what it says: "Then cometh the wicked one and catcheth away that which was sown in his heart. This is he which received seed by the way side." Here He says, "If you don't understand it, you don't get to keep it." Now you know why Solomon said in Proverbs 4:7, "In all thy getting, get wisdom, and get understanding."

You have to get understanding; you can't just hear it. You don't get brownie points for just sitting and hearing. "Well, I was there. I was in church, and I heard." No. You have to understand; it's important that you understand. He said, "This is he which received seed by the way side."

Verse 20,

> 20 But he that received the seed into stony places, the same is he that heareth the word, and anon with joy receiveth it;

21 Yet hath he not root in himself, but dureth for a while: for when tribulation or persecution ariseth because of the word, by and by he is offended.

"Yet hath he no root in himself." Now, get that: "He hath no root in himself." Right there, we would think, "Well, that doesn't even sound like a Christian term, "root in yourself."

Some might say, "You shouldn't have root in yourself; you should have root in Christ." Well, that's a good religious answer, but you have to realize that the only thing you bring to the table is the commitment, the will to stick, the ability to stick, and the ability to endure.

Don't back off, don't back down, and move on into it.

"Yet had he no root in himself, but dureth," or endures, "for a while: for when tribulation or persecution arises because of the Word." Why does tribulation or persecution arise? It is because of the Word—to steal that Word. It tells you right there, "…tribulation or persecution arises because of the Word." People say, "I started going to church, and it was good truth, but then all hell broke out against me." Guess what happened? People were hearing the truth, and the enemy came to steal it.

All of the DBI students were saying, "Get hold of it and stick. Don't back off, don't back down, and move on into it." I heard one preacher one time say, "If you're going through hell, don't stop, because then you just stay in hell. Move through it." The idea is to pass through it.

Over and over again the Bible says, "And it came to pass…" Anything you're going through will pass—unless you stop. You don't want to stop. You want to keep on going.

> 21 …when tribulation or persecution ariseth because of the word, by and by he is offended.

What does *"offended"* mean? It can mean *mad or angry*, and it does have that connotation, but it also means *to quit, back off, or not show up*. If you get offended, you quit.

Well, that's exactly what it said about the people in the hometown of Jesus. They heard the Word, and they got offended.

The Word in your life can become unfruitful because of the "deceitfulness of riches."

> 22 He also that received seed among the thorns is he that heareth the word; and the care of this world, and the deceitfulness of riches, choke the word, and he becometh unfruitful.

You can have the Word in your life, and it can become unfruitful because of the cares of this world and because of the deceitfulness of riches. "I would love to be at church on Sunday, or attend a Life Team, or enjoy home fellowship, but they offered me this overtime. It's a holiday, and it pays double time and a half. I just can't pass that up." That's called the deceitfulness of riches.

23 But he that received seed into the good ground is he that heareth the word, and understandeth *it;* which also beareth fruit, and bringeth forth, some an hundredfold, some sixty, some thirty.

That was "The Parable of the Sower," and He explained it. If you want the answer to "The Parable of the Sower," there it is. It is really simple.

A parable about what the kingdom of heaven is like:

24 Another parable put he forth unto them, saying, The kingdom of heaven is likened unto a man which sowed good seed in his field:

In other words, "Let me give you an illustration of what the kingdom of heaven is like." Then He told them: "The kingdom of heaven is likened unto a man which sowed good seed in his field."

Notice: "His enemy came and sowed tares among the wheat." The tares are not of God; God didn't plant them.

25 But while men slept, his enemy came and sowed tares among the wheat, and went his way.

26 But when the blade was sprung up, and brought forth fruit, then appeared the tares also.

> 27 So the servants of the householder came and said unto him, Sir, didst not thou sow good seed in thy field? from whence then hath it tares?

We know that the wheat and the tares are people. I'm not saying to change this around, but I want you to notice that this is what people do. The first thing they say is, "God, didn't you sow good seed? God, I thought You were a good God. How can there be bad things in my life? God, where are You? God, why did You let this happen to me? You're the one that's supposed to be sowing the seed. You're the one that's supposed to be in charge of everything. Why am I having tares in my life? Why isn't my life just all wheat?"

Many people ask, "God, why is this happening? Why don't You do something?" He goes on here to give God's answer.

> 28 He said unto them, An enemy hath done this. The servants said unto him, Wilt thou then that we go and gather them up?

He said, "An enemy has done this." "The servants said unto him, "Wilt thou then that we go and gather them up?"

> 29 But he said, Nay; lest while ye gather up the tares, ye root up also the wheat with them.

The wheat and the tares grow up together.

We know that the wheat and tares are people, and they grow up together. They both show up at the same time. When they saw the tares (the people), they said, "Lord do you want us to take these out?" and the householder said, "No. No, don't do it, because if you do, you might tear up the wheat, also."

I said this before, and this is what this is getting down to. If you tell me you're a Christian, I take your word for it, because this is the realm of profession. You profess as a Christian. Unless a gift operates, where I can discern your spirit and discern whether you are of God, or whether by your accumulated actions you prove that you're not, then I have to go with what you say.

I've told God before, "We need a tenth gift in 1 Corinthians, and that would be the gift to be able to look at a person and say, "Born again" or "Not born again." That would make evangelism so easy. Wouldn't it? You could just walk down the street and say, "No, I don't need to talk to you. You've got it; you're good." You could just go right on to the next person.

With this being the realm of profession, we have to take people's word for it, then watch their lives, and then see if their fruit bears witness to their words.

We know there is a universal Church. It is what is called the invisible Church. That is the true Church. Those are people that are actually born of God, and they're united with Him. We also know that there are people who are in church that are not born of God, and yet they say, "Oh, I'm a Christian. I go to church, I'm in church, and everybody in church says I am a Christian," but we don't know. There are some that are and some that are not.

Just because you are in church doesn't mean you're a part of "the Church." To be in "the Church" you have to be born of God. Anybody can walk in here, sit down, and say, "Oh yeah, I'm a Christian," but that doesn't put them in "the Church," into "the Body of Christ." There are some that only profess.

The "wheat" are those that are truly the children of God, and they are born again.

The "tares" are those that attend church and are not born again.

Maybe the "tares" never intend to be born again. We know that we have wheat and tares in the church, and many times, even if the tares know they are tares, they think that the wheat doesn't know that they're tares.

All church discipline is to be geared toward reconciliation.

The reality is that many times God does reveal and show you things about people. Then people ask, "Don't you know this about…?" I say, "Yes, I know that." "Why don't you do something about it?" I tell them, "If I do, it could hurt other people," so we just let it go. It's also called giving a person enough room to hang themselves. If a person is a tare, it will show up.

You don't have to tear them out, and you don't have to do anything about them. You can keep preaching truth. I would like to think that the tares could become wheat. The bottom line is, even if they don't, they are hearing the Gospel, and they will have no excuse when they stand before God. However, if you kick a tare out, then all you've done is reinforce their old idea of God.

You also have to make sure that you know that the tares are not infecting the wheat. That's where church discipline comes in. That's when you have to start saying, "No. This will not happen."

We're a little different. We do Matthew 18. We'll talk to you, we'll say what the problem is, and if it goes beyond that, then we'll bring another person with us. We'll share with you and say, "This is what we see. Here it is." Then, if you still don't listen, then there will have to be some church discipline.

Some would say, "Hey, come here a minute. This person right here has absolutely refused discipline and has absolutely refused to listen to truth. They're living in open sin. They are infecting the rest of the church with their false doctrine. They are a heretic. They're trying to pull people off to the side, so this person is to be treated as a heathen to you." Think about that. Have you ever seen that in a church?

It hasn't happened often, but it has happened. That's what Dr. Sumrall did. That's the way he ran things, so I have no problem with that, but here's the difference: we say, "Treat them like a heathen," and how do we treat the heathen? We love them.

All church discipline is to be geared toward reconciliation. It is not just kicking somebody out; that's ridiculous. We are to love, but we are also to know that they can't be trusted with anything spiritual. They're carnal, because they're a tare. We're not going to say, "Excuse me, Mr. Tare. Would you come forward?" We're not going to do that, but there has to be an aspect of church discipline, which very honestly, you don't see anymore.

The key is to love people, and try to win them. That's what Matthew 18 is about. It's about loving people. It is going to them and saying, "Fix this; just change."

Let's read on. In verse 28 He said, "An enemy has done that." The servant asks, "Do you want us to go gather them up?" In verse 29, He said, "No, lest while you gather up the tares, you root up also the wheat with them."

> 30 Let both grow together until the harvest: and in the time of harvest I will say to the reapers, Gather ye together first the tares, and bind them in bundles to burn them: but gather the wheat into my barn.

This parable likens the kingdom of heaven to a grain of mustard seed, which grows into a large tree:

This is the third parable in this passage. This whole chapter of Matthew 13 is just parable after parable. He was likening the kingdom of heaven to so many different things. He was saying, "Sooner or later,

I'll give an illustration where you get it." He just kept telling the parables, and each one brought out a different facet of the Kingdom.

> 31 Another parable put he forth unto them, saying, The kingdom of heaven is like to a grain of mustard seed, which a man took, and sowed in his field:
>
> 32 Which indeed is the least of all seeds: but when it is grown, it is the greatest among herbs, and becometh a tree, so that the birds of the air come and lodge in the branches thereof.

He goes on with other parables.

Understanding leaven:

> 33 Another parable spake he unto them; The kingdom of heaven is like unto leaven, which a woman took, and hid in three measures of meal, till the whole was leavened.

I brought this out, specifically, because I want you to realize that many times I will make reference to the *"leaven"* aspect of the kingdom. I will be talking about going into an area, just getting in there, then letting it grow, and letting it bring forth fruit. Many times I use the term *"leaven"* and people automatically think of the warning that Jesus gave against the leaven of the Pharisees.

I wanted you to see in your own Bible that Jesus said, "The kingdom of heaven is like unto *leaven*." Every time you see the word *"leaven,"* it doesn't mean something bad. Here it means something good. It means that it *permeates with an altering or transforming element.* It is *something that spreads or something that grows.* Yeast is a good way of saying it. *"Leaven"* was just simply the *yeast.*

Jesus said, "The kingdom of heaven may start as the smallest of all seeds, but it's like leaven. If you put it in something, it will take over. The nature of the kingdom is domination; it is to take over. It is to reestablish dominion in believers.

> 34 All these things spake Jesus unto the multitude in parables; and without a parable spake he not unto them:

Let me just interject here. I know this isn't always as exciting as a testimony or different things that we have, but you have to understand this, because this is the basis; this is what Jesus taught. This is straight from the Master's mouth.

If you get this, nobody will be able to fool you. All I'm trying to do is inoculate you against wrong teaching, wrong doctrine, and against hirelings and wolves. I'm trying to bring truth to you straight from the mouth of Jesus, so you can say, "This is what the Kingdom is like."

Understand what Jesus said about the Kingdom and what He was trying to accomplish:

I pray that you will start to understand His plan, His program, and how He wants to accomplish it. Like I said, it may not be very exciting; you might not be cheering, or waving handkerchiefs at me. I'm not trying to get you excited. I'm trying to get you grounded. You've got to get grounded into the Word and into the truth of the Word.

We need to look at these things and be accountable, but make sure we stick to the truth. We don't just want to get the hype and get something exciting; we want to get truth. When you get truth, and it gets grounded, then the thing that truth produces gets exciting. Amen?

> 35 That it might be fulfilled which was spoken by the prophet, saying, I will open my mouth in parables; I will utter things which have been kept secret from the foundation of the world.

Jesus was talking about the Kingdom. It all goes back to who you are and what you can do in the Kingdom.

Understanding the parable of the tares of the field:

> 36 Then Jesus sent the multitude away, and went into the house: and his disciples came unto him, saying, Declare unto us the parable of the tares of the field.

You'll notice that He had already given two other parables since that one on the tares. They said, "We want You to explain that parable about the enemy coming and sowing. We want to know about that."

> 37 He answered and said unto them, He that soweth the good seed is the Son of man;

Who sows the good seed? Jesus (the Son of man) sows it. Here, He was explaining it, so you don't have to guess.

> 38 The field is the world; the good seed are the children of the kingdom; but the tares are the children of the wicked *one;*

How many of you know that you can have children of the wicked one sitting in a church service? That's where they should be. You have to realize that everybody was a child of the wicked one until they weren't. That's why we don't run them off; we want them to be there. We want to infect them with the Spirit of the living God.

> 39 The enemy that sowed them is the devil; the harvest is the end of the world; and the reapers are the angels.

That's as clear as you can get. He spoke to them in parables, but then He explained it in such a way that they couldn't get it wrong.

> 40 As therefore the tares are gathered and burned in the fire; so shall it be in the end of this world.

You can refer to the kingdom of heaven and not be referring to the Kingdom of God.

> 41 The Son of man shall send forth his angels, and they shall gather out of his kingdom all things that offend, and them which do iniquity;

"They shall gather out of his kingdom…" The children of the devil are in the kingdom of Christ. Isn't that something? What did Jesus preach? He preached the Gospel of the kingdom of heaven all through Matthew. We're in Matthew, and He was referring to the Gospel of the kingdom of heaven. You can refer to the kingdom of heaven and not be referring to the Kingdom of God.

Jesus came to put down rebellion on the earth and to destroy all the works of the enemy.

The earth was given to man, and it was operating under the dominion of God. When the enemy rebelled against God and was kicked out of heaven, he came to the earth. Then, the earth was given to the enemy.

The enemy then set up this rebellion, and the earth became a pocket of rebellion against the Kingdom of God. Based on that, this rebellion was ongoing.

Then the Father said to Jesus, "We've got rebellion on the earth, and I want you to take care of it. I want you to go, and put down the rebellion. I want you to go and destroy all the works of the enemy." That is what Jesus came to do. God said, "I want you to go and do that," so Jesus came and did it.

Notice: the earth is one part of the overall Kingdom of God.

When we refer to the kingdom of heaven, it is almost exclusively talking about the kingdom over which Jesus is King, and it is referring specifically to the work of God on this earth.

Jesus said, "If I heal the sick, if I cast out a devil by the finger of God, then you would say that the Kingdom has come." When Jesus referred to acts of power, He was referring to the Kingdom of God, not the kingdom of heaven, because the kingdom of heaven is the realm of profession. In other words, we profess that we're walking in this.

Both wheat and tares are in the kingdom of heaven. However, within the Kingdom of God, there are no tares. The Kingdom of God is the true Kingdom of God.

To get into the kingdom of heaven all you've got to do is say, "I want in. I'm here; I'm part of it," and no one will say anything.

To get into the Kingdom of God, you must be born again. Do you see the difference? People in the Kingdom of God are in the kingdom of heaven, but everybody in the kingdom of heaven isn't in the Kingdom of God. I'll prove all of this as we go on.

Are you possibly hearing something that might be a little surprising to you as compared to the way that it has been taught before? I know it is different from the way I was originally taught years ago.

He says here that the field is the world, the good seed are the children of the kingdom, but the tares are the children of the wicked one. The enemy that sowed them is the devil. The harvest is the end of the world, and the reapers are the angels. Therefore, the tares are gathered, burned with fire, and it shall be at the end of the world. I am just trying to recap here.

> 41 The Son of man shall send forth his angels, and they shall gather out of his kingdom all things that offend, and them which do iniquity;

Listen to that. There are people doing iniquity in the kingdom of heaven, and they shall be gathered out. That's the problem with tares; they think they're getting away with it. God is blessing them. God is there. He helps them, He heals them, and He blesses them.

That is all amazing, but that doesn't show that they're getting away with it. It just shows how good God is. However, there will be a time when those that do iniquity shall be gathered out of the kingdom of heaven.

> 42 And shall cast them into a furnace of fire: there shall be wailing and gnashing of teeth.
>
> 43 Then shall the righteous shine forth as the sun in the kingdom of their Father. Who hath ears to hear, let him hear.

There are two different kingdoms: the Kingdom of God and the kingdom of heaven. You have the Son of Man (Jesus) over His kingdom (the kingdom of heaven), and you have God the Father over His Kingdom (the Kingdom of God).

If you find the kingdom of heaven, you'll sell everything, because it's worth it.

He gives another parable that likens the kingdom of heaven to a treasure.

> 44 Again, the kingdom of heaven is like unto treasure hid in a field; the which when a man hath found, he hideth, and for joy thereof goeth and selleth all that he hath, and buyeth that field.

That's all He said about it. Do you realize that He just said this is how good the kingdom is? If you find the kingdom of heaven, you'll sell everything, because it's worth it.

> 45 Again, the kingdom of heaven is like unto a merchant man, seeking goodly pearls:
>
> 46 Who, when he had found one pearl of great price, went and sold all that he had, and bought it.

You can tell what these last two parables were all about. They were about selling out to God about everything. In other words, we are to go for it 100 percent and not let anything else get us off track. It's worth it for the kingdom. This actually goes into proving some of the things I've already said.

> 47 Again, the kingdom of heaven is like unto a net, that was cast into the sea, and gathered of every kind:

> 48 Which, when it was full, they drew to shore, and sat down, and gathered the good into vessels, but cast the bad away.

The kingdom of heaven is like a net that has good and bad in it. However, the bad gets cast out of the net (out of the kingdom).

You say, "What's this got to do with anything?" As you move forward, you have to see what Jesus was teaching and what He was proclaiming with an authority, a gravity, and a solemnity that had to be obeyed. You have to see what He was saying and what He was laying out for the people to see as the kingdom that He preached.

The kingdom is why we are here.
We are here to preach the kingdom as Jesus preached it.

We have to walk in fullness, realizing that finally we are coming into the reason why we are here. Everything before the kingdom is not why we are here. Anything outside of the kingdom is not why we are here. The kingdom is why we are here.

> 49 So shall it be at the end of the world: the angels shall come forth, and sever the wicked from among the just,
>
> 50 And shall cast them into the furnace of fire: there shall be wailing and gnashing of teeth.
>
> 51 Jesus saith unto them, Have ye understood all these things? They say unto him, Yea, Lord.

I am guessing here, but it's just hard to believe that they understood all of those things that He said, because this was in Matthew 13, and they still didn't understand a lot of things from Matthew 13 all the way to Matthew 28. They were still lost half the time in their understanding.

None of them just wanted to look stupid. They said, "Oh yeah, Lord, we got it; we got it." When they walked off they probably said, "Did you get that? See if you got what I got. Tell me what you got, and I'll tell you if I got it." It is human nature.

If you're instructed in the kingdom, you'll have understanding.

This is another parable. He says in verse 52,

> 52 Then said he unto them, Therefore every scribe *which is* instructed unto the kingdom of heaven is like unto a man *that is* an householder, which bringeth forth out of his treasure *things* new and old.

Jesus was saying, "If you're instructed in the things of the kingdom of heaven, you are going to be able to bring forth old things and new things. You're going to be able to look into the Old Testament and say, 'That's pointing to this. Yes, look at this. This is a reality. In the Old Testament it was a type and a shadow. That means that it wasn't as good as this.'"

He was saying, "We have the reality, and I can show you how these two fit together. If you're instructed in the kingdom, you'll have that understanding."

Notice, also that the man is likened unto a householder, the owner of a house. What does that mean? It means that the man is likened unto a steward. We will see a parable later that the man is likened as someone that has a responsibility to do something with what he has authority over.

> 53 And it came to pass, *that* when Jesus had finished these parables, he departed thence.

The people in the hometown of Jesus heard the Word, and they got offended.

> 54 And when he was come into his own country, he taught them in their synagogue, insomuch that they were astonished, and said, Whence hath this *man* this wisdom, and *these* mighty works?

Do you see where this event took place? He taught them in their synagogue.

> 55 Is not this the carpenter's son? is not his mother called Mary? and his brethren, James, and Joses, and Simon, and Judas?

Notice: Jesus was the son of the carpenter, Joseph, and Jesus was a carpenter.

> 56 And his sisters, are they not all with us? Whence then hath this *man* all these things?

> 57 And they were offended in him. But Jesus said unto them, A prophet is not without honour, save in his own country, and in his own house.

"And they were offended in Him." This is exactly what I was referring to earlier. Jesus predicted this. He just went in and sowed seed in the synagogue, and they didn't get it, and immediately, they were offended.

The kingdom of heaven in this age is the realm of profession.

> 58 And he did not many mighty works there because of their unbelief.

I said all of that to get to this point: there's a difference between the Kingdom of God and the kingdom of heaven. It's very simple. The kingdom of heaven in this age is the realm of profession. Anybody can enter the kingdom of heaven. If you get this message then you will understand.

This is where the once saved, always saved doctrine and the other doctrine, you can lose your salvation if you have a bad thought, come in. This is what fixes both of those. Both of those are wrong. They're both ditches.

You would say, "Well, he that endures to the end, he shall be saved." Yes, but then it says, "All that call upon the Name of the Lord shall be saved."

"Yes, I was saved at one point, but I'm being saved, and I must end up being saved, but he that endures shall be saved." When you call upon the Name of the Lord, you're saved, but you've still got to endure. It wasn't a one-time deal, just to get your ticket punched and that was it.

The one doctrine, the once saved always saved, is technically, unconditional eternal security. Eternal security is not unconditional. There are conditions to eternal security.

If you just get an idea of God, you will understand that God is a faith God. By that, I mean that He has faith in us more than we do. God says, "I have provided the most amazing opportunity that mankind has ever had." Why would anybody that gets in ever want out? Then, He says, "But, knowing man, some will."

For God to be perfect, He has to put forth a perfect expectation. His perfect expectation is that once you're in, you're in, and you should just move right on. That's what He desires, but we know that there are people that won't do that. The reality of that is the fact that He was able to provide provisions for that.

Hopefully, this is answering some questions and making things come into focus, because we're preaching the Gospel of the Kingdom here.

The kingdom of heaven in this age is the realm of profession, as we just saw in the kingdom parables. It's all about professing and coming into the kingdom, wherein the wheat and the tares (the good and the bad) are in the kingdom of heaven. Do you see that? The good and the bad, the wheat and the tares, are <u>all</u> in the kingdom of heaven.

The Kingdom of God is the realm of God in the vast universe. The kingdom of heaven is only upon this earth.

The Kingdom of God is everywhere. It is this entire universe and any other universe. It goes as far as whatever there is that's out there.

The kingdom of heaven is one part of the Kingdom of God, and it is relegated to the earthly realm at this time.

The kingdom of heaven is only upon this earth. He said, "Thy will be done on earth as it is in heaven." The idea is to make earth look like heaven in all of its actions. The kingdom of heaven is only one part of the universal Kingdom of God. The Kingdom of God is the realm of God in the vast universe.

Texas is one state in the Union. The idea here is that the kingdom of heaven is one part of the Kingdom of God, and it is relegated to the earthly realm at this time.

The church is the wheat part of the kingdom of heaven, and only a part of the true servants of the universal Kingdom of God.

In other words, the tares in the kingdom of heaven, the angels, and other subjects of God in the Kingdom of God are not part of the church.

UNDERSTANDING THE KINGDOMS

"The Kingdom of God is within you."

Let's go to Luke 17. If you were to look for Scripture that would summarize everything that JGLM, this church, or anything else that we are a part of represents, it would be the following verses. Verses 20 and 21 summarize the essence of everything we teach.

Luke 17:20,

> 20 And when he was demanded of the Pharisees, when the Kingdom of God should come, he answered them and said, The Kingdom of God cometh not with observation:

"The Kingdom of God comes not with observation," because it is of the Spirit. The results of the Kingdom of God can be seen, but the Kingdom itself is not seen, because it is spiritual.

> 21 Neither shall they say, Lo here! or, lo there! for, behold, the Kingdom of God is within you.

It talks about us being in the kingdom of heaven, but it talks about the Kingdom of God being in us. There are the two different kingdoms.

When you see this, you begin to realize that the Kingdom of God has invaded this world by being in God's people.

The kingdom of heaven is the demonstration of the Kingdom of God.

The kingdom of heaven is the demonstration of the Kingdom of God, but it's in the realm of profession. In other words, anybody can profess it; anybody can say they're a part of it.

When it comes down to it, how do you know if a person is in the kingdom of heaven or in the Kingdom of God? How do you know they're not just professing? How do you know they actually have it? That's because people in the Kingdom of God are able to put forth their finger and say, "Come out! Be healed!" Wheat can do that; tares can't, because they are of the wicked one.

That is not to say that if you're not flowing or functioning consistently in power that you're not in the Kingdom of God or that you're not born again. I'm not saying that, but I do have to put forth the perfect expectation of God's Word. Otherwise, I'm just a man making excuses like anybody else. If I represent God, I have to say what God has said. God said that if you are a believer, these signs will follow you. It's that simple.

"The Kingdom of God is within you." I don't know of any other Scripture that better encapsulates what we preach as a whole than Luke 17:20-21.

We don't have to call Him down; we don't have to call Him up.

Romans 10:6-8 says,

> 6 But the righteousness which is of faith speaketh on this wise, Say not in thine heart, Who shall ascend into heaven? (that is, to bring Christ down *from above:*)
>
> 7 Or, Who shall descend into the deep? (that is, to bring up Christ again from the dead.)
>
> 8 But what saith it? The word is nigh thee, *even* in thy mouth, and in thy heart: that is, the word of faith, which we preach;

We don't have to call Him down; we don't have to call Him up. Why? That's because He is in us. The word of faith is in our hearts, and in our mouths, which we preach.

Romans 10:10,

> 10 For with the heart man believeth unto righteousness; and with the mouth confession is made unto salvation.

We have an anointing.

We don't have to wait for an anointing; we have an anointing. We are anointed of God. We have that anointing, and it abides within us, which is the Holy Spirit who teaches us all things and leads us into all truth.

What determines the waiting time is how much you've grown up into Him, and the more grown up, the faster things happen.

After the rebellion is put down, the kingdom of heaven will be submerged into the Kingdom of God.

The Kingdom of God on earth now is mainly spiritual and in a sense includes only those who are willingly subject to doing the will of God. The kingdom of heaven takes in those who are not subject to the will of God, in the same sense that any kingdom includes rebels.

God's purpose in establishing the kingdom of heaven and sending His Son with an expeditionary force from heaven to invade the earth was literally to put down rebellion in this earthly part, which is a part of the universal Kingdom of God. Jesus was sent here to put down rebellion.

I'm giving you an overall view—after this is done, the kingdom of heaven will be submerged into the Kingdom of God. At that point He will turn the kingdom of heaven over to God, and it will all become part of the Kingdom of God. The kingdom of heaven will be submerged into the Kingdom of God, and God will become supreme over all, as He was before the rebellion started in the universe.

People say, "But God is God, and He's in control." There is not one verse in the Bible that says that. There is not one verse that says that He is absolutely in control of everything and that everything that happens is His will. It does not say that.

UNDERSTANDING THE KINGDOMS

As in any kingdom, during a rebellion, rebels cannot be considered a part of the kingdom or subjects of the king that they are rebelling against, until they become reconciled or submissive again.

When the Messiah puts down all rebellion and every enemy is destroyed, then everyone in the universe, except the rebels who are confined to external hell (meaning those outside the true Kingdom of God), will be willing subjects of God. God becomes all in all, as He was before the rebellion. The Son will then become subject to the Father, but will continue to reign with the Father forever and ever.

Both the professed sons and the true sons of God are in the kingdom of heaven at this time, and the rest are in the universal Kingdom of God. God recognizes only the true sons of God as being in the Kingdom of God. Do you hear the difference? That is why one must be born again in order to become a willing subject of God and to be a part of His Kingdom.

We are being born again into the Kingdom of God. The natural connotation of that would be the naturalization process of immigration. Adoption is also the same thing. This is why one has to be born again to be in the Kingdom of God. One does not have to be born again to be a part of the kingdom of heaven.

In Matthew Jesus told the Jews at that time, "The kingdom will be taken away from you and will be given to others of a different tongue." Just because you're in the kingdom of heaven doesn't mean that you're going to be there all the time. He very clearly said, "Don't think that just because you have Abraham as your father that you're good and that it is all okay." He said, "God can make sons of Abraham out of these rocks."

There are places, as we mentioned earlier, where the two terms kingdom of heaven and Kingdom of God are used in parallel passages of Scripture. Any time those are used in parallel passages it would be as if I were saying, "I'm in Texas," but then I could also say, "I'm in the United States." However, if I say, "I am in the United States," it doesn't mean that I am saying I'm from any one state. Do you see the difference? It's exactly the same way. The kingdom of heaven is the earthly realm of the Kingdom of God.

Here are some contrasts between the two terms, the kingdom of heaven and the Kingdom of God:

1. The kingdom of heaven has the Messiah as its King. The Kingdom of God has God as its King.

2. The kingdom of heaven is from heaven, under heaven, and upon earth. This is talking about during the millennium. The Kingdom of God is in heaven and over the earth during that time, so there are definite distinctions between the two. Then the kingdom of heaven becomes submerged into the Kingdom of God.

3. The kingdom of heaven is limited in its scope. The Kingdom of God is unlimited.

UNDERSTANDING THE KINGDOMS

4. The kingdom of heaven was technically Jewish, because it was offered to the Jews first, but they rejected it. In this earthly realm, it is still the kingdom of heaven. We have accepted the kingdom of heaven that was offered to the Jews, but we also get born again into the Kingdom of God.

The kingdom of heaven was Jewish and exclusive in its character—the Kingdom of God is universal and inclusive in its character.

The kingdom of heaven is national in its aspect—the Kingdom of God is universal in its aspect.

5. After the Jews rejected the kingdom of heaven, then it went to the Gentiles. Because it went to the Gentiles, it went to every other nation. It wasn't just one nation; it was any nation.

6. The kingdom of heaven is dispensational in its duration or time period. In other words, there is a time when it started and a time when it will end. The Kingdom of God is eternal.

7. The kingdom of heaven includes only a portion of time in eternity. The Kingdom of God includes all time in eternity.

8. The kingdom of heaven had a beginning. The Kingdom of God had no beginning.

9. John the Baptist and then Jesus began to preach or proclaim that the kingdom of heaven was at hand. The kingdom of heaven started at that

point on the earth. The Kingdom of God had no starting point, because it was always with God.

10. All who profess are in the kingdom of heaven in this age. One must be born again to be in the Kingdom of God.

11. The kingdom of heaven comes with an outward show. The Kingdom of God does not come with an outward show. Do you see the difference? These cannot be two terms talking about the same thing, because one comes with an outward show and one does not.

12. The kingdom of heaven is inherited by flesh and blood. The Kingdom of God is not inherited by flesh and blood. They cannot be the same.

13. Men were never told to seek the kingdom of heaven. It was offered, but they were never told to seek it. They were told to seek the Kingdom of God, His rule, and His reign over their lives.

We're not taught to seek the kingdom of heaven, meaning a religio/political rule per se, but we are to seek the Kingdom of God in our hearts. When God rules in our hearts, then whatever we do will have the character of God in it.

You cannot legislate morality. You can legislate to protect the victims of immorality, but you cannot legislate morality. However, if you put righteous men in rule, then the character of God will be seen in the rules and regulations that they legislate.

14. Finally, if you go back to Daniel 2 and 7, you will see that the kingdom of heaven was prophesied for a future time. It was postponed for a time and came back in. The Kingdom of God is now, in the sense that God rules and reigns in and through us now.

Do you see the difference between the two? You say, "Okay, I see the difference," but I don't want to leave you thinking, "Well, that was informational, but it didn't tell me anything. How am I supposed to live?" You do have to go in and study. It took some time for me to study it. When I was studying it out, I had to look at the differences. They are quite different.

The key is to demonstrate God who lives in us.

By demonstrating the Kingdom of God, we will be showing the kingdom of heaven. The kingdom of heaven can be seen, in some sense, as the result of people living in the Kingdom of God. It wasn't that way in the beginning, but it can be now, in the sense that the Kingdom of God has to do with an inner rule. However, the kingdom of heaven has to do more with an outward show of that Kingdom.

That's the reason you can't just accept a person that has power or gifts. You can't just take their word for it, because they can be operating in the kingdom of heaven and not be speaking for God. They can have these things. Then it is up to you to decide. The Bible says that the closer to the end we get, the more there will be lying signs and wonders, so even the tares can be walking in power.

There was a man I heard of who went to prison. He got hold of Kenneth Hagin's sermons, and he started reading them while he was in there. He read them and thought, "This is pretty good stuff." He didn't get born again, but when he got out, he went to preaching and had signs and wonders. Then he started talking about it saying, "This is what I did." He exposed himself, but he was really exposing the spiritual blindness that was in the church. He talked about how all of these other churches would invite him in. He said, "They never knew I wasn't born again." They never knew it.

We cannot go just by signs and wonders. We should have signs and wonders, don't get me wrong, but signs are to follow believers; believers shouldn't follow signs. We have to recognize that and always know that what we do, we do because we love God and want to help people, not just to have a sign and wonder. Amen.

"Father,

"We thank you for clarity and understanding, and Father we desire to see your Kingdom advanced. Father, in Jesus' name, let this understanding settle into the peoples' minds, let them get a clear understanding of it, and let them see that the kingdom comes with power, and that it is to set the captive free.

"Our job here, at this point in time, is to exercise Your authority and Your power, to set the captives free, to heal the sick, cast out devils, and raise the dead. Father, we know that there's coming a time when this kingdom will be submerged into Your overall Kingdom, and there will be no need for power, no need for healings, and no need for deliverances.

"At that point, our opportunity to share in that part of Your work will be over, so we thank You that now is our time to work. While we're in this world, we are the light of the world, and we thank You for it.

"We thank You for bodies healed and blind eyes opened. We thank You for sickness and diseases eradicated. Father, we thank You, and we bless You for it. In the name of Jesus, we thank You that the Kingdom of God is within us. It is with us, and it goes everywhere we go, at all times. Father, we thank You that the Kingdom is always nigh at hand. In the name of Jesus. Amen."

KEYS OF THE KINGDOM

Sermon given by Curry R. Blake

**Jesus came to introduce God to us
and to create a relationship between God and man.**

When Jesus came, He did not come to start a religion. He came to introduce God to us, and to create the relationship between God and man in the same way that He had a relationship with His heavenly Father. If you go back and look at the Garden of Eden, there was no religious aspect to it. It was just man walking with God.

Religion didn't come in until later on, and even then, it wasn't religion. It was simply because man messed up, and there were certain things that had to be done because of the mess up. Man took those rituals and turned them into a religion, thinking that doing those rituals would make him right with God. It didn't. If it had, Jesus wouldn't have had to come.

We are going to look at what Jesus preached and what He talked about. Some of the things that we are going to talk about, I have already mentioned, but I really want to be able to bring it to you in a slightly different way than I did before.

In the last session, we were talking about "Understanding the Kingdoms" and we were talking about the differences between the kingdom of heaven and the Kingdom of God. There are overlaps, so you really have to look at all of it together to really see the whole picture. We did it in one session. Very seldom do you do justice to any biblical truth in one session, but we took the best shot at it that we could. We're going to be talking about this off and on, as the Lord directs.

In this session we're going to be looking at another aspect of the Kingdom, and I'm going to try to tie two things together. I really feel that the Spirit of God is bringing this out. Just remember: sometimes true ministry doesn't always look polished; everything doesn't always fit together just like you want.

War a good warfare with prophecies.

For years, I was right on the verge of actually doing something the Bible says not to do in this particular area. Specifically, the Scripture says, "Despise not prophesying." I was right on that verge, because I'd seen so much of the "flake" and the "fake" that I had just gotten to a point where I said, "I don't care. I'll just avoid it altogether." I was at the point where I was ready to start despising prophesying because of the way I saw it.

Then, I was blessed, because I was actually called to minister out in Santa Maria, California, and there was a man there who truly operates as a prophet. My daughter was with me and we were in one of the front rows. I had never met him before; he didn't know any details.

I'm sure there were some things he could have found out by way of the internet and by reading our webpage, but a lot of things he spoke over us he couldn't have read.

He actually called both of us up front. They had a group there, kind of a presbytery, and they began speaking into our lives. They gave my daughter a specific word. Actually, several other people operated prophetically there, also.

At that time, my son and daughter-in-law were about to have their first child and they were going to name him Josiah. This prophet was giving me a word, which I didn't ask for. I've never pursued or gone to somebody and asked, "Do you have a word for me?" I have never done that. I am like Dr Sumrall was. People would always come to him and say, "I have a word for you from the Lord." He would say, "Well, if you know Him so well, you go do the word." He said, "God knows where I live. He can talk to me if He wants to." He didn't let just anybody walk up and start saying things to him.

When we were there, they began speaking into our lives. This prophet spoke to me and said, "I am bringing you a Josiah generation." As I said, my son and his wife had just found out that their child was going to be a boy, and they were going to name him Josiah. This prophet had no way of knowing this, because I had just heard it myself. When he spoke that, I perked up. I thought, "Okay, he's hitting pretty close here." He began to proceed and actually spoke for some time.

One good thing about that particular group is that they're always ready with some type of recorder, and they record. They're very adamant about recording prophetic words, because they don't believe in people just saying things. They believe that you ought to be able to go back, listen to them, and check them.

One of the things that Paul told Timothy was to pay attention to the prophecies that had been put out upon him. He was told to war a good warfare with the prophecies that had been given. Honestly, I've been around a lot of Christians, and most Christians don't know how to war a good warfare with prophecies.

I had to study the prophecy out, and then I started doing some research. I asked God about it, and He said, "This is what I meant."

Some prophecies are just going to come to pass, but some of them are conditional. In some of them there are aspects where you do this, and then God does that, and until you do this, God doesn't do that.

There are aspects of prophecy that you have to judge.

The Bible says in the New Testament that we are to judge the words of a prophet or of prophecies that come forward. We're not supposed to take them just as they are. We are to judge them. I wouldn't say to analyze them, but check them out. Make sure that they line up with

Scripture. We started doing that, and in many ways, prophecy was the foundation of this ministry.

Back in 1934, Dr. Lake gave a prophecy and that prophecy is the reason I am in the position I am in today. Dr. Lake's family had heard the prophecy. We made contact with them, and eventually, they decided that I was the person that this prophecy was talking about. The very reason I am in this ministry is because of a prophetic word, yet for years, like I said, I was on the verge of despising prophesying. You can see the work of the enemy there, trying to take us away from it.

We've always been sticklers for the Word and making sure that what we say lines up with Scripture and keeping it on Scripture. You can fall into a ditch on either side. You can either become so "pseudo-prophetic" that you get weird and just say anything, or you can say, "Next week is going to be a bigger prophecy than last week." Then you have a stack of prophecies that never come to pass and nobody judges them.

You can say whatever you want to say in the church today and nobody will call you on it, or you can go to the other side and just get so legalistic and dead that the Spirit of God can hardly even move in your midst. We don't want to be in either ditch. We want to make sure that we are in the middle. We want to be right where God wants us.

I want to show you a couple of things here, and we're still going to be talking about the Kingdom. It is a high privilege to pastor this fellowship and to pastor people around the world. It's a high privilege, but it's also a great responsibility. I hear from people all the time saying, "Your teaching on this has changed my life." I hear people say, "We've taken this teaching, and we're doing this."

I recognize that the words that come out of my mouth alter people's destinies, and so I'm very cognizant of what I say. I'm very aware, and I always want to make sure that I am right, not for the sake of being right, but because I just don't want to lead anybody off in a direction that is not right. Therefore, I'm very careful about things.

In saying that, if you're hitched to this wagon, then where I go, you go. That's another reason why I'm so careful about where I go, because I want to make sure that I don't take you somewhere you don't need to go. In these prophetic words, if they were spoken to me and they're accurate from God, by the Spirit of God, then because of that and because of where I'm going, as I said, you will go, too.

I think it only right that you should know some of the things that have been said and put forth, so I'm going to bring some of those things out. They directly tie in with what we're talking about right now and what we have talked about.

Go to Matthew chapter 13. We are talking about the "Keys of the Kingdom," so we're obviously going to Matthew 13, and then we're going to go to Matthew 16. In Matthew chapter 13, we'll start with verse 10.

> 10 And the disciples came, and said unto him, Why speakest thou unto them in parables?
>
> 11 He answered and said unto them, Because it is given unto you to know the mysteries of the kingdom of heaven, but to them it is not given.
>
> 12 For whosoever hath, to him shall be given, and he shall have more abundance: but whosoever hath not, from him shall be taken away even that he hath.

Notice, He had been speaking to the people, but He was speaking in parables.

It is not given to them to know the mysteries of the kingdom of heaven.

He said in Matthew 13:13-14,

> 13 Therefore speak I to them in parables: because they seeing see not; and hearing they hear not, neither do they understand.
>
> 14 And in them is fulfilled the prophecy of Esaias, which saith, By hearing ye shall hear, and shall not understand; and seeing ye shall see, and shall not perceive:

He even said that, in hearing, they wouldn't hear and in seeing, they wouldn't see; they would not perceive. He was saying, "I'm putting it out there, but they're not getting it."

It is given unto you to know
the mysteries of the kingdom of heaven.

Matthew 13:10-11, says,

> 10 And the disciples came, and said unto him, Why speakest thou unto them in parables?
>
> 11 He answered and said unto them, Because it is given unto you to know the <u>mysteries</u> of the kingdom of heaven, but to them it is not given.

The disciples had come to Him asking, "Why are you talking in parables?" He said, "Because it is not given to them to know the mysteries of the kingdom of heaven, but to you it is. You are to know the mysteries of the kingdom of heaven."

The word, *"mysteries,"* in verse 11 is from the Greek word *mustērion*. It literally means *something hidden*. It means *hidden in terms of a secret*. It even talks about being initiated into something that is a secret. Those are just different ideas of the mysteries.

In a previous session, we ministered on Paul's revelation, which was the mystery of the ages. I want to be very distinct. Here, Jesus was telling Peter and the disciples that there were mysteries, plural, of the kingdom of heaven that they should know. The amazing thing is that He talked about all of these mysteries right in the next few passages. He talked about what we call the kingdom of heaven parables. He gave all of these mysteries and laid them out.

These mysteries were not the mystery that Paul said had been hidden from the beginning of the ages. Remember: they are two separate things.

The one mystery that Paul talks about is the mystery of the ages, which is "Christ in you, the Hope of glory." Without that mystery, there is no Church. We also look at these mysteries of the kingdom, and we know that if you are in the Church, you're in the Kingdom.

The kingdom of heaven is something you can see, but the Kingdom of God is something you cannot see.

The Kingdom of God is said to be within you. The kingdom of heaven is something you can see, but the Kingdom of God is something you cannot generally see, but you can see the results of it. I would almost say that the Kingdom of God is in you, and the kingdom of heaven is the physical representation of the Kingdom of God that is in you. I wouldn't want to make that a doctrine, but it's close to being an accurate way of saying it.

Jesus talked about these mysteries of the Kingdom, and I will be reading some things to you about these mysteries.

I have been looking at this over the last couple of weeks, but last night, it all came together. My wife stood and looked at me several times, and she asked, "Okay, what's going on?" I said, "I'm getting this; I'm seeing this!"

As I was going back and looking at this, she started trying to talk to me, and I said, "Hang on." She said, "Hello. You're not even here, are you? You're not even here." That was because I was, as we would say, "Getting a download." It was just coming, and as it came, I was just thinking, "Okay. That fits with this and that goes there."

All of a sudden, it was like, "Okay, I need to get a Bible. I need to start going through this." I got my I-Pad and started looking up Scriptures. Then, I took my physical Bible and started going through different Scriptures. I started seeing these prophecies that had been given to us. Some of them go way back, but the ones that I'm specifically referring to right now go back to 2003.

You can see how some are coming to pass right now. Some have already come to pass, and then there are some that are coming to pass, yet there are parts of it that are still for the future. You can tell it's for the future, but it's all happening. That's why I want you to know what's going on, because this will help you to know where we're going.

One of the things that I really don't like to do is get into a car and have someone take me somewhere without telling me where. I ask, "Where are we going?" They say, "We're just going somewhere." I ask, "Well, how long is it going to take?" They say, "Well, it won't take long." That tells me absolutely nothing. I hate sitting in the back of a car or in the passenger seat and wondering where we are going. Tell me where we are going. I don't even care if I don't know where it is; just tell me where we're going.

I want to know my destination. I want to know where I'm headed; that's just my personality. I'm trying to tell you, ahead of time, where we're headed so that you can get an idea. If you know where you are and you know where you're going, you have a pretty good idea of how to get there. If not, you can usually figure it out. That's what we're going to do in this session.

In Matthew 13:10-11, He told them, "Unto you it is given to know the mysteries," plural, "of the kingdom of heaven, but to them it is not given."

Go to Matthew 16:13. It starts with what Jesus was asking His disciples:

> 13 When Jesus came into the coasts of Caesarea Philippi, he asked his disciples, saying, Whom do men say that I the Son of man am?
>
> 14 And they said, Some *say that thou art* John the Baptist: some, Elias; and others, Jeremias, or one of the prophets.

Jesus asked His disciples, "Whom do men say that I the Son of man am?" They said, "Some say that thou art John the Baptist." It could have been a real trick, because they were both in the same place at the River Jordan.

> 15 He saith unto them, But whom say ye that I am?

He was saying, "Who do you say I am? I hear you saying what they say, but who do you say I am?"

The first revelation that Jesus was the Christ, the Son of the living God:

> 16 And Simon Peter answered and said, Thou art the Christ, the Son of the living God.
>
> 17 And Jesus answered and said unto him, <u>Blessed</u> art thou, Simon Barjona: for flesh and blood hath not revealed *it* unto thee, but my Father which is in heaven.

Peter was the first one to answer. He said, "Thou art the Christ, the Son of the living God." Jesus looked at him and said, *"Blessed* art thou." The word *"blessed,"* means *spiritually prosperous*. He called him Simon Barjona. The word *"Barjona"* means *son of Jonas;* his father's name was Jonah.

Jesus said, "Simon Barjona, you are blessed (you are spiritually prosperous), because flesh and blood has not revealed this to you." In other words, you didn't figure this out. He said, "…but my Father which is in heaven." This is the first revelation, so to speak, where we see a reference to Jesus being the Christ, the Son of the living God, spoken by somebody other than Jesus.

Jesus was saying, "I'm going to build My Church upon this revelation of Who I am."

> 18 And I say also unto thee, That thou art Peter, and upon this rock I will build my church; and the gates of hell shall not prevail against it.

Notice, Jesus was talking to Peter here. The word *"Peter"* in the Greek is the word *petros,* and it means *a piece of a larger rock.* One translation even says, *"...a pebble,"* and another one says, *"...a stone."* Here He was saying, "I say unto thee, that thou art Peter, and you are a piece of a larger rock," and then He said, "...and upon this *rock* I will build my Church."

Now, the word for *"rock"* there is the word *petra* and it means *the larger mass of rock.* What He was saying was, "Upon this rock (larger mass), of which you are a piece (smaller piece of this larger mass)..." Notice what He said, "...and upon this rock (larger mass), I will build my Church, and the gates of hell shall not prevail against it."

You have to realize what He was talking about here. He was talking about this revelation of Jesus being the Son of the living God and that Jesus was the Christ. He was saying, "That's the revelation."

Jesus didn't say, "I'm going to build my church on you, Peter." That's not what He was talking about. He was saying, "What I'm going to build my Church on is the fact that my Father reveals to people who I am, the revelation that I am the Christ, the Son of the living God."

That is the basis of the Church. I know that's not revelation to you; it was at one time, but it's not now.

Jesus said, "I will give you the keys of the kingdom of heaven."

In verse 19 He says,

> 19 And I will give unto thee the keys of the kingdom of heaven: and whatsoever thou shalt bind on earth shall be bound in heaven: and whatsoever thou shalt loose on earth shall be loosed in heaven.

"I will give you the keys of the kingdom." What kingdom? It was talking about the kingdom of heaven. It has a lot to do with the visible kingdom on this earth. He said, "I'm going to give you some keys that are going to open up certain things. They are going to allow things to be seen here, physically.

Remember, He said, "The kingdom of heaven is at hand," and He said, "Go and preach the Gospel of the kingdom of heaven, and when you go and preach, you say, 'The kingdom is at hand, and heal the sick, raise the dead, and cast out devils.'" Here He was saying, "I'm giving you keys that will allow these manifestations."

**The keys of the kingdom of heaven
have to do with binding and loosing.**

After that, He says, "Because of that revelation, I am going to give unto you the keys, plural, of the kingdom of heaven." Watch what these keys are going to do: "And whatsoever thou shalt bind on earth shall be bound in heaven." These keys have to do with binding things on earth. One translation even says, going back to the original Greek, "You will bind and anything you bind will have already been bound in heaven."

I've heard that preached a lot of different ways, but you have to realize that your Heavenly Father knows what you have need of before you ask. Whenever you bind something and it says it's already bound, it doesn't mean that you're finding what is bound. There would be a truth to that, but He was saying, "By the time you ask, it's already done, because your Heavenly Father already knows what you need. You're just making the requisition and Heaven has already granted it."

This is where I actually got the idea that I tell people, "When a son of God speaks, heaven hears and agrees, and hell hears and obeys." This is the verse that I got that from.

Matthew 16:19 says, "And whatsoever thou shalt bind on earth shall be bound in heaven: and whatsoever thou shalt loose on earth shall be loosed in heaven." You will notice that this is in the exact same Scripture where it talks about these keys, so the keys of the kingdom of heaven have to do with binding and loosing and have to do with you being in contact with heaven and heaven backing you up so that what is seen on the earth is representative of heaven.

The keys of the kingdom of heaven have to do with binding and loosing, but that means allowing and forbidding things to happen.

If you have the keys of the kingdom of heaven, then you can open things that are locked.

Remember the term, "mysteries;" remember the term, "keys." Think of this: a key is something that opens something that is locked. We know that keys throughout history have represented that one main thing, but usually they represent some form of authority. If they give you the key to the city, there is some privilege or benefit, and it represents some form of authority.

If you have the keys of the kingdom of heaven, then you have some type of authority in the kingdom of heaven, and that means that you can open things that are locked.

This goes right back to what we talked about before. Things that are locked tend to be mysteries to us. That's exactly what it goes back to when it talks about mysteries. It was saying that these things are hidden, they're secret.

We see that in Matthew 13 where Jesus spoke to them in parables. He said, "The reason I speak in parables is because these things are hidden. They're locked away from these people, but they are given to you so that you might understand the mysteries of these things that are locked."

Jesus told the disciples: "You understand who I am, but these people don't know who I am." At the beginning of these passages, He asked, "Who do they say that I am?" The disciples said, "Well, some say that

You are John the Baptist." John the Baptist was a prophet. "And some say Elias, and others Jeremias, or one of the prophets." What did the people think? They weren't coming to him to be healed because He was the Christ. They were coming to Him, because they saw that a great prophet had arisen in Israel, which is exactly what it says about Him in one place. They had this idea that He was a prophet, but they did not have an understanding of who He was.

His disciples knew Him. They started seeing Who He was. They said, "You're somebody different. You are the Messiah. We believe that; we're staking everything on You. We've already been run out of the temple; we can't go in there and worship anymore, because they know that we follow You. Every time we go in there, You heal somebody and then they run us out."

This idea that they had was this knowledge of the mysteries. This is one of the mysteries, and because of that, the mysteries were opened, and they could understand the other mysteries of the kingdom of heaven. These keys opened things.

Let's go on. I'm going to read, and then I'm going to come back to these keys. Remember the keys of the kingdom, and remember the keys and mysteries. Remember those two words.

Then in verse 20,

> 20 Then charged he his disciples that they should tell no man that he was Jesus the Christ.

That verse proves that Jesus didn't go around healing just to prove He was the Christ, because He just said, "Don't go and tell anybody I'm the Christ." Even demons said, "You're the Christ, you're the Son of the living God." The demons realized that Jesus was the Christ before some of these disciples did. He told them, "Hold your peace," because He didn't want them to tell who He was.

Jesus was not healing to prove who He was. He was healing because of compassion. He was healing because of who He was—not to prove who He was. Now, remember that.

> 21 From that time forth began Jesus to shew unto his disciples, how that he must go unto Jerusalem, and suffer many things of the elders and chief priests and scribes, and be killed, and be raised again the third day.

Jesus told them these things from Matthew 16 on. Matthew has 28 chapters, so more than halfway through, they found out who He was. From that point on, He started saying, "Here's the plan: I've got to go, I've got to suffer, I've got to die, and I've got to be raised." He pointblank told them that. Even after He died and was resurrected, many of them didn't even believe that He was raised from the dead.

If His ministry lasted from three to four years, based on the chronology of it, then somewhere between a year and a half to two years is probably when He told them this. For a year and a half they had time to think about it, hear about it, and ask questions about it. Yet, even after it happened, they were all hiding and thinking, "What are we going to do now? Our Rabbi, our Master is gone."

Then, Jesus showed up and asked, "Why do you doubt?" Think about that. You're not as bad off as you thought. They were with Him, and they had those kinds of thoughts. You think, "Why is God allowing this?" or "Why is that happening?" You're not that much different from them, and they had a lot of personal contact with Jesus. He was physically in their presence. Don't be too hard on yourself when you ask questions like that.

Jesus showed the disciples that
He must be killed and raised again on the third day.

> 22 Then Peter took him, and began to rebuke him, saying, Be it far from thee, Lord: this shall not be unto thee.

"Then Peter took Him, and began to rebuke Him." Notice: as soon as He started talking about being killed and raised, Peter rebuked him. Imagine rebuking Jesus.

> 23 But he turned, and said unto Peter, Get thee behind me, Satan: thou art an offence unto me: for thou savourest not the things that be of God, but those that be of men.

Now, that's strong language. Jesus just turned around, and said, "Get behind me, Satan." Satan means adversary. He said, "Get behind me. You're an offence to me." Why? That's because Peter was trying to convince Jesus that He didn't have to go and die.

If you know your purpose and someone tries to tell you that is not your purpose, it offends you. That's the reason you have to make sure that you don't offend someone by telling them, "You'll never amount to anything; there's no hope for you." Believe me, if there's breath, there's hope.

Jesus said, "Thou art an offence unto me because you savor not the things that be of God, but those that be of men." Peter had just said, "You are the Christ, the Son of the living God." That was a revelation from God, a revelation that nobody else had at that time, except for the demons who knew it.

Imagine here: Peter had just given this great revelation, this great statement, and then Jesus said, "I'm going to build my church on this revelation of who I am." Then Jesus turned around, and Peter said, "No, it's not going to happen that way, Lord. We're not going to let you die," and Jesus said, "Get behind me, Satan, because you're not thinking like God. You're thinking like man."

Just because someone gets a revelation does not mean that the way they think about everything is right.

Here was this man that had just received a great revelation one minute, and the next minute he was operating totally carnal, totally after the things of the flesh.

I'm just trying to show you that you can have great revelation, you can have great victories, you can have great faith for things, and yet, in a moment, in a second of time, switch and be thinking carnal.

You shouldn't always take as gospel every word that comes out of somebody's mouth, because one minute they could be talking about revelation, and the next minute they could be trying to figure out revelation from a carnal mindset and give you a totally wrong conclusion.

I've read books where the people laying down their argument seemed so right on, and I thought, "Yes, this is good, this is good." However, after laying all of the pieces out and putting the puzzle together, the conclusion was so far off, that I started thinking, "How did they get that? How did one plus one equal sixteen? How did they do that?" They were just that far off.

It shows that you can get revelation and truth of the Word of God, and yet, in a split second, because of previous teaching, you can think wrong and put a wrong connotation to it or come to a wrong conclusion. Just because you got a revelation that does not mean that the way you think about everything is right. You can still think carnal. That's why our minds have to be renewed in every area, and every area has to work together with the others. That's one of the main things.

We ought to be able to take apart and put back together anything we say, and it ought to line up and not violate any principles. That's the

Word of God—the Word of God fits together seamlessly, regardless of what topic you're talking about.

If you are on the topic of healing and you're talking about healing in the Atonement, and then you talk about God not healing a person because of this thing in his or her life, those two cannot sit together. You are violating the very basic principle of the Word of God.

Jesus said unto his disciples, "If any *man* will come after me, let him deny himself, and take up his cross, and follow me."

> 24 Then said Jesus unto his disciples, If any *man* will come after me, let him deny himself, and take up his cross, and follow me.

The disciples knew that if they took up their cross, the end was going to be death. Leonard Ravenhill used to say, "One thing for sure, when you saw a man carrying a cross out of Jerusalem, you knew he wasn't coming back." Think about that. When Jesus talked about taking up one's cross, that's what they knew. He was saying, "You're taking up My path, and it leads to one place—death to yourself." In other words, "You will not come back this way again."

> 25 For whosoever will save his life shall lose it: and whosoever will lose his life for my sake shall find it.
>
> 26 For what is a man profited, if he shall gain the whole world, and lose his own soul? Or what shall a man give in exchange for his soul?

27 For the Son of man shall come in the glory of his Father with his angels; and then he shall reward every man according to his works.

Notice His words. When Jesus returns is when He will bring His rewards. Healing isn't a reward. Jesus is going to bring His reward with Him to give to every man according to his works when He returns. Anything you see in life is not a reward. There is an aspect of sowing and reaping, but let's get specific. Anybody can sow and reap.

28 Verily I say unto you, There be some standing here, which shall not taste of death, till they see the Son of man coming in his kingdom.

I want you to hear some of these prophetic words that have been given, because I want you to see what is going on, even in what we're doing here now and what we've been doing here for almost a year now. It is an answer to some prophetic words, some of which I had not recognized until now.

Some of these things aren't written down, but some of them are in the back of the DHT manual. You can go in and read them there. I'm going to tell you about two that we don't have written down. We'll get them transcribed, because we do have them on tape.

Prophecy by woman in South Africa:

One was by a woman that was in South Africa the last time we were there. We were in the church that John Lake founded in 1908. I had been there several times before, and after a service, we went into a backroom to have a meeting, and we had lunch back there.

There was a woman who came up; we had run into her a time or two. She was a sweet lady, but we didn't know how prophetic she was. After we finished eating, she came up and said, "I've got a word for you." I was acting like Dr. Sumrall, and I said, "Okay. You talk and we'll see. I'll judge it, and we'll go from there."

She began talking and she began laying these things out. My wife actually got her phone out and recorded it. I will show you why I tie this into what's going on right now, because we talked about this last week.

In this prophecy she said, "I see you going into a room and opening this old chest." It was like the type that they used to carry. They called them steamer trunks, back in the day. They would use those huge trunks to travel with.

She said, "I see you opening this old chest and pulling out these clothes that were very neatly folded. They were all really old, but they were perfectly folded, perfectly clean, and pure white. You were taking these old clothes out, but they looked brand new." She said, "As you were taking these clothes out, you were putting them up to these people. You were helping people get dressed in these old, old white clothes."

As I was looking at this, I started thinking of all these things together. She said, "There are things that you're bringing out." She also said, "You had two keys that you were using to open this trunk." As I was looking at this prophecy, I began to see what had been going on.

Last week we talked about the kingdom, and how Jesus said that every scribe that is instructed in the kingdom of heaven brings forth treasures both old and new.

Matthew 13:52:

> 52 Then said he unto them, Therefore every scribe *which is* instructed unto the kingdom of heaven is like unto a man *that is* an householder, which bringeth forth out of his treasure *things* new and old.

All of these things started coming together. There were more things to the prophecy with details, but essentially, that was the prophecy that she had.

Prophecy by David Wagner:

A couple of months later, I went over to a meeting in Denver, Colorado. We were having our JGLM Board of Directors meeting for the year. Most of my directors lived there in the Denver area, so I went up there, and we spent a full week in one of our director's home. We would get up in the morning, start talking, and talk until evening. We went over things that God was doing and where He was taking JGLM. It was really a great time just to fellowship.

One night they said, "The church that we've been working with is having a meeting on a weekend, and the speaker's name is David Wagner. He is known for being a prophet." I had never heard of him; I didn't know anything about him.

We went into the meeting and we got the entire JGLM board of directors in two pews. We were sitting right in the center, but back a few rows. This man, David Wagner, started to minister. Finally, he said, "I understand that we have the John G. Lake Ministries' Board of Directors here." I don't know where he got the information or who told him, but he said, "Alright, if I could just get all of you to come forward."

We had been in places where people who knew us would call us out. They would call us out, lay hands on us, and try to give us a double portion of something, or they would try to give us the new mantle of John Lake. They would do all kinds of different of things.

Have you heard of "guilt by association?" A lot of times it is "photo-op by association." They will call you out, so they can say, "Yes, I laid hands on him. Miracles happened after I laid hands on him." That kind of thing goes on where people want to be seen as somebody who helped start something. I'm just not big on that.

I remember I was sitting on the very end, and my wife was sitting next to me. We had all of our Board of Directors there, and as I've said before, "I can be extremely stubborn. It's called 'sanctified perseverance' now, but it was 'stubborn' when I was younger."

David Wagner said, "Would all of you come up; everybody come on up here." I was just sitting there, and they all looked at me. I was like, "I am not going up. I'm not going to do it." The pastor was there on the other side, and he turned around and looked at me, and I looked at him. I was like, "I'm not getting up there; I'm not going to do it." I don't know if you realize how awkward that can be. Again, he said, "Yes, if you all can just come right up here and stand." You know, 30 seconds of silence is long.

He just stood there for a few seconds, and nobody was moving. I was looking around at all of my Board of Directors, and they were looking at me like, "Are we going to go up?" and I was thinking, "Nope, we're not going up; not going to do it." There was a long silence.

You can tell a lot about a person by how they handle things like that. He stood there for a few seconds, saying, "Yes, just the JGLM Board of Directors; if you will, just come right up here; come right up front here, because I have a word for you." I was thinking, "Nope, not moving. If you are really of God, you would know that. You would know how I am, and you would know that I am not moving." It wasn't comfortable for anybody, especially for him I'm sure, but it wasn't comfortable for me either.

We were sitting there, and I remembered what Dr. Sumrall said. He said, "If God gives you a word, you have to give it." He said, "You have to, and if it doesn't work the way you want it to, you will find a way to deliver that word, because you have to. The word is there, and it will be on you until you do give it." I was still just sitting there.

Then, he walked down the aisle right next to me. I had never met him, but he walked right up next to me.

I also don't like for people to just walk up and lay their hands on me. It is an act of submission for you to allow someone to lay hands on you. I will "defer one to another," but I'm very careful about submitting to another. If I don't know you, and if I submit to you laying hands on me, then that gives you permission to put into me whatever you've got, and if I don't know you, I may not want what you have. That's why I'm very careful about who I allow to lay hands on me in that type of situation.

I know we train people to go into all the world and lay hands on the sick everywhere. You say, "Well, what if they are as picky as you?" Then they probably wouldn't be sick either, and they wouldn't need your hands. We understand that the people we lay hands on don't always understand in regard to transference or inputting.

I was sitting there thinking, "We're really going to find out if he's of God, because if he comes and puts his hands on me, I'm probably going to get up and walk out." I am not going to say I'm stubborn, but I held my ground. He walked over, and I could tell he was about to lay hands on me. He said, "The Lord says," and then he stepped back.

He didn't touch me, which was the first sign that this guy might actually hear from God. He began to prophesy, and he said, "I see you. You're supposed to be writing some books," and he mentioned these five books. I thought, "Okay," because I had heard of these books from this other prophet from five years before that.

He said, "These books are going to bring forth these two keys." I had heard about these two keys just a couple of months before that from this other lady, so God was putting all of this out there.

Then, I began to listen, thinking, "Okay, this guy could be for real." He went through this whole thing, and he said, "These keys are going to open this up and bring forth revelation. You're going to look at this, and you're going to think, 'Can this be true?' You're going to bring revelation out." There are a lot more details to it, like I said, but I don't have it written down. I will get it transcribed and written down, and then I will put it out.

After he finished, he went back up to the front, and he said, "Now, we're going to begin to minister." He said, "If you need healing, or if you need something different, come forward." It was very awkward, because I never really acknowledged anything. I just sat there and listened to what was going on.

He started to minister to people, and he had an amazing graciousness in him. He even called my name and said, "If I can, I'm going to get Brother Blake to come up and help me minister healing."

Very honestly, if somebody had just done that to me, I probably wouldn't have invited them up to help me minister healing, but he did. When I got up there, he handed me the microphone, and said, "Would you pray for these people?" I said, "Yes, but before I do, I want you all to know this man is of God. I want you to know that when I sat there, I wasn't trying to be rude, or mean, or anything," and I told them some things. I said, "This is the way I was raised, spiritually."

I told them who I had studied under, and I told them how we did things. I said, "Very honestly, the way he handled that proved to me that he was of God, because he didn't lay hands on me, and he didn't do certain other things, yet he had to get that word out."

He was standing there saying, "Yes," and started laughing. I said, "So he did. He found a way to get it out, even though I didn't come forward and didn't do what he wanted me to do. He still had to deliver that word." I said, "It was right," and I went through all of these things. I said, "What he has said is exactly right. He hears from God," and I told them about the details of the lady in South Africa. I was basically just verifying his whole ministry.

Prophecy to Curry Blake by Bishop Bill Hamon:

I want to show you the following prophecy that was given to me before those other two prophecies were given. I'm not going to read all of it, but I am going to read the parts that apply now.

First he said,

> *"Son, you have some things set before Me that have been a cry in your heart for a number of years that you have not voiced or shared*

> with other people, but you are going to begin to see that the answers that I have for you are going to become a real living revelation to you. You have had a measure of revelation, even in healing, but I am taking you to deeper places of revelation that is even going to begin to blow your mind.
>
> "But as it comes forth you are going to say, "God, this is what I have been crying out for. This is what I have been looking for." And even as the books are written, each will be a piece to the puzzle that you are trying to solve."

Here he was talking about these books that I'm supposed to be writing.

Now think about that. Only God can say that you're going to write books and that each book is going to be a piece of puzzle that you're trying to solve. That shows that the books are going to be by revelation and not by knowledge, per se.

He said,

> "You have been putting together here and pieces together there. You'll begin to see the pieces all coming together in greater unity. And even as you step out into deeper places of healing and step into places where you will see even more people raised from the dead just by you walking past them.
>
> "Son, there are also some relational things that you've set before me that I am going to begin to resurrect from those dead places and

bring into a place of life and purpose and destiny in Me and even those people that you thought would never come into the Kngdom will come in and they will even work alongside of you, those who many years ago did not understand what you were doing; they turned and walked away. This is the day of reconciliation, this the day of restitution, this is the day where you will begin to see them coming back to you, repenting for their attitude and repenting for the fact that they misunderstood and they will ask you to mentor them and to train and equip them."

This part of the prophecy relates to the prophecy that Dr. Lake gave. One of the things that Dr. Lake said was that we would not be understood or accepted by our brethren and that we would be rejected by our brethren. We have seen clear cases of that; we have seen outright, blatant rejections. I want to say that it is almost like being ignored in a way, but it is the fulfillment of prophecy. It's hard to get offended if it's fulfillment of prophecy.

"Son, you will raise up many people who will be the reproducers of reproducers and you will see that the work will be a quick work and it will be an even quicker work than you have had to labor to do because you have ploughed the ground and made the way and now is the time for that next generation to step in."

Years ago, a word was given that one of the reasons why God chose us was because we would raise our children correctly, and even though we buried one physical child, God would bring forth spiritual children, and even spiritual grandchildren into our ministry, so a lot of this goes together.

> *"Even as your grandchildren begin to step into places of healing, you will see healing and deliverance and great victory, even in nations, will come forth from the words of your grandchildren because of the anointing upon them will be more than double of what is upon you. It will be greater than even you would envision. But Son, it will be greater than all that you have ever wanted.*
>
> *"'For surely,' says the Lord, 'Son, this is a season, a time that you are coming into that you are going to reap the harvest of seeds that you have sown in your late teens and early twenties.' The roots of the seeds that you have sown have grown and become this huge thing and it is a blessing that is not only going to impact you in your soul, mind and spirit. I see it being something that will restore the energy and restore the things in the areas where you may have grown tired. Part of the benefit and the reaping of the harvest that you are getting is a physical reaping even in your body's rejuvenation but also where you have seen miracles with people in the physical realm and have seen miracles happen before your eyes."*

All of this is going to be increasing, and we are going to see rejuvenation.

The prophecy continued:

"The Lord says, 'Son, I'm going to supernaturally bring money and finances into your life.' I see someone coming into your life that is of great financial stature who will connect with your ministry and your call and your purpose and your plan. He will know the root of what you're trying to do in the ministry and the obedience that you walk in with the Father. The Lord says, 'Son, this person is going to be someone that supports you in whatever you need.' I see checks after checks being written, finances being there.

"The Lord says, 'Son, I am opening new doors for your family, even as your family starts to travel more and more with you.' The Lord says, 'Son, I am bringing a new, deeper, fresh relationship between your family, and what is going to happen.' I see a zeal within your children rising up, a passion to receive that double portion anointing, and the plowing, and to see their eyes being opened to the sacrifices you have made throughout your life where you have set things aside, where you have wanted different things at different times and you said, 'Lord, I receive your will and I am going to be obedient to You no matter what is I set aside right now.'

"I see your family's appreciation growing for seeing your sacrifices and what it is you have given up and sacrificed. Even though you have done that since you were a teen, this is the time when you are going to reap the harvest, not only financially but physically and relationally with your family. I see where there have been estrangement between family members where they have had questions and the answers have not been right according to what they wanted to hear.

> "The Lord says, 'Son, you are going to be back in that situation again, and Son, just lay it all on the line with them. I see the situation turning around and even them doing the partnering in with you that you thought would never have been possible because of the way they presented themselves. Son, sit back, just receive from Me. This is a time of joy; this is a time of reaping the harvest for the seed sown and the sacrifices made.'

> "'Son, receive it. Sit back and relax for I am going to bless you, I am going to bring what you need. This is the time to ask for even great, great bigger things than you can imagine.'"

The prophet continued:

> "I don't know if it is airplanes or whatever it is that comes into the ministry but the Lord says, 'Now is the time to ask for that but it is in the Spirit that now is the time for the release of that. Son, I am there for you and I am going to bring it and now is the time for the reaping of the harvest.'"

You can keep hearing this thing over, and over, and over again.

> "The Lord says, 'My Son, I sense the urgency within your spirit because I have placed that urgency there.'"

Again, this goes back to a prophecy that was given by Dr. Lake where it talks about what was put in me and this urgency.

> *"The Lord says, 'Even though, Son, there are things that you have done that no one else has done, there are still things you know you can do. There are even teachings that you have done that you have not even released yet because in your study of people that walked with Me, twenty, thirty or forty years, a hundred years ago, you saw some things there that are not ready to be revealed yet. Son, now is the time to reveal those teachings. Now is the time to reveal those revelations. And even though the disappointment in your relationship has come about here in the last two years, it is going to be taken care of. It is not going to have to be a burden on you. Son, release that burden on you. That is not your burden, my Son; that is My burden. I took that burden from off your shoulders. I am taking it off your shoulders.'*
>
> *"Son, you are a man in integrity. You have people who have been looking at you for the past five years who are not sure where you are standing, but now they are sure where you are standing and now your finances will be coming in and the plane that was spoken of will be brought to you because Son, your time in travel has to be decreased and your time teaching has to be increased, and that is the way it is going to be done.*
>
> *"You will be going, not just from country to country, but you will be going from nation to nation. You will get phone calls from presidents and princes wanting you to come to their nations. They*

will be Muslim nations. They will be radical nations. They will be nations that don't even know who Jesus is. But they are going to be hearing from you and people who they trust and they have some things and issues and physical issues that need to be healed. You will be able to turn around nations and make decisions in the Spirit that will change the political direction of different nations."

This is very similar to what Dr. Sumrall also walked in.

"'Although you are going to be looking for things to do further, I will have people walking side by side with you. It has been spoken before that your children and grandchildren will be doing marvelous works. It will set within you the desire to keep doing more, but there are times when I will hold the reins on you and will pull you back, because if you go too quickly, you will be bypassing people. There are things that have to come across your path slowly.'

"'The calling on your life will be increased and your strength, your vitality and purpose will be revealed.'

"'I have a purpose for you that is going to be revealed. You have had a taste of it. I have not told you about it, but you have sensed in the Spirit that I am going to speak to you. When I speak those words and I give you that unction, there is going to be a quick move and you will be staying within a country for three months and during that stay there will be a change within that country that you

will know what your new calling is and that you will know what needs to be done.'

"'I've searched the whole earth through. I've gone to places with you. I have found your heart. I've seen your heart. I know your heart is true, for My eyes are upon you my Son. I've come to support you my Son.'

"'I'm clothing you this day,' says the Lord, 'for My angels have come to you. I'm strengthening you. I'm restoring you. I'm causing you to be strong.'

"'You will have what you need. You will ask what you need. You will have what you need,' says the Lord. 'Look up and see My face. Look up and see My face, for you have My attention. You have My voice. You have My will. You will have My way. Look up,' says the Lord your God, 'for I have shaken the systems of man. I am enabling you, my Son. Look now and see for I have redeemed. I am yours this day. You are mine in every way. You have given your heart, now I give you My best. I give you My best,' says the Lord.

"The Lord says, 'Just as I have searched and looked and looked and looked and found you, I am also jealous for you. You are not even jealous for yourself and with other ministries and the competition thing has not taken root in your heart, and I am pleased with your heart and how you have kept the garden of your heart and the garden with the weeds being torn out so that the *weeds do not go down into any kind of bitterness or infection within,' says the Lord.*

"The Lord says, 'Son, I am going to be taking you to what it looks like to you.' 'God is this necessary?' 'Don't argue with me Son.'"

The Lord knows me well.

Here, the Lord was speaking, talking about a particular thing. This would definitely be relevant to this current church family, so I will definitely have to deal with it.

"'I'm giving you that land that is prime where people will say, 'Oh, no, this just can't be. This is too prime a piece of land for people to build a house on.' 'You build My house, and I'll build your house. The plans are going to be there.'

"'It will be timely given to you; you will know what to do with it.'

"The Lord says, 'Not only will it be a home, but there will be provision for the training center.' The Lord says, 'You go to people, now I am bringing them to you. You have been free to give out that which I have given to you and I am giving you more. You can't even imagine the depths, the mysteries and the keys that are going to be coming to you.'

"'I'll bring the entire family and they will have a peace that will enable because I will give them sharpening tools. I am taking the scales off the eyes of some, there will be greater vision and acuity

and you will be surprised. Yes, you will marvel because you thought, 'Can this happen?' and the Lord will say, 'You better believe it.'

"'This season is good. This season is fast. This season is for the future. You will see this season is for the very thing that I have placed in your heart. It is bigger; it is more, because you just can't see it all. It is here,' says the Lord.

"Doctors are going to begin to come and ask how to cure a specific disease or illness because they have heard of your reputation as a doctor and that all these people are healed. As they come and ask you how you would treat or cure this, God will give you the medical terminology that will surprise you because you aren't familiar with the words. They will sense or feel that you have the information and as they are open to receive it, you will say, 'Now let me show you a better way,' and you are going to bring many of the medical profession into the Kingdom of God as you do that.

"'My Son, even as you set your feet on this property [the place we went to minister], *I began to do a deepening work in the midst of your heart and I am doing an enlargening work in the midst of your spirit. You have deposited a thing here because it is the earnest of the multiplication getting ready to happen. For surely you have come into the prophets and even this day you are receiving the mantle of prophet and you will prophecy more than you thought was possible and you will have dreams and visions that are going to begin to open up to you. 'There will be third heaven revelations,*

like John the Revelator. I will cause you to be caught away in measures of My Spirit that are even unfathomable in your mind that you thought could be possible.'

"'For this is the season that I am opening up the gate of divine revelation and you will see a release of My Spirit to show Himself to you in a way that you have not seen. I am opening your eyes. I am opening up your heart and I am opening up your spirit, and this day My divine deposit is going within.'

"'Now even as you put the seed in the ground, there has been a measure of dying for you, though not only to get here but to process what had to happen here. This has been a springboard and you will begin to count down, ten, nine, eight, seven, six, right on down. For surely as it is established in My Word, I tell My secrets to My prophets. I tell you now that which I tell you secretly, that which I read to you secretly, that which has been behind closed doors and hidden for a season, will burst open and be revealed by My Spirit and you will see a worldwide impact.'

"'You have stepped into a worldwide thrust of My Spirit going forth, sent by the prophets even unto the nations. You will begin to release a demonstration of My Spirit that is beyond your imagination.'

"'Son, I am partnering with you in this hour because the last days are coming quickly. I am calling My bride forth and I am preparing My warriors in this hour. I am going to put a trumpet to

> *your mouth, for surely within the midst of you I put an Amos 7 plumb line.'"*

Actually, I had to go in and study that.

> *"'I have put within the midst of you a line of demarcation; I put within you, within the midst of you, My Spirit of Truth. Now it will come out with forcefulness.'*

> *"'You will be in a situation where you will speak words that will come out of your spirit that you will want to put back in your mouth.'"*

That has actually happened many times. This next part was the hardest thing for me to believe. The prophet continued saying,

> *"The Lord says, 'Don't hinder the process of what I am going to do through you in this hour. I am going to cause you to be a man who will articulate in a way that will astound you. For surely the command of the English language, the pearls and poetic ability that come out of your mouth will even be a shock to you.'"*

Well, it certainly will be. If I can articulate the English language that will truly be a work of God. Then He said,

> *"'I am going to show you signs and wonders of My love. I am going to show you signs and wonders of My heart.'*

"'I spoke to you and said I would give to you some hidden mysteries and there has been some measure of that come forth within the midst of your life. This has not been the fullness. There is getting ready to open up to you, an open heaven revelation that will reveal to you the armies of My heavenly realms. I am going to show you My battle strategies and plans. I am going to give you, as it were, CIA secret information that will reveal what I am going to be doing. Son, you will go forth establishing a thing, where your foot will trod, there will I establish My Kingdom.'

"'Son, this thing will be bigger, broader, stronger, higher and greater than you can possibly think in your mind, for this is My heart, not just for you, but My heart through you and to others. I am going to bring round about you people of divine revelation, those who are raising up as apostolic prophetic authority in this hour, and you are going to link arms. There will be a gathering of eagles. There will be a rising up of My divine last days 'Ark of the Covenant' and there will be a shouldering of the priesthood that will come underneath the Ark of the Covenant. You will begin to demonstrate some wonders of the fulfillment of My divine plan that was established in the Old Testament and fulfilled in the New Testament.'"

There's that old and new thing again.

"'And it is a heart cry of the proclaiming of the soon coming King.'

> *"'There is coming a royalty upon your head and shoulders. I am clothing you and you have no idea what the garment looks like.'"*

There's that first mention of the garment we were talking about earlier.

> *"'Son, as I begin to reveal the demonstration of this to your spirit, you will begin to weep and cry at the glory of My mighty mysteries. For surely you have no idea what My heaven and My Kingdom in fullness is like.'"*

> *"'I'm getting ready to pull back the veil. I'm getting ready to pull back the eyes. I'm getting ready to show you some things that you have cried out for. You will see this in the thrusting of the wings of the eagle that will begin to spread and begin to soar with heights in Me. You will demonstrate that ability of discernment that you have been asking for. It will settle and rise in your heart and spirit like it has not happened before.'"*

> *"'This is the day and the hour that I am standing up in the midst of My throne. I have told you that I am sending you on a journey. I've called you a mighty Warrior. I am raising you up as a General. I am also telling you right now the power that I have in the midst of Me to establish, to dethrone and enthrone, to release and bind, to establish new developmental orders of government and tear down old forms of government is being put in your hand. A sickle is being put in your right hand.'"*

> *"There are going to come visitations to you personally. Things that I am going to do that are private experiences between you and Me. There will come the appearance of angels. There will come the revelation of seeing Me. There will come the revelation of seeing the divine order of seeing heaven. There will be moments when you will feel like saying, 'Oh, God, this is so majestic, so beautiful and so huge; I don't want to leave, I just want to stay here.'*
>
> *"The Lord says, 'Son, I have a work for you to do. I have a commission that is being placed upon you. I have a release that is coming forth out of the midst of you. There will be a joining of family. There will be a joining of teams. There will be a networking of people around about you.'"*

You have to remember, all of this was given in 2003 before we were doing Life Teams and before a lot of the things we have now were actually established.

> *"'For surely it is time to expand the tent pegs. It is time to enlarge the tent and to establish the fullness of it. This is the hour in which I am raising up My eternal government. I am releasing to men and women the mantle, the scepter and the authority in this hour to establish My Kingdom in the midst of the hurling of hell itself.'*
>
> *"'Now, Son, I am causing you to come to a place of full stature.'"*

Those in the Bible School have been hearing about fullness of stature and growing up.

> *"'To standing up tall and straight as an ambassador of royalty for Me. For even as you come to the house of prophets, you will leave this place with My cornerstone put in place in your spirit. I have set the foundation. I am getting ready to ramp up the beams and build the building. For it is an appointed time and season and a time to cross over and move through the gate.'*
>
> *"'I am releasing a new dispensation.'*
>
> *"'There is coming a fast change and a ripping of the wineskins that the second and third party revelation has had a measure of fire and difficulty to it. I am releasing an enabling of adjusting and grace that is supernatural. There will be a visitation that will draw you together for the purposes of My ordained eternal destiny for all of you that will cause you to flow in harmony of divine orchestration, releasing a new song.'"*

You have to go through all of this and look at it, even this idea of releasing a new song. Every move of God has a song, and it has its own sound. Very honestly, that has been the one thing that we have been lacking. We have not been able to take the words of this message and put it into song so that we don't have to sing the old songs. The new songs should come forth and literally take people to a higher level of revelation.

"'For this is the hour, son, for you to rise and proclaim; this is the hour for you to rise and declare. It is the hour for you to set in order and to position for surely have I placed upon you the apostolic authority of the last days Prophet, Apostle.'

"'I am releasing inside of your heart. I am releasing within you right now a supernatural divine network because My hand is releasing you to a place of demonstration that I might be able to rise up in My throne. For I am standing now, says God. For I am with you and I have put My mind in you. I have placed My purposes in your heart. And you shall accomplish My will.'

"'You will lead this last day army into battle, into victory. Your time is now at hand.'

"'You will continue to travel but you shall travel from a base. The Training Center shall be your launching place. You will produce those who will also be mighty warriors.'

"'You must not fear. You must not back off. You must move forward. You must attack, attack, attack.'"

That's code, and it is surprising that God would use that, because a lot of people wouldn't catch that. The words, "Attack, attack, attack," are a direct quote from General George S. Patton, Jr. He said, "When in doubt, attack, attack, attack." When this person said this, it was like, "Oh, yeah; okay," because I had questions about the path I was on, and this just confirmed some of those things.

> *"There will come a burst as it were of writing and the books you produce will change dead traditional Christianity into a living practical lifestyle that will produce victory.'"*

There is a lot more on this; I'm not going to read it all right now. There are other pages of this prophecy. One of the things that it actually talks more about is the revelation that is coming forth. Actually, in the last couple of days in the Bible School, we have completely broken the mold as far as teaching courses like we planned to. Instead of following through the course, we have stayed on the "new man." We've been teaching this "new man" to the Bible School students here and just going through it, and going through it.

Half of the time we will read a Scripture, start to comment on it, and immediately it's like, "How did you get that out of that Scripture?" Well, I wasn't trying to get that out of that Scripture. It was revelation coming forth that we have since gone back and checked out. This is part of that process of revelation.

As we move forward, there are a lot of things that are beginning to happen, even here in the ministry and where we're going. We are worldwide now. We are getting invitations to some other countries for conferences. Things like that are going to be major aspects of what we are going to be doing.

The reason I'm telling you this is because, like I said before, if you're hooked to this wagon, that is where you're going. I think it is only fitting that you know where you are going. We will always have people that come in for ministry and come in to be prayed for; that's just a given.

The next generation (the second generation), is the generation that will follow the generation that is putting out this message.

You heard that a lot of what was said in this prophecy had to do with the next generation. I believe that the next generation does have to do with an age, but I also believe that is because God usually speaks to a person in a language that they understand.

When I first got interested in martial arts, I wanted to study directly under Bruce Lee. By the time I started my studies, he had passed away. All I could do was find his students to train under, so I went and found them. Training under them was the closest I could get to Bruce Lee. That was a second generation, so when I hear second generation, it has nothing to do with age.

When it talks about grandchildren, I do believe it has to do with my grandchildren. I believe it is for them, but I also believe that it also talks about spiritual children and spiritual grandchildren. I believe that it talked about the next generation being the second generation of whoever gets this message. In other words, if God pours it through me, then you would be the second generation, regardless of who you are. I believe that's what is going forth.

Our purpose: To grow up believers into Him (Christ Jesus), in all things.

Ephesians 4:11-15,

> 15 But speaking the truth in love, may grow up into him in all things, which is the head, even Christ:

We will always have people who come in that just want to hear; they just want to go to church on Sunday. They come in, maybe they like the message, so they keep coming back, but they never get involved. They just show up and leave. We will always minister to them.

We obviously wouldn't treat new people any differently than we do anybody else. If you have ever watched a mama bird feed the baby birds, it's the one that sticks its head up the farthest with the mouth open that gets fed first. I have to be very judicious in how I spend my time.

We will share with anybody, and we will talk with anybody. I meet with people, go to eat with people, and just fellowship. That's always good and I enjoy it, but at the same time, the purpose of this place is not just to give people a place to worship. The purpose of this place is to train up believers so that people don't feel like they always have to meet with me. Until we get that taken care of, this is still going to be a man-centered thing, and that's definitely not what we are trying to do.

We really want this ministry to be Christ-centered so that people can realize, "If I can reach any of those people, they can get the job done." The purpose is to "grow up" believers.

You can ask anybody around here: if you hang around very much, we'll put you to work. That doesn't mean a paycheck from me or the ministry, but that means we will find things in the Kingdom of God that need to be done and see if you will do them. If you do them, God will pay you; He will take care of you. God doesn't rip people off. If you work for God, He will take care of you. That's just the way it is.

The whole idea here is to get people active. What most of you are looking for, you won't ever learn by sitting there. You've already heard the message; you've already heard what you need to know. What you think you need to learn now, you're going to learn by doing it. That's where 90 percent of my growth came from. It wasn't from just what I read, but what I started putting into practice. We will have opportunities for you to get involved and for you to step up. You will actually be put into a place where you can be used by God.

Going on Sunday afternoons with the Feeding Jesus Outreach program is a great birthing place for you to minister to people. Going to the senior care facility is a great place. The Feeding Jesus Outreach is where we go out and take care of people, feed them, clothe them, talk to them, minister to them, and pray for them. That's good because it gives you a chance to practice. In the business world, they call that cold calling. You just walk up to a person and minister to them.

The senior care facility is the same way, but you can also establish a relationship where you actually start to pastor these people. You find out what they need, take it to them, and then you start to have relationships with them. Honestly, a lot of these people are very close to death, and they'll never see outside that building that they are in, so it is very important that we make sure that they know Jesus as their Lord. This is a vital thing.

It's the same thing on the streets. People die every day, so we need to make sure that we are touching lives. This is your chance. It is not all about pulpit ministry. It's not about you having a title or business card. It is about you touching lives anywhere and everywhere. That is the essence of it.

My job here is to train you up, and this is the first chance we've ever had to literally train people up, from start to finish. God is giving us the information, the plan, and what we need to get that done.

I will tell you just very plainly: I cannot do all that I need to do. We need people to take on things and to start being available to do things; that is part of the growth. This is not just a place for singing and entertainment. You can go to any one of a hundred other churches for that. That's not what we are about. A lot of things around here don't look all polished and professional, because we are actually trying to really touch lives with the power of God.

To those of you who have been around, you can tell that a lot of these things that we've talked about in the last couple of weeks can be seen in these prophetic words. A lot of these things I didn't even try to put together, until last night. I was looking at these prophecies and thinking about some of these things.

The two primary keys that God has given us are the keys that open up the mysteries of the kingdom of heaven.

These two keys that we have been talking about just kept coming up over and over again. There are more than two, but the two primary ones that God has given us are the keys that open up the mysteries of the kingdom of heaven, and these keys are very simple.

To you, they may not seem dramatic, but it's because you're used to them. However, if you took what you have been hearing here, or if you took our CDs or DVDs, or any of our material from the last couple of years to most other church congregations, it would be a revelation to them. In many cases, they would absolutely just stop, back off, and say, "Whoa! That is so far out there."

Until we started presenting healing as warfare, it was not presented as warfare. People started accepting it about ten years ago. Although it is not totally accepted, to a large degree people are starting to see that there's a warfare aspect to it.

The two main keys: The aspect of dominion (authority), and the aspect of obedience to the Word.

The keys that we're talking about here predominantly have to do with dominion and authority. I would say that dominion and authority run together. I could look at it from several different viewpoints, but if I had to pick two, I would say that at this point, the two main keys that we have brought to people are: the aspect of dominion, and the aspect of obedience to the Word. Just do what it says. Most people don't think they can, because they don't think they have the authority, or they don't think they have that level of responsibility.

What I hear at almost every DHT is that we bring a level of freedom and a new level of life. We bring this dominion, this authority aspect, but we also bring a responsibility that we are our brother's keeper. That goes from food and clothing, all the way to getting them healed, and getting them born again. It's the full realm. We have to see that we are members of this Kingdom, and that we are part of this Kingdom, and wherever we go, the Kingdom is advanced.

As a body here, we have to begin seeing ourselves as a Kingdom outpost, a colony of Kingdom saints and citizens. That it is not going to look all spiritual, because there is a political aspect to it.

Isaiah 9:6-7,

> 6 For unto us a child is born, unto us a son is given: and the government shall be upon his shoulder: and his name shall be called Wonderful, Counsellor, The mighty God, The everlasting Father, The Prince of Peace.

> 7 Of the increase of *his* government and peace *there shall be* no end, upon the throne of David, and upon his kingdom, to order it, and to establish it with judgment and with justice from henceforth even for ever. The zeal of the LORD of hosts will perform this.

Here in Isaiah it did not say, "On His shoulders shall be a new religion." It said, "The Government will be upon his shoulder," and that Government is the Kingdom of God. It is a different type of government.

That is exactly what this person prophesied. A while ago, when I was reading, he said, "There is a new government, a new way of moving into things that I am beginning to bring forth and reveal to you." It is very simple. The Kingdom of God is the Government, and it is operating in that Kingdom; it is not operating under natural principles that we have in this world. To those of us in this Kingdom, these keys have been given.

Another key: Understanding. Jesus said that what you understand can't be stolen from you.

We studied last week in Matthew chapter 13. We're going to be building on these things as we go along. The keys of this Kingdom are used for understanding these mysteries, and they are the keys that open these mysteries. Jesus made that very clear in Matthew chapter 13. When He started explaining the parable of the "sower," He made a big point of this. He said that what you understand can't be stolen from you. Well, that understanding is a key. It's not one or two keys; actually, the bigger a kingdom is, the more keys there are attached to it. These keys have to do with this understanding.

If I teach something, or anybody here teaches anything, I highly encourage you, "If you don't understand it, talk to us; let us know." Tell us, "I didn't get that; I didn't understand that part." Let us know. Don't hesitate, make an appointment, and come in. Let's sit down; let's talk. It doesn't just have to be with me. It could be any one of our staff here. They understand these things. We will talk with you if you have a question. Write it down, get it to us, or make an appointment. Don't go with your questions unanswered. We will help you to get understanding.

That's the whole purpose of having this training center. It's not to give me a place to preach. If we didn't have this, I could be preaching anywhere in the world. We have thousands of open invitations. I don't need a place to preach. I am here to sow into your life and to pastor you, "to grow you up" so that you look, talk, and act like Jesus. The way for you to do that is to understand the principles of the Kingdom of God. If you don't understand those principles, you will never walk in the fullness.

Jesus used the parable of the sower as the principle. He said about this parable, "If you don't understand this one, how are you going to understand any of the rest?" You have to get understanding.

Once you have that understanding, the devil cannot steal it from you. Get understanding, whether it comes by healing, by the Baptism of the Holy Spirit, or by the Kingdom; get understanding. Keep going after it until you get those questions answered. If we have to say the same thing a hundred different ways, we will do it, because it is not enough that we preach it. You've got to get it.

Jesus demonstrated how to live in the Kingdom.

We have to look at all of this. We can't just look at it from a point of here's a topic, and there's a topic. Those are just pieces. That's the way it has been. The church has been too big on just topical preaching and they give out pieces.

A lot of people don't understand the overall plan of God. The Kingdom is what Jesus preached. He preached the Kingdom and how to walk in that Kingdom. Everything He did was an exhibition; it was a demonstration of how to live in the Kingdom.

Healing the sick is not a gift. You have to understand that there are gifts of healing, but you don't have a gift so that you are able to heal. You are a believer. Healing is walking in the Kingdom.

Here in America, we look at driving a car sometimes as a right. It's not; it's a privilege. That's why they give you a license that can be revoked. It is a privilege unless you show yourself to be a danger to yourself or somebody else.

We have laws, but we also have rights here in America. That is how we live in this culture. There are different ethnic groups that have different cultures within their ethnic group, yet all of those cultures come together to make this country.

The Kingdom of God is like that. In other words, there are all different ways that people do things, but we all have to abide by the same principles. We all live under the same principles, and they are very simple. Those principles are the ones that Jesus laid out.

Those principles are the beatitudes that we talked about previously. He said, "This is the attitude you will be having in the Kingdom." He said, "If it's not on earth the way it is in heaven, fix it." These are principles.

A Kingdom principle: Set the captives free.

We have things that we take as natural for us. If I want to go down to the store I could walk, ride a bicycle, or drive a car, but I have the right to go. There is that aspect. In the Kingdom we have the right to set the captives free. That is a Kingdom principle.

We have to change our minds to think in line with Kingdom principles. We have to begin thinking along the line that we are ambassadors of a Kingdom and we are in a foreign country. We are ambassadors sent to a foreign country to convince the people how much better it is to live in the Kingdom of God than it is to live in the kingdom of darkness.

For the people in the kingdom of darkness, it's dark; that's the reason we have to bring light. How do we bring light? We bring light by preaching truth, healing the sick, and setting the captives free, because that's what it is like to live in this Kingdom. In this Kingdom, there is health.

You don't need a health plan; you've already got one. I see people saying different things about insurance, but that doesn't concern me one bit, because I've got none of it. I've got Psalm 91 brought over into Luke 10:19. That's how I live. Based on that, there are principles in the Kingdom of God that are your right. You have the right to live a certain way, but you have to get used to it.

When you go to foreign countries, there is a period of adjustment when you get there. You have to remember which side of the road to drive on. You have to remember how they do certain things, and it is different from how we do them here. I don't go over there and say, "Well, back in America, this is how we do it." They don't care; you're not in America.

We, as the people of God, have to begin walking this out.

We have to think according to the Kingdom. Our job is to cause this Kingdom that we live in to be established in this new place, this new place being where this new Kingdom has not been established. We're talking about getting this into the hearts of people so that it can come out in their lives.

The first ground you need to take is other people's hearts. You need to win their hearts, because until you win their hearts, you're not going to see much of the Kingdom lived out through their lives. We can demonstrate it "on them," but it won't be demonstrated "through them" until we convert them.

We're talking about colonizing; we're talking about going into a new area, planting the flag of Jesus, and causing those people to see truth. In order to do that, we have to walk in it. We can't walk two sides. I know there are some countries where you can have dual passports. That's not the Kingdom of God. The Kingdom of God has one passport—it is the blood of Jesus. We need to understand that we walk in this Kingdom, and therefore, we walk on these principles. We have to get it drilled into us to the point where we start walking that out, and we start living in the Kingdom.

The other day I saw a book that told how the best leaders lead. I thought, "I don't even need to read it. It's called, 'By example.'" There are a lot of other details there, but bottom line, it comes down to some point where you can't just describe it; you have to demonstrate it. We, as the people of God, have to begin walking this out.

The first reaction you're going to get is going to be a negative reaction from religious people. That's going to be the first thing, because you don't act holy enough or spiritual enough.

There were some people who got kicked out of some healing rooms. They were not our healing rooms. They got kicked out, because the people running them said, "You're not relying on the Holy Spirit's anointing enough." When asked what results they were getting, they said, "Oh, people were getting healed left and right."

They were probably relying on the anointing enough, but it just didn't look the way that those running it wanted it to look; it didn't fit in with their culture. Why? That's because their culture is trying to build something that is not biblical.

The more spiritual you get when walking in the Kingdom of God, the more natural you're going to look in how you do these things. You're not going to look weird; you're going to look normal.

Someone might say, "Oh, this is horrible! I just got a phone call and someone is on life support." You're not going to sit there, do the same thing they did, and say, "Oh really? Oh, no! That's horrible." No, it's going to be natural for you to say, "Well, get them on the phone." "Well, I can't get them on the phone; they're on life support." "Okay, call somebody who's next to them. When you get them on the phone say, 'Take the phone and put the phone near them or point it toward them.'" Then you say, "In the name of Jesus, I command you to wake up! I command you to be healed!" They will ask, "Okay, are you done?" You say, "Yes, I'm done."

After you have done that, you will go back to eating and being normal. The people that are with you will look at you and say, "That was weird. Do you think that really worked? I mean, don't we need to stop eating and fast?" "No, it's too late now to fast; you were already eating."

We have to realize that this is who we are, and this has to be normal to you. Until it is normal to you, nobody else is going to want it. They have to see that this is part of who you are. When people see you walking in this, and they ask, "When everybody else got scared and nervous, why didn't you get scared and nervous?" you can say, "I didn't get scared, because nothing is going to touch me. I don't care if everything falls apart; I'm going to walk out into the midst of it."

I firmly believe that if I had been at the World Trade Tower on 9/11, I would have walked right out. Either that or it would have collapsed around me, and I would have been standing there looking at the pile of rubble. You say, "That sounds crazy?" No, that is what it sounds like when you are walking in the Kingdom.

You have to realize who you are; you are not the same as you were before. You have access to power, you have access to knowledge, and you have access to wisdom that has not been revealed before. You are a new creation, a new species. You have to realize that.

We are not just sinners saved by grace. We are a new creation, righteous before God. The prayers of a righteous man avails much, not the prayers of a sinner saved by grace. You are righteous in Christ Jesus. It is not because of what you did, but thank God you got in it, and because you got in it, now you are righteous. Now, act righteous.

KEYS OF THE KINGDOM

In 1 Corinthians 15:34 it says,

> 34 Awake to righteousness, and sin not; for some have not the knowledge of God: I speak *this* to your shame.

He said, "Beloved, awake unto righteousness and sin not." In other words, quit wasting your time with things that shame you. Get busy about Kingdom business. Show people what it is like to live in the Kingdom, because it is good in the Kingdom. What that means is that we are going to do things differently. We are going to act differently and talk differently.

If you get around me and talk cars, I won't have a clue. If you were to ask me about different kinds of cars, I wouldn't be able to tell you the difference. Cars may impress you, but I would be standing there looking at you like, "Yeah, so?" Why? It's not my world.

We need to get to the point where the Kingdom is our world and to where we talk and people say, "What are you talking about?" "Don't you understand? Here let me explain it to you. It's like this…"

What are you doing? You're throwing out a parable, because that's the way Jesus taught, and you begin to explain the Kingdom. Everything is about the Kingdom.

Everything we are going to be doing here, especially over the next few months, you're going to hear it more, and you're going to see it more. We're going to start living out the Kingdom here. You're going to see it functioning in ways that you've never seen it function before, because I believe that this is the time; this is what we have been waiting for.

Honestly, what I like about this place is that we are not under any type of denominational thumb so that we have to do it a certain way. We can just see what the Bible says, and do it the way the Bible says to do it, and by the Spirit of God, we will establish the Kingdom of God in this place. People that come here can walk through those doors and get healed. They don't even have to get prayed for. It's all fine and good to pray, but we don't have to. We can just begin to minister the Kingdom of God.

After going through some of these prophetic words, the hardest thing to believe is that God knows you well enough that He can speak prophetic words to you and say, "This is what I have for you." When I got called to the ministry, everybody told me that I wasn't fit for ministry or couldn't be used by God. I heard all of that. If I had not answered the call to ministry and stepped out, I would not have been on that platform the day that God had a word for me. Every step you take today puts you somewhere else tomorrow.

When people say, "That's never been done before," I say, "Well, nothing has ever been done before until you do it." Basically, that's what it comes down to. It is time for us to do some things that have never been done before. Let the world marvel at it, and when they ask, "How did ya'll do that?" we will just say, "That's just Kingdom. That's just normal; it's how we live."

THE GOVERNMENT OF GOD

Sermon given by Curry R. Blake

Jesus preached the Gospel of the Kingdom and healed all manner of sickness and disease.

Recently, the Lord has been really pressing on me to begin teaching more along the lines of the Kingdom. We have taught on the Kingdom for years now, but we want to bring more and more emphasis to it.

When we first started, we started predominately in the area of divine healing. That led us to a greater study and hopefully a greater understanding of what we call the "new man" or the "new creation."

It's because of what Christ did in and through us and what He did for us. It's as if I keep going farther and farther back, and healing is just one spoke on the wheel of salvation, so to speak, and of God's overall plan.

Healing works because of the "new creation."

As I started studying the new creation, I realized that the reason healing worked was because of this new creation.

The new creation works, because of what God did in us, and because of what He did through Jesus at the cross. We moved into a new time at that point, especially with His resurrection.

In studying the new creation and the new man, we looked at this. Paul literally spent his entire ministry teaching this new creation, and every time there was a problem in the church, he always answered that problem by teaching them about the new creation. We will continue doing that. Paul spent his entire life doing that, so I don't have any real hope of doing it in a few days of teaching, but we can at least head you in the right direction.

I'm going to give you some Scriptures here, and I am going to give you a major piece of what we're going to be talking about in this session. Then I'm going to break it down and hopefully give you some nuggets that you will be able to use.

We have to have our minds renewed.

As I said, first we did the DHT (Divine Healing Technician training). Then God took us back and said, "The new creation is why the DHT works." We started studying out the new creation, and we are still studying it out. We are still having our minds renewed to it, but even in the midst of that, God has gone back and said, "Now, look at this," and He took me back to the Kingdom. He told me about the Kingdom and how it works. There has been a whole lot of information that we have had that has caused misunderstanding, even misguidance, concerning the Kingdom.

There is a real danger in Christianity for people who have been around the church for a very long time, in that they get "religionized." When somebody says the Kingdom, they automatically switch modes of thinking to religion.

We're going to go to Isaiah chapter 9. This actually ties into some of the Scriptures we're going to be looking at next.

Isaiah 9, starting with verse 2,

> 2 The people that walked in darkness have seen a great light: they that dwell in the land of the shadow of death, upon them hath the light shined.
>
> 3 Thou hast multiplied the nation, *and* not increased the joy: they joy before thee according to the joy in harvest, *and* as *men* rejoice when they divide the spoil.

Notice: it says that these people walked in darkness, and they saw a great light. This is exactly the Scripture that was later quoted about Jesus when He showed up in the flesh and began walking through Galilee and began doing the works of God.

> 4 For thou hast broken the yoke of his burden, and the staff of his shoulder, the rod of his oppressor, as in the day of Midian.

Notice it is talking about breaking this rod and breaking this yoke. We talk about that when we talk about the anointing. There is a teaching where He said, "You have broken this yoke from off your shoulder and the burden from off your shoulder." It was talking about the day of Jesus, specifically about when He showed up. He was talking here about breaking the yoke. Look at verse 5:

> 5 For every battle of the warrior *is* with confused noise, and garments rolled in blood; but *this* shall be with burning *and* fuel of fire.

Notice: verse 5 was a strange verse to put in just before verse 6:

> 6 For unto us a child is born, unto us a son is given: and the government shall be upon his shoulder: and his name shall be called Wonderful, Counsellor, The mighty God, The everlasting Father, The Prince of Peace.
>
> 7 Of the increase of *his* government and peace *there shall be* no end, upon the throne of David, and upon his kingdom, to order it, and to establish it with judgment and with justice from henceforth even for ever. The zeal of the LORD of hosts will perform this.

Let's go back to verse 5. Notice what was being said here.

> 5 For every battle of the warrior *is* with confused noise, and garments rolled in blood; but *this* shall be with burning *and* fuel of fire.

I brought this verse out, because here it was talking about the battle, and the warrior, and the rod of the oppressor being broken.

Then it goes into verse 6 which is usually the most peaceful verse, because it's always spoken at Christmas. It is always spoken in a most peaceful way.

6 For unto us a child is born, unto us a son is given...

At Christmas, people want to give you the idea of how peaceful and how good it is going to be. They talk about the child, Jesus, who was a baby in a manger and all of the other things that you hear. Yet they never go back and find out that in the verse just before that peaceful one, he talked about warriors, breaking the yoke, the clothing rolled in blood, and all of that. It almost sounds like violence, and then it says, "For unto us a child is born." You would think that would be the antithesis of violence.

When I say, "Kingdom," people from the UK (United Kingdom) will think differently from those of us here in America. In the UK, they would think of Kingdom as a place or a country. Here in the US, especially if you are in church, you would think of "Kingdom" as a religious idea, or you would think of it in a religious mode. Here it says, "For unto us a child is born, unto us a son is given: and the government shall be upon His shoulder." It is speaking of a government.

BEHOLD THE KINGDOM

The kingdom of heaven is a tangible, literal empire; it is a government.

I want you to realize that when we talk about kingdom of heaven, we're not talking about just a concept or even an idea. We're talking about a tangible literal empire, even to the point where you would call it a government.

Usually, when we talk about the Kingdom of God and the kingdom of heaven, we don't think in terms of the Government of God or the government of heaven, but that's what it means, because a kingdom is a government. We are going to be talking about what is required for there to be a kingdom.

I don't know if you realize it or not but a person can't just go out in their front yard with their own special flag that they've hand sewn, stick it in the front yard and say, "We're a kingdom." I know that people say, "A man's house is his castle," but that doesn't make his front yard his kingdom. There's more to it than that.

There are some legal requirements for a kingdom to exist. There has to be a certain territory, and there has to be a provision. The people that live there have to be subjects of the kingdom, and there has to be an army to protect the kingdom. There has to be a governing body to actually operate in the kingdom.

THE GOVERNMENT OF GOD

When you go to back and look at it, it is amazing how God used those terms specifically, both kingdom and government, referring to His own way of doing things.

The Word says that Jesus was born in the fullness of time, and the empire that most closely resembled the way that the Kingdom and the Government of God operated was the Roman Empire. That was one of the most corrupt empires ever in existence. It just shows that once man gets hold of something, he usually messes it up. If an empire was done the right way, it would be in God's keeping and in His will.

Going back to Isaiah 9, notice the point of his Kingdom, of his Government. In verse 7: "Of the increase of *his* government and peace *there shall be* no end." Verse 6 said, "And unto us a son is given and the government shall be upon his shoulder." It didn't say Kingdom, but we know that it meant Kingdom.

Here He was talking about this in more specific terms, so I want you to think in terms of government. Don't think of it as some wispy idea of the Kingdom of God being here, as in it's here…it's there…it's everywhere. Don't think of it that way. You need to think of the Kingdom of God as the Government of God and that the Kingdom is wherever God's will is being done.

Wherever you put your foot, the Kingdom of God is there.

If you are a subject of that Kingdom, if you're a subject of God Himself, then wherever you put your foot the Kingdom of God is there, as long as you are doing the will of God. As you go out and do the will of God, you are advancing His Kingdom.

I want you to see that there is a Government. I want you to get away from the religious idea and start thinking in more concrete terms, because most people never think that way.

In Matthew it says that He began to teach and began to preach the Gospel of the Kingdom.

Matthew 4:17,

> 17 From that time Jesus began to preach, and to say, Repent: for the kingdom of heaven is at hand.

Jesus began to teach and He didn't stop. Everything that Jesus taught was Kingdom, all the way through. He was basically showing us how God's Government operates. Start thinking more along the lines of the Kingdom being Government rather than thinking of it as just an idea.

Don't think of the Kingdom in terms of religious thought, because there will be a point where people, religious or not, will bow their knee to King Jesus. They will be in subjection to His Kingdom again, whether they like it or not.

That's government; that's not freewill in that sense. In other words, there is going to come a time when Jesus is going to rule with a rod of iron, and He's going to put down all rebellion. There are going to be things going on, so there is an aspect of this that you need to realize, because the Government, the Kingdom of God, is going to cover the earth at some point.

We can be the "advanced force" to help bring that into being, or we can wait. If we wait until He arrives, we're not going to get what He has promised to those who actually advanced His Kingdom. It's really simple.

He was preaching the Kingdom, so He was telling you how the Kingdom would operate.

In Matthew 6:19, He said,

> 19 Lay not up for yourselves treasures upon earth, where moth and rust doth corrupt, and where thieves break through and steal:
>
> 20 But lay up for yourselves treasures in heaven, where neither moth nor rust doth corrupt, and where thieves do not break through nor steal:

When He said, "...treasures in heaven," He was referring to laying up your treasures in the kingdom of heaven which is in heaven and is of heaven. He never mentioned anything but the Kingdom, so anything He was talking about always went back to how the Kingdom operates. Part of it is spiritual, and part of it is physical. You'll see both as we go on.

> 21 For where your treasure is, there will your heart be also.

BEHOLD THE KINGDOM

Remember: "…where your treasure is, there will your heart be also."

We need to be single-minded: "No man can serve two masters."

> 22 The light of the body is the eye: if therefore thine eye be single, thy whole body shall be full of light.
>
> 23 But if thine eye be evil, thy whole body shall be full of darkness. If therefore the light that is in thee be darkness, how great *is* that darkness!

You can have light, and it can be dark. Notice the essence of what He was talking about here. He was talking about being single-minded.

> 24 No man can serve two masters: for either he will hate the one, and love the other; or else he will hold to the one, and despise the other. Ye cannot serve God and mammon.

"*Mammon*" means *riches or material wealth*, or *a personification of riches as an evil spirit or deity.*

"Take no thought for your life, what ye shall eat, or what ye shall drink; nor yet for your body, what ye shall put on."

> 25 Therefore I say unto you, Take no thought for your life, what ye shall eat, or what ye shall drink; nor yet for your body, what ye shall put on. Is not the life more than meat, and the body than raiment?

Understand that He was not saying not to think about it. He was saying, "Take no thought." The word *"thought"* there actually leans toward *a concerned thought*, in other words, *a worry*. We have to realize that He was trying to say, "Don't put all of your time into thinking and making sure that you're going to be taken care of."

> 26 Behold the fowls of the air: for they sow not, neither do they reap, nor gather into barns; yet your heavenly Father feedeth them. Are ye not much better than they?
>
> 27 Which of you by taking thought can add one cubit unto his stature?
>
> 28 And why take ye thought for raiment? Consider the lilies of the field, how they grow; they toil not, neither do they spin:
>
> 29 And yet I say unto you, That even Solomon in all his glory was not arrayed like one of these.

What was He saying over and over again? He was saying, "Don't worry about what you're going to eat, or what you're going to drink, or what you're going to put on." He wasn't saying, "Don't think about it." He was saying, "Don't worry about it. Don't let that be the reason you live." You have to realize that this is one of the first generations to potentially have so much leisure time.

Almost every previous generation spent most of their time just working toward making sure they had a roof over their head and making sure that they had food to eat. If you think about it, before supermarkets and refrigeration and all of that, they had to go out nearly every day and get food for that day; they had to gather it. The whole day was spent either in going and getting it, or preparing it, building a fire, and getting everything ready. There was a lot involved. Your whole day was wrapped around just existing.

Some people would say that's how we are today; we're having problems in paying our mortgage and this bill or that bill. Very honestly, most of that we brought on ourselves. Many times we (Americans, especially), tend to try to live above our means. At some point, you have to choose to cut back on spending. Unless you have a money printing machine, you can't just make more money. You have to learn to cut back on some things.

Most of what we have today are not necessities. They are luxuries, and we've gotten so used to them that the luxuries have become necessities, or at least we think they have.

Jesus was trying to tell them, "Don't get hung up on all of those things so that that's all you think about and live for."

Have faith in your Heavenly Father.

Matthew 6:30,

> 30 Wherefore, if God so clothe the grass of the field, which to day is, and to morrow is cast into the oven, *shall he* not much more *clothe* you, O ye of little faith?

Notice He calls them, "O ye of little faith." He was talking to those who were concerned about surviving on a day-to-day basis or at least the way we would think of surviving. He was saying, "Don't be worried about these things. Don't you have faith in your Heavenly Father?"

The church has gotten far away from the Bible and from the teachings of Jesus, what He actually did, and what He said. It has gone to this other extreme from what the Bible teaches. The way the world operates is the opposite of everything in the Bible. The hardest thing is to take that first step across and start operating the opposite of the way the world operates. Most people never get there, and that's where religion comes in.

Religion comes in and says, "Live like the world, and pay your penance for living like the world." Religion is based on: "You can never be good enough and since you're not going to be good enough, you must always pay the price of not being good enough. If you pay a big enough price, you can continue to live while not being good enough. It won't matter, because as long as you pay the price, God will overlook what you're doing wrong." That's what religion does.

That's not what God said. Jesus was telling us right here, "Don't be like the world; don't think like the world. You have to do the opposite."

Know that God will take care of you.

> 31 Therefore take no thought, saying, What shall we eat? or, What shall we drink? or, Wherewithal shall we be clothed?

In other words, "Don't be worrying about those things, and don't let that be your topic of conversation."

> 32 (For after all these things do the Gentiles seek:) for your heavenly Father knoweth that ye have need of all these things.

"For after all these things do the Gentiles seek." He could have put in there the word heathen or godless. He could have said, "People that don't have God think like that, however if you have God, you shouldn't think that way." He was telling them, "You have to remember that you have a God who will take care of you. You're not going to starve; you're not going to do without."

He went on to say, "…for your heavenly Father knoweth that ye have need of all these things." He knows what you need. He knows you need to eat, He knows you need a place to stay, and He knows you need clothing. He knows you need these things.

I specifically put this part in at the beginning, because if you get an understanding of this, then your life can change. Then these other things you can pick up as you go along, but you need to get this. You have a God; He will take care of you. Quit worrying, quit fretting over it, quit wringing your hands, and quit being like people that have no hope. We have a God who loves us so much that He gave His son; we all know that Scripture.

Romans 8:32,

> 32 He that spared not his own Son, but delivered him up for us all, how shall he not with him also freely give us all things?

We have to realize: He gave His Son. What in the world would He hold back if He was willing to give His Son? Is there anything He would not give us? If you gave up your son, you would give up anything else, too. The Scripture even says, "If He gave us Jesus, will He not with Jesus give us all these other things that we need?"

Matthew 6:33,

> 33 But seek ye first the kingdom of God, and his righteousness; and all these things shall be added unto you.

That's just the opposite of what the world says. The world says, "If you want it, you've got to go get it. If you want it you've got to grab hold of it, you've got to take it, you've got to exert yourself, assert yourself, and you've got to step up, even if that means stepping on somebody else. If you want something, you've got to go after it."

Here He said, "If you want to be clothed, if you want to be fed, and if you want to be taken care of, the way to do that is not to think about being clothed and fed and taken care of, but to seek first God's Kingdom." Let me just paraphrase this: "If you take care of God's business, He'll take care of yours. If you make other people your responsibility, God will make you His responsibility." Amen?

It's like mercury. Have you ever tried to put your finger on a little spot of mercury? You try, but you can't; it always slips away. That's the way chasing all of these things are. The more you try to catch them, the more they just slip away from you.

Have you ever tried to sneak up on a dog or a cat? The best way to do that is not to walk toward them; it's to turn around and walk backward toward them, because then they don't realize you're coming toward them. They will lay there and let you just walk right up to them, but only if you are backing up. You can't act as though you're going after them, because they'll run or do whatever else they might do, but if you act like you don't want them, you can catch them.

It's the same thing with all the things that we were just talking about. The best way to be taken care of is not to put your mind on being taken care of, in the sense of trying to get this and trying to get that.

The Scriptures say that if we will humble ourselves, then God will exalt us.

There are only two positions: the humbler position and the exalted position. You get to choose which one you want. If you choose to be your own exalter, then you will automatically put God in the humbler position. You don't want God humbling you. However, if you take the humbler position and you humble yourself, then God will exalt you.

That's what you want, because God is a good exalter. God can exalt you better than you can.

You're going to have to decide: who is your provider? God has already said, "I am Jehovah Jireh, the Lord who provides." You have to decide, "Is that what He is to me?" If He is not and if you are your own provider, then God isn't your provider.

If you are going to provide for yourself then you are going to go back under Adam. You're going to toil, you're going to sweat, you're going to have to work at these things, and it's going to be hard to get it all done. However, if you take God as your provider, and you start taking care of other people, then God will take care of you.

"Seek ye first the Kingdom of God."

Matthew 6:32-33,

> 32 (For after all these things do the Gentiles seek:) for your heavenly Father knoweth that ye have need of all these things.
>
> 33 But seek ye first the kingdom of God, and his righteousness; and all these things shall be added unto you.

"All these things…" God's not against you having things. He said, "…and all these things shall be added unto you." God's not against you having things; He's against things having you. You've heard that before. It says here that He will add these things to you. I don't know about you, but it's much better to have them added to you than you having to chase them down.

If you understand this, you will find out how to have things delivered to you, rather than you having to go and chase them down and provide for yourself. This is the way the Kingdom operates—this is not the earthly way. The earthly way says, "Well, you've got to sow, and then you will get it back." It's not like that in the Kingdom. It's amazing!

God is well pleased in you when your faith is in Him.

Before Jesus ever did one miracle, even when He came up out of the water and saw the dove, He had never done any work, yet He heard the Father say, "I'm well pleased in you." Isn't that amazing? Now according to most Christians' way of thinking today, that would only have come at the end of His life after He had done all the works and then God could look at the works and say, "Yes, yes, yes, that's good. I'm well pleased. Well done."

People look at it like it should come at the end of His life, but Jesus heard it at the beginning. Jesus heard that before He ever did a thing, so God being well pleased cannot be based upon what you do.

Faith pleases God, and you can have faith. We know that faith without works is dead, but you have to realize that when Jesus pleased the Father, He was already living in faith. That pleased the Father and He said, "In whom I am well pleased." He had to be living by faith, and yet had not done a thing.

Don't think that you're not pleasing to God just because you haven't raised the dead or healed 1,000 sick people. You have to realize that God is well pleased in you when your faith is in Him. You have faith in Him by trusting Him to take care of your daily needs.

It pleases God for you to have faith in Him that He's going to give you things and that He's going to take care of you. Why? It is because He is your heavenly Father, first and foremost.

He's still a Judge, but He's not your Judge today. Today He is your Father, and even when you stand before Him as your Judge, you're going to stand there with Him as your Father. Remember that.

Blessings will overtake you.

Notice it said in Matthew 6:33, "Seek ye first the Kingdom of God and His righteousness and all these 'things' shall be added unto you." In Deuteronomy 28 it talked about going back under the Law, the blessing of the Law.

Deuteronomy 28:2,

> 2 And all these blessings shall come on thee, and overtake thee, if thou shalt hearken unto the voice of the LORD thy God.

Matthew 6:33 wasn't some brand new thing. Jesus was just "cutting to the chase," you might say, and getting right back to the blessings. He said, "If you will listen to God and listen to His voice, then all these blessings will be added to you." In other words, these blessings will overtake you. You won't chase them; they will chase you down. You cannot run fast enough to get away from the blessings of God, and that was under the Old Covenant.

All Jesus was saying here is this: "Seek first the Kingdom, God's Government; seek first His rule in your life and through your life. Seek first how He does things."

The way you were in the world cannot be the way you operate in the Kingdom of God.

Do you know that the government of America operates differently than the government of Great Britain, or different than the government of Australia or South Africa or any of those other countries? Different governments operate in different ways, and that is the main reason why we generally need lawyers.

You could represent yourself, but lawyers know laws, and they know when to make certain motions and when to say certain things that are supposed to help your case. You have to have a license and have passed the bar to operate in a court of law in almost any country.

Every country will tell you that you have to go through their school and generally, a lawyer in one country cannot operate in another country without having gone through law school there. That is mainly because the laws are different and the ways of operation are different.

THE GOVERNMENT OF GOD

God's Government, His laws, His regulations, and His principles of operation are different. You can't just walk in off the street and say, "Oh yeah, I'm going to do things the way I've always done them," because that will not pass the bar, so to speak. God has a different Government.

The way you were in the world cannot be the way you operate in the Kingdom of God. It's a different system. The best rule of thumb is very simple: whatever you used to do, just do the opposite. That is generally the best way. If you do the opposite, you're going to be in keeping with the way God does things.

Let's look at these two Scriptures again:

Deuteronomy 28:2,

> 2 And all these blessings shall come on thee, and overtake thee, if thou shalt hearken unto the voice of the LORD thy God.

Matthew 6:33-34,

> 33 But seek ye first the kingdom of God, and his righteousness; and all these things shall be added unto you.
>
> 34 Take therefore no thought for the morrow: for the morrow shall take thought for the things of itself. Sufficient unto the day *is* the evil thereof.

He told them, "Seek first the Kingdom of God, and His righteousness and all these things will be added to you."

You've heard these Scriptures before. I generally like to break them up a little in a way so that you won't think about them religiously or the way you've heard them before. I want you to actually read them. He was saying, "Seek first the Kingdom of God, and these things will be taken care of. Don't worry about tomorrow because you have a heavenly Father."

Don't be like the heathen who think that you have to take care of yourself. You have to think in terms of, "I have to take care of other people." That's the exact opposite of the way the world thinks. The world says, "I'm going to get mine; it's too bad you didn't get here sooner if you wanted to get it. You should have gotten here before I got here, because now I'm getting it." That's the way the world thinks.

The Kingdom of God says, "I've got this, and I want to give it to you. I want to help you, because I cannot exhaust the resources of heaven. The more I give you, the more blessed I get."

Think in terms of this: Jesus was telling them how to operate according to the Kingdom, according to God's Government, and how it operates. He said, "Don't worry about tomorrow, don't worry about things, and don't worry about your daily needs."

I started thinking about when I was in the military. I never thought about food, in the sense of wondering if there was going to be any food tomorrow. I always knew they were going to take care of me. We were going to have chow, it was going to be open at the right time, we were going to go down to eat, and it would be there. What that did was allow me to be free to concentrate on my job and on what I was doing.

I didn't have to worry about things. If I needed a uniform, they provided it. If I needed food, they provided it, If I needed transportation from one place to another, they provided it. They provided everything I needed so that I could effectively do my job.

When I started looking at that, I started seeing the correlation between it and the way the Kingdom operates. That's the way that the Kingdom of God, the Government of God operates. If you will quit making sure that you are provided for, trust your Heavenly Father and start making sure others are provided for, you will always be provided for. Why? It is because there is a Government, and at the head of that Government is a King who happens to be your Father who will take care of you.

Get busy about your Father's business and everything will start to fall into place.

Right at this moment, many have situations going on. There may be financial situations or health situations going on within a family; there might even be social situations. Many would say that their lives are in an uproar. The more they focus on it, the more their lives will be in an uproar.

However, the more they focus on the Kingdom of God, on the Government of God, and on how God does things, the more they will start applying that into everyday life. All of those things will just begin to shape up and begin to fall in place.

We've got one of those little coin counting machines. You turn this lever and every coin goes into the right slot. That's the way things work, as long as you try not to focus on the coins. You start pouring those coins in and you may try to watch them going into the slots, but you can't. You just pour them all in there, turn the thing on and they go into the right slot. That's the way the Government of heaven is. You just get busy about your Father's business and everything will start to fall into place.

That's not to say that everything in my life is in place. It doesn't mean that all things in the ministry are in place and that everything is just perfect; it's not like that. We are like anybody else. We have family things going on, and we have ministry things going on; we have all kinds of things going on. The amazing thing is that I've learned to just take my hands off and trust God.

I was raised over in Mesquite, east of Dallas, most of my early life and I went through high school there. During that time, I went to Larry Mahan Bull Riding School and rode bulls with Donny Gay. I always enjoyed it. I was just an adrenaline junkie, so I liked the adrenaline rush of it.

We used to make bets about who was going to get thrown the first and how quickly. The key was being able to tell the riders who were uptight that they were the first ones to go. The first thing you have to learn about bull riding is that you have to relax. You have to relax, and then you have to get what they call the rhythm of the bull.

Admittedly, you only have eight seconds or less to do that ride, so it happens quickly. The idea is that if you get on, you have to get a good grip, because you're holding yourself on there. You have to really hold that rope. It doesn't latch in; it's not like a belt buckle. You actually have to hold it, so you have to have a really good grip, but at the same time, you have to be totally relaxed.

If you're not relaxed, the ride will pop every joint and every bone. Those who are uptight are the people who will get hurt, so you have to learn to relax. Hold on tight, relax and listen for the buzzer. That's all you have to do. Lean back, and as they say, "Rake the spurs." The farther you lean back, the higher your score goes. The whole idea is to relax.

Have the peace of God and the joy of God in the journey.

Jesus said several times, "They're going to know you because of your love." He said, "I'm leaving you a peace, not like the world has, but My peace. They're going to know you because of your peace." He said, "You're going to have a joy that no one else is going to be able to understand." Well, joy comes out of peace. If you don't have peace, you are not going to have joy. Love and joy are the things that we are supposed to be known for.

Jesus didn't say that you were going to be known for your power. Power has to do with signs to show people that God is with you. He said that you would be known because you love people.

Jesus was saying, "People are going to know I'm with you, because you love them. People are going to know I am with you, because you have joy that they cannot explain. They are in the same situation you're in, but you have joy, and they don't. In the midst of that, you're going to have a peace that they're not going to understand. The reason is that you understand that you have a Heavenly Father, and they don't." Think about that. The things you seldom see in the lives of Christians are love, peace, and joy, all of which are fruit of the Spirit.

There has to be a place where we actually make that conscious decision that we are going to live differently. There is no "chance" involved, because you're relying on God, which is the strongest position you could ever be in. There comes a point where you just have to let go. Quit being all uptight; have the peace of God and have the joy of God in the journey.

People will watch someone ride a bull and ask, "How can he do that? That's so dangerous." The rider will say, "Are you kidding me? It's so much fun." "How can it be fun? It's dangerous." "That's why it's fun. You get that adrenaline rush, but once you get past that, then it becomes an art."

Somebody that has ridden a bull before, or someone that is familiar with bull riding, knows that when a guy gets on a bull, people watch the guy; they don't even watch the bull. They don't think of the danger wondering, "Oh, what is going to happen? Is he going to get hurt? Is he going to get trampled?" No, they watch the rider, and say, "Oh, look! He's leaning back, his hands are up, and he's in perfect form! Look at how he's raking those spurs! Man, this is going to be a good score." They are not even judging it from the same viewpoint of somebody who has never been on a bull. Someone that has ridden a bull has been there, so they look at it differently.

As Christians, that's who we have to be. We cannot be like the world looking on the outside saying, "Oh, what are we going to do? It's terrible; it's awful! The economy is in the tank. It's bad, and it's going down. What am I going to do?" We can't be like that. When people ask, "What is so different? How are you happy? Don't you see what's going on? How can you be so peaceful? Haven't you heard what's happening?" then you can turn around, and say, "Oh, I'm not worried about that. I've got somebody else backing me."

You have to realize that paper currency is unstable, because they can value it or devalue it at will. I would say the most sure things are gold, silver, and precious metals. Even that fluctuates, but still it is more solid than just paper money. If you have paper money, it's usually in a bank somewhere, and even if it's not, the value goes up or down, it doesn't matter whether it's in a bank or in your mattress. When you pull it out, it isn't worth what it was before, and it usually isn't going to go up. However, if you have precious metals, most of the time those stay solid, and they become something you can trade with.

Have faith in God that He will to do what He has said He will to do.

The Kingdom of God, the Government of God, has a different currency than paper money. It has a solid value all the time, and we call it faith. As long as you can maintain faith, you can maintain stability. You have to be able to have faith in God that He will do what He has said He will do. That is having faith in the Government of God, having faith in the Kingdom of God.

The other day I was at the bank and on the window was a sign that said, "This is backed by the full faith and credit of the United States." I looked at that and asked the teller, "Does that make you nervous having that thing on there? Do you ever get any comments on that sign?" The girl started laughing and said, "Yeah, we get a lot of comments on that now, because people don't have very much faith in the stability of the United States government. A lot of people are concerned about it." She also said that people came in all the time to just check their balance as if that would make a difference. How much balance you have in the account is not how much you have in there.

In the Kingdom of God, your faith in God will enable you to relax, to enter into His rest, to trust that you have a Heavenly Father who will take care of you under all circumstances, no matter what you're going through and no matter what's happening. You know that there may be ups and downs, but at the end you're going to come out all right.

That's the main aspect of what God is trying to get across through His Kingdom.

Remember what He said in Matthew 6:33: "If you seek first the Kingdom of God and His righteousness, these things shall be added to you." It doesn't say you will pursue them. As a matter of fact it says the opposite. He says if you want them, don't pursue them. You go after the Kingdom of God, and these things will be added to you. If you go after those things, you're acting like a heathen. Go with me to Philippians 4.

Philippians 4:19,

> 19 But my God shall supply all your need according to his riches in glory by Christ Jesus.

"His riches and glory by Christ Jesus" are immeasurable. We can talk about them, but they are immeasurable. You could never deplete "His riches in glory by Christ Jesus." It is a bottomless bank account. I'm not just talking money. Hopefully, I'm just giving you a visual.

Notice he said, "My God shall supply all your need according to His riches in glory." Notice that it doesn't say it is according to your good works or according to the way you sow. Now, admittedly, when he was talking to the Philippians, the people of the Philippian church had sacrificially supported Paul. When nobody else did, they had partnered with him so there was an aspect of that that they were walking in.

Paul was writing to them saying, "My God." He didn't say, "Their God." Obviously, it was the same God, but he said, "I'm not even talking about how much you believe in God. I'm telling you my God will take care of all your need by His riches in glory by Christ Jesus." Paul had faith in God for the Philippians. He told them that God was going to take care of them.

In Matthew 6:33, Jesus said, in so many words, "Seek first the Kingdom, seek first the Government of God, seek first God's way of doing things and His righteousness, and all the things you need shall be taken care of." Then, in Philippians 4:19, Paul said, "My God shall supply all your need." Wasn't he saying the same thing that Jesus said? Jesus didn't brag on Himself, but he did say that God would supply all your need. Jesus said, "Your Heavenly Father knows that you have need of these things, and He's going to take care of you."

James 4:1,

1 From whence *come* wars and fightings among you? *come they* not hence, *even* of your lusts that war in your members?

2 Ye lust, and have not: ye kill, and desire to have, and cannot obtain: ye fight and war, yet ye have not, because ye ask not.

"You lust, and have not." The word "*lust*" and the way it is used today usually has a strong, sexual connotation to it, but all it means is *an insatiable desire.* That's all it means.

"You lust, and have not." Notice what it was saying: "You desire to have things, you strongly want things, and don't have them. You desire to have them, and cannot obtain them." That's the old carrot and stick thing, which refers to a policy of offering a combination of rewards and punishment to induce behavior. It's always out there. They pay people just enough to keep them from quitting, and the people will work just enough to keep from getting fired. Generally, that's the way business is.

He says, "You lust, and have not: you kill, and desire to have, and cannot obtain: you fight and war, yet you have not, because you ask not." Do you hear that? He was saying, "You want it, you desire it, you go after it, and you fight for it. You go after those things, you lust after them, you try to get them, and you can't get them, and the reason you don't have them is because you didn't ask." Isn't that simple?

You say, "You mean I don't have to struggle, and fight, and war, and go after these things? Are you telling me business isn't cutthroat? I can't go out there and step on the other guy? That's not the way it's done?" James said, "You're doing all that you think you're supposed to do, and it is not working." He said, "Do it the Kingdom way; do God's Government; do God's principle."

Ask for the things that you strongly desire, not for the things you need.

In Matthew 6:33 Jesus didn't say anything about asking. He said, "If you seek first the Kingdom of God and His righteousness, these things will be added unto you." Your focus is on the Kingdom; your focus is on the Government of God. Then in Philippians it said, "My God shall supply all your need according to His riches." He didn't say according to how you ask. Both times, in Matthew 6:33 and Philippians 4:19, it was talking about needs. Your needs will be taken care of by God without you asking.

Then what do we have to ask for? According to James 4, you have to ask for the things that you strongly desire, not for the things you need. You ask for what you want. You don't have to ask for what you need.

When my kids were at home with us, they didn't have to ask us for food; we fed them. They didn't have to ask us for clothing; we clothed them. They didn't have to ask. We did it for them automatically. As a matter of fact, sometimes we had to make them eat when they didn't want to. We had to make them wear clothes when they didn't want to. Those things can be provided. Are you seeing the picture here?

I am trying to get across to you that what most people do is spend all their time begging God for their needs. You're wasting your time begging God for your needs because He said, "I'm taking care of your needs. If you are going to talk to Me, if you are going to ask Me for something, ask Me for what you want, ask Me for what you strongly desire. The wants are what you ask for. The needs are handled, so don't waste your time."

You can spend time thanking God for meeting your needs. You can spend time worshiping God. What most people end up doing is spending all of their time chasing after their needs. If they talk to God, it's usually about things they need. It is sometimes about what they want, but they spend so much time trying to get things that they never really fellowship with God. I can tell you, "I am blessed, and yet I don't ask God for anything."

Transparency here: my biggest thought toward anything is that I always want to make sure that what I have promised our employees is there, and that there is enough money to pay them. I'm not worried about it. I don't say, "Are we going to make budget this week? Are we going to be able to make payroll day?" I don't think that way. It's always there. On my list of priorities, that is my number one priority.

Honestly, everything else could fall apart, but I've promised people by hiring them that we are going to pay them. Therefore, to me that's a big thing, because if it isn't there, that's a family that is going to do without. That's the way I see it, because I have taken them on as a responsibility. God has blessed us all through the years. Even before we had employees, God blessed us. We had abundance, and we were able to do things and help other people.

As I take employees on as responsibility, I have never said, "Okay, God. We are going to need an extra X amount of dollars this week, because we hired this person or we hired that person." I've never done that. Whatever we promised, the increase was there the next week, and it has always been there. I am not preaching theory here; this is reality.

If you make other people your responsibility, then the increase will come through you. You've just got to remember it's coming through you, and it's not just for you. Then, you start to give it out. I hope you see that God takes care of your needs. If you have some wants, you can tell Him about that.

James 4:3,

> 3 Ye ask, and receive not, because ye ask amiss, that ye may consume *it* upon your lusts.

He says, "You ask, and receive not." There's a stipulation here, "…because you ask amiss, that you may consume it upon your lusts." What He was saying here is, "I'm going to take care of your needs. I'm going to take care of what you need here, and if you ask, then I will give you the things you want. However, if what you want is moving into an area where you're putting your attention on those things rather than seeking first the Kingdom, then you're not going to get it, because you're getting your attention off the Kingdom. It is your attention on the Kingdom that actually causes all of these things to come to you."

> 4 Ye adulterers and adulteresses, know ye not that the friendship of the world is enmity with God? whosoever therefore will be a friend of the world is the enemy of God.

He was speaking to adulterers and adulteresses, asking them, "Don't you know that friendship with the world is enmity with God?" If you are a friend of the world, then you are the enemy of God.

> 5 Do ye think that the scripture saith in vain, The spirit that dwelleth in us lusteth to envy?

Do you hear that? "The spirit that dwells in you lusts." It puts a strong insatiable desire in you and is envious and jealous over your time. God wants you to focus on Him. He wants to be "All in All." He wants to be "El Shaddai" to you. He wants to be everything that we need, yet we make everything else our need.

Lean on God and not to your own understanding.

Proverbs 3:5 says,

> 5 Trust in the Lord with all thine heart; and lean not unto thine own understanding.

Why would we make other things the answer to our need rather than God? It is because when we make other things the answer to our need or we go after these other things, then we're not leaning on God. We start to lean to our own understanding.

We start to go down our own path, and it's like, "Well, I can believe God for this, or I can buy it. It's easier to buy it than to believe God for it, because I'm not really sure that God wants me to have it. I really want it, so I'm just going to buy it."

It has been amazing that God has known what our needs were going to be before we knew that we had need of them. Whenever I recognized that I had need for something, I just told God, "This is what we need. I know that You already know it, so I thank You for it." I didn't fret over it, as we would say. I told Him exactly.

I have retired two Tahoes with over 400,000 miles on each of them. They were still holding up, still running, still decent cars, but not good enough for going across the country. I told God, "I need a new vehicle and it needs to be bigger than a Tahoe. I'll take a Suburban or a Yukon, either one, I don't care which, and I don't want to pay for it." I said, "I'm going around the country preaching Your gospel, doing Your business, and I'm not buying this for a personal car. This is Your business car, so You provide it."

Within a week, the money came in for that vehicle. When we found a vehicle, the money was to the dime, exactly. My wife and daughter went online, found a vehicle, and said, "Here it is." I said, "How much is it?" They said, "X amount of dollars." I said, "Okay." Now, could we have paid for it? Probably, but I would have had to divert funds from somewhere else where I had need of it. I shouldn't have to pay for what I have a need for. He said that He would provide that. I'm not telling you theory here; I'm telling you what works.

Relax and trust God.

I really want you to get understand that you need to relax and trust God. He loves you. He is your Father, and He will take care of you. If you are going to use faith, don't be in stress. If you're in stress, you're not in faith. Some people talk about being in faith when they're really in stress, and you can usually tell the difference. Just relax. I'm not saying don't push, but you can push relaxed. It's one of those weird things about the Kingdom.

Matthew 3:1,

> 1 In those days came John the Baptist, preaching in the wilderness of Judaea,
>
> 2 And saying, Repent ye: for the kingdom of heaven is at hand.

"The kingdom," the government of heaven, "is at hand."

We've talked about the Kingdom of God and the kingdom of heaven, and I am going to be clarifying some things that we have said throughout this teaching, because I want to be specific about these things.

I want you to realize these things about the Kingdom, but I don't want you to take these things and make them into some hard and fast rule. Don't try to use them as a formula. Formulas are what you use when you are trying to work things out for yourself. Trust God. God's not a formula. There are ways that God works, but don't try to play God; don't try to work God.

There are some people that will come up to you, and they will try to play you; they will try to con you. You're not going to con God. It's like worship. Sometimes when you have worship, it's not really worship. It is you trying to convince God to show up to do something.

Don't try to manipulate God. It doesn't work. He knows what you're planning.

The Kingdom of God is within you. The kingdom of heaven is merely the manifestation of the Kingdom of God that is in you.

Notice that when we talk about the kingdom of heaven, with only one or two exceptions, the kingdom of heaven is always referred to as being at hand. The Kingdom of God, with only one exception, is always referred to as being within you.

The Kingdom of God is within you, and the kingdom of heaven is at hand. The kingdom of heaven is merely the manifestation of the Kingdom of God that is in you. Because the Kingdom of God is within you, when you put your hands on someone, you are manifesting the Kingdom of God. That manifestation is called the kingdom of heaven. This Government of God in you shows how things are supposed to be in heaven.

When you lay hands on the sick, you're showing the earth Who is in you and what is in you; you're showing earth how it is supposed to be and how it is in heaven. The Kingdom of God is within you; the kingdom of heaven is at hand.

Many people have the Kingdom of God for years. They have it within them, but they never have the kingdom of heaven, because it is never at hand for them. It's always within, but it's not always at hand for some.

The manifestation of the Kingdom of God that is in you is causing earth to look like heaven. I'm trying to say it every way I can so I can get it across to you. When you reach out your hand to touch a life, the Kingdom of God is being made manifest, and that manifestation is called the kingdom of heaven. Hopefully that will help clear some things up.

He said in verse 2, "Repent, for the kingdom of heaven is at hand."

Matthew chapter 3,

> 3 For this is he that was spoken of by the prophet Esaias, saying, The voice of one crying in the wilderness, Prepare ye the way of the Lord, make his paths straight.
>
> 4 And the same John had his raiment of camel's hair, and a leathern girdle about his loins; and his meat was locusts and wild honey.
>
> 5 Then went out to him Jerusalem, and all Judaea, and all the region round about Jordan,
>
> 6 And were baptized of him in Jordan, confessing their sins.
>
> 7 But when he saw many of the Pharisees and Sadducees come to his baptism, he said unto them, O generation of vipers, who hath warned you to flee from the wrath to come?

Don't become a Pharisee and let someone remain in pain just so you don't violate what you see as a biblical principle.

You have to remember the differences between the Pharisees and Sadducees. Christians today, especially charismatic Christians, when compared to religious Jewish sects of that time, are closest to the Pharisees. The Pharisees believed in the spirit realm, they believed in the resurrection of the dead, they believed in power, they believed in the accuracy of the Word of God, and they believed in the divine inspiration of the Word of God. It was amazing.

The Sadducees were just the opposite. They didn't believe in angels, didn't believe in gifts, and didn't believe in power. They didn't believe in anything really, which is why they were "Sad-you-see." Now, just to give credit where credit is due, that expression came from Charles Capps. Some of you might remember him. I remember when he first said that, I thought, "That is a good way to remember the difference between the two groups."

Always remember: it is very easy for a Spirit-filled Christian to become a Pharisee, because they are so close. The way you become a Pharisee is when you allow someone to remain in pain, to remain hurt, just so you don't violate what you see as a biblical principle. That's what the Pharisees did. They didn't want Jesus healing on the Sabbath because keeping the Sabbath was a law—yet all of the Law was given to help man, not to put man down. The Pharisees turned it around. We cannot be that way.

There are times when you do things that you wouldn't normally do in order to help somebody, even though you might not agree, on a general basis, of what they are doing. You say, "What in the world are you talking about?" Maybe you would go into a place you would never go, but you know that there is a person there who needs help. You go there even though you wouldn't go there on your own, because you don't like it. I'm just giving you an example.

I'll tell you this too: if your car is such that you are unwilling to pick up a drunk who's passed out on the gutter because you're afraid he is going to throw up all over your leather or carpet, that car is an idol to you. People are more important than things. If God gave you the thing, you need to use it for God. Amen?

If you truly repent, you should have some fruit to prove it. Repentance is not in word only.

8 Bring forth therefore fruits meet for repentance:

9 And think not to say within yourselves, We have Abraham to *our* father: for I say unto you, that God is able of these stones to raise up children unto Abraham.

10 And now also the axe is laid unto the root of the trees: therefore every tree which bringeth not forth good fruit is hewn down, and cast into the fire.

We know that he was not talking about trees.

11 I indeed baptize you with water unto repentance: but he that cometh after me is mightier than I, whose shoes I am not worthy to bear: he shall baptize you with the Holy Ghost, and *with* fire:

12 Whose fan *is* in his hand, and he will throughly purge his floor, and gather his wheat into the garner; but he will burn up the chaff with unquenchable fire.

The fire here is in context with burning up the chaff.

Again, I'm going to try to break some religious thinking. If you're going to study the Bible, you have to take it in context. Here he said, "He shall baptize you with the Holy Ghost and with fire." Then he said, "He will purge His floor, gather His wheat, and He will burn up the chaff."

Notice that wheat and chaff are two different things: wheat is good, chaff is bad. Chaff gets burned up but not the wheat. He says of Jesus, "He that comes after me…is going to baptize you with the Holy Ghost and fire." Notice: He was mentioning fire with being burned up.

People say, "He's going to baptize us with the Holy Ghost and fire. I want that fire." Actually, the fire here is in context with burning up the chaff, so the fire isn't always a good thing. It's good to be purged, but this fire is not a pleasant thing, because purging is never a pleasant thing.

When people say, "He's going to baptize me with the Holy Ghost and fire. I want the Holy Ghost fire," they're talking about the purging. He will be purging them, chopping things off, burning things up, and purging their lives.

THE GOVERNMENT OF GOD

Jesus preached, "Repent: for the kingdom of heaven is at hand."

Matthew 4:17,

> 17 From that time Jesus began to preach, and to say, Repent: for the kingdom of heaven is at hand.

John the Baptist preached the kingdom of heaven is at hand, also. Both Jesus and John the Baptist had the same message, basically. What it says here is that from that time on, Jesus began to preach and to say, "The kingdom of heaven is at hand." It never says He stopped. Everything Jesus preached was the Kingdom.

People talk about these great teachings, these great philosophical, moral, and ethical teachings that Jesus did. They were none of those things. They were not philosophical in the sense of what we would think of as philosophy. They were not great moral teachings. Jesus was not trying to make bad people act the right way. He was trying to tell them, "This is how God operates in His Government. If you are going to be in the Kingdom, if you are going to be in God's Government, this is how you will operate; this is how you will function."

You could be seeking citizenship here in the United States, and we could do a citizenship class and teach you all the basics that you need for citizenship. From what I understand, they still teach in these naturalization classes about the three branches of government and how they operate. Unfortunately, there are many people that are being naturalized that know more about how our government operates than some of our native-born citizens.

If someone wants to be naturalized into another country, take on citizenship of another country, they will have to be trained in how that country operates. They can't just go there and say, "I want to be a citizen," and those people say, "Okay, raise your hand. You're in. Go ahead and live anyway you want." No, they say, "Here's the way we operate here. This is our culture here. You can bring your culture with you, but there are rules you have to abide by here. There are ways that we do things." There is a right way to go about it.

Everything in the Bible has two aspects---legal and vital.

The legal aspect is the governmental aspect. The vital aspect is the dynamic; it's how you function in it. As you read the Bible, I want you to start thinking differently. I don't want you to think religiously, I want you to think Kingdom; I want you to think the Government of God. I want you to think from a legal standpoint. Don't think legalistic or legalism, but think about if from a legal standpoint.

We are even told that we are citizens of heaven. That means that we're not citizens here, per se. Admittedly, we apparently have dual citizenship; we're here, but we're not of here. We are born of heaven, therefore, we should know how heaven operates. That's what church generally is about, or what it's supposed to be about.

The church is supposed to be training you how to be good productive citizens in the kingdom of heaven. It's supposed to be teaching you how the Government of God operates and how to function by the principles and laws of the Government of God. Don't think in just religious terms; think in terms of governmental actions.

When you pray, you are an ambassador making a requisition to headquarters.

Once you start thinking in governmental terms, then you start realizing that when you pray, you are an ambassador making a requisition to headquarters. You just simply tell your Heavenly Father what you want. He already knows what you need, so you let Him know, "We want this," then He will provide that for you.

A church should be an embassy. It should be training ambassadors for the kingdom of heaven; that's what a church is supposed to be. It is a family, but it is predominately an embassy.

The Kingdom of God is wherever you are.

This Kingdom that Jesus talked about is not a physical kingdom in the sense that it has a locale, a certain land, so to speak. The difference is that the Kingdom of God is wherever we are. If we're here, then this is the Kingdom of God. If we all left here, this wouldn't be the Kingdom of God. If we were to become scattered, anywhere we put our feet would be the Kingdom of God.

BEHOLD THE KINGDOM

My body is a temple, because it houses the Spirit of God. It's a temple because we're talking about a theocracy; we're not talking about just a physical government in terms of a secular government. We're talking about a Government whose King is God, so instead of a courthouse, we would have a temple, because God is the King, not a judiciary.

My body is a temple of God. Wherever this body goes, wherever I put my foot, this body is technically an embassy. The Kingdom is wherever I am.

When you drive by embassies in other countries, they have guards, especially American Embassies. They have Marines standing guard, and it's usually heavily fortified. It's a fort, yet you look at it and think, "Why would you want to guard this place?" The answer would be that it keeps people from overrunning it. They don't just have an open door.

When you go to an embassy, they stop you at the gate, because that embassy and the grounds around it are the sovereign territory of the nation it represents. If you climb the wall of that embassy and drop to the ground, the minute you touch that ground, no one outside the wall, no one in that country where the embassy is, can touch you. That embassy has to kick you out or you have to leave on your own before that country where the embassy is can have jurisdiction over you.

America abides by that. That is the reason we have guards at the front gate of an American Embassy. We don't want anybody just walking in and saying, "I'm in America now; here I am."

THE GOVERNMENT OF GOD

In an American Embassy in other countries, American laws are observed, but if you go outside that embassy, the laws of whatever country you are in are observed. We also know that ambassadors have what is called diplomatic immunity, meaning that even though they are in another country, the rules of that country there have no rule over them. Generally speaking, the worst they can do is make them leave the country.

We are ambassadors for the Kingdom. The kingdom of this world can't touch us, because we have diplomatic immunity.

That is the reason the enemy has fought Kingdom teaching for so long. You start to realize, as an ambassador, that wherever you go is an embassy. All you and I have to do is put out the invitation, and anybody who jumps into this Kingdom becomes an ambassador, also.

That outside kingdom, the kingdom of this world, can't touch them, because they have diplomatic immunity. That means that sickness, disease, poverty, fear, any mental problems, habits, addictions, or anything like that have a right, but all of those operate under the system of the world. Not one of those things will be in heaven. The Kingdom of God dwells in us, and wherever we are is an embassy. Our body is a temple and because of that, wherever we go we can set the captives free. We can take the Kingdom to them. That's what we do.

I've done a little research on this. Marines who are guarding an American Embassy can actually go out as a unit, as a contingency, and take somebody off the street who has a threat from a crowd against them and take them into the embassy. The minute they are surrounded by the Marines, they are protected by the governmental forces of the United States. Once they get them inside the embassy, the United States can offer asylum.

They can rescue someone who's in danger of imminent harm and take them into the embassy. Once inside, they are given the opportunity to decide, "Do I want to go back out there, or do I want to seek asylum in the United States?" We have that same ability as ambassadors of the Kingdom.

I really want you to see that this is not about some religious thing; it is about a governmental aspect. God says, "This is how My government operates."

God's health care system/God's provisional system:

Divine healing is God's health care system. Jehovah Jirah is God's provisional system; that is God's economy. The way you operate in it is the exact opposite of the way you would operate in the world.

This is so vast and so big, that it is going to take some time to go through it. You need to take it piece by piece, and take the Scripture references we have for you and go through them. Everywhere you see the word "Kingdom," write Government. Write that, and you will start to get a different idea of it.

Thank God that the head of our Government is the King of the universe, and He is our Father. At the same time, He is a King, and He is the head of a Governmental Entity, so we can bring this to pass. Amen? Our job is to show the Kingdom to the world. We are to manifest the Kingdom of God that is within us by bringing the kingdom of heaven to hand. Amen?

Dignity is an element of the Government of God. Jesus walked with dignity.

If you get this message, and if you start walking the way we are talking about here, you will walk like T. L. Osborn. T. L. Osborn walked around with dignity. He gave people dignity, because dignity is an element of the Government of God. Jesus walked with dignity.

Dr. Sumrall used to tell us, as his students, "The devil always wants to make man lose dignity and make man look bad, so he does things to denigrate man. God always gives dignity back to man." The devil will always cause man to walk around with his shoulders slumped, his head down, and afraid to look people in the eye. Jesus comes and lifts our head and says, "Look on us; look at us." He gives man dignity. You don't have to be ashamed.

If you ever face a Christian, you never have to face them with your head down, because the heart of a Christian is to show people respect and to give them dignity. It is never to put them down and definitely not to put condemnation and shame on them. If you ever go somewhere and people put condemnation and shame on you, get up and walk out. Don't listen to them.

Jesus died for us, and those that trust in Him will never be ashamed. He died to give you dignity. He died to lift you, not to put you down. He is the only One who has ever had a right to put you down. He didn't. He lifted you up.

**Kingdom living brings all of the
Kingdom provisions to you and to your life.**

As we go out, let us be ambassadors for the Kingdom of God. Let's go out and be "walking embassies." Let's manifest the Kingdom of God and bring the kingdom of heaven to hand. Let's give people dignity, let's lift people, and let's bless people. Let the people in the world see in us a peace, a joy, and a love so that they will know us by our fruits.

This is what Jesus taught. The "new man" is the result of you coming into the Kingdom. It literally gives you the ability to live out this Kingdom life. You can do this; you can live this life. You were born to live this life. Kingdom living will bring all of the Kingdom provisions to you and to your life.

In Matthew 6:33, Jesus said, in so many words, "Seek first the Kingdom, seek first the Government of God, seek first God's way of doing things, and His righteousness and all the things you need shall be taken care of."

KINGDOM ADMINISTRATORS – PART 1

Sermon given by Curry R. Blake

The last shall be first, and the first shall be last.

Matthew chapter 20,

> 1 For the kingdom of heaven is like unto a man *that is* an householder, which went out early in the morning to hire labourers into his vineyard.

You can already see what Jesus was talking about. There is a spiritual connotation to this, a spiritual application.

> 2 And when he had agreed with the labourers for a penny a day, he sent them into his vineyard.

A "penny" wasn't just a penny as we know it. Obviously, it was a day's wages.

One of the things I always do when I read a passage is to put myself into the situation. We think in pictures, so I picture it. I picture this first century type village. Even today, there are places that you can go where people who do day labor type work are just waiting for somebody to come along and hire them. That's exactly what this was like.

They had this opening in the middle of the city or village, and they would go to this area. They would hang out there to see if there was any work, and if so, then somebody would come along and hire them.

He was likening the kingdom of heaven to a man who is a householder; he was over a house, over his fields, and over his household, as we would say. He went into the city, looked at the people standing around, and he hired them. He hired everybody. That's the main thing I see about this. He hired everybody there for a set wage. Then he sent them into his vineyard, and he went back home.

> 3 And he went out about the third hour, and saw others standing idle in the marketplace,
>
> 4 And said unto them; Go ye also into the vineyard, and whatsoever is right I will give you. And they went their way.

He went back in the third hour, and there was a whole new group of people just hanging around.

Notice: this was twice that he went into the city market and found people who were just standing around idle. He hired them all. Every time he went in, he hired everybody who was standing around.

> 5 Again he went out about the sixth and ninth hour, and did likewise.

Every three hours, he went back to the city. He looked in the marketplace to see if anybody was standing around. He hired everybody there, every time.

> 6 And about the eleventh hour he went out, and found others standing idle, and saith unto them, Why stand ye here all the day idle?

Notice: this time it wasn't three hours later; it was only two hours later. He went back into the town, looked at them and asked, "What are you doing here? Why are you all just standing around idle?"

> 7 They say unto him, Because no man hath hired us. He saith unto them, Go ye also into the vineyard; and whatsoever is right, *that* shall ye receive.

He didn't seem put out necessarily, but he was asking, "Why are you just standing around?" They said, "Well, nobody has hired us." He said, "Well, just go on out to the vineyard, and I'll pay you what is right. I'll take care of you. Just go out there and get busy."

Notice that he was not upset, but he definitely didn't agree with the fact that somebody had to hire them and send them out. He was thinking, "You should have just gotten busy."

> 8 So when even was come, the lord of the vineyard saith unto his steward, Call the labourers, and give them *their* hire, beginning from the last unto the first.

Did you hear that? Start with the last. Why? That's because the last will be first, and the first will be last. He said, "Start with the last, and then work your way to the first; pay them what we agreed to pay them."

> 9 And when they came that *were hired* about the eleventh hour, they received every man a penny.
>
> 10 But when the first came, they supposed that they should have received more; and they likewise received every man a penny.
>
> 11 And when they had received *it*, they murmured against the goodman of the house,
>
> 12 Saying, These last have wrought *but* one hour, and thou hast made them equal unto us, which have borne the burden and heat of the day.

They were expecting more money even though they had agreed to work for a certain amount. What they were trying to do was limit the householder, the employer; they were trying to limit his generosity. They were telling him, "It's not right that you give them the same that you gave us. We worked longer so we should get more."

> 13 But he answered one of them, and said, Friend, I do thee no wrong: didst not thou agree with me for a penny?

He was saying, "That's what you're getting. What is it to you what I pay somebody else?"

14 Take *that* thine *is*, and go thy way: I will give unto this last, even as unto thee.

15 Is it not lawful for me to do what I will with mine own? Is thine eye evil, because I am good?

We know who Jesus was talking about, because one time they came to him and said, "Oh, good Master…" Jesus had said, "There is none good but God." Jesus in this parable called this man good, so we know He was talking about God.

Few are chosen.

16 So the last shall be first, and the first last: for many be called, but few chosen.

That has tripped up a lot of people over time, and in keeping with the illustration of the Kingdom, I just wanted to bring this out to you.

For instance, for people to get into the presidential cabinet, they generally have to be in some other area of government, or in a good business, or be in a place of prominence. Maybe it is wishful thinking on my part, but there should have been a point where those people should have developed some skills to get them in there.

Now, all of the people who work in this kingdom/government that I'm talking about are all working; they have all been called. They've all answered the call for Civil Service, but then out of that Civil Service pool, there will be a few that are chosen. The chosen means that they are in, but they will have certain assignments.

"Make your calling and election sure."

The Word doesn't really say much about making sure that you were chosen.

In 2 Peter 1:10 it says,

> 10 Wherefore the rather, brethren, give diligence to make your calling and election sure: for if ye do these things, ye shall never fall:

Peter said, "Give diligence to make your calling and election sure."

"Don't judge yourself according to other people."

In the parable the householder said, "It is right that I pay the last as much as I pay the first, and it's nobody's business how much I pay anyone." However, that's not the key here. It's obviously telling you, "Don't judge yourself according to other people. Don't look at what they get."

You think, "Well, they haven't been a Christian as long as I have, and look at how God is blessing them. I've been in church faithfully. I've been Sunday School Superintendent for 25 years, and I have to fight to get any healing; I have to fight to get any blessing. Here this guy comes in, and last week, he was a drug addict, a drunkard, and a whoremonger. He stumbles in here high, and gets saved, and God delivers him, and now look at how God's just blessing him. That is just not right; he ought to have to pay some dues."

Jesus said, "That's not how you get healed. That's not how you get any blessing from God. It is not by paying your dues." It is all by the mercy and grace of Jesus Christ. If you had been there in that situation, and you had been what you claim to be, then when you saw this younger Christian come in, then you would have been walking in love and you wouldn't have been envious. You wouldn't have been jealous. You wouldn't have been wishing them harm by wishing that they hadn't been blessed as much as they were.

Our attitudes and our thought processes have to be conformed to the image of Christ.

I am trying to show you some kingdom attitudes, because our attitudes, our thoughts, and our thought processes have to be conformed to the image of Christ. Amen? It's great to talk about power, it's great to talk about miracles, healings, and different things, but we also have to realize that we're being conformed to the image of Christ. That includes power, but your path as a Christian has to be the path of character, it has to be the path of nature, and it has to be the path of fruit. Amen?

Everybody wants to prophesy. Everybody wants to speak into somebody's life, and very honestly, most of the time they don't have the right to speak into other people's lives. If you want to speak into other people's lives, you have got to show some fruit, not gifts.

**If you get a prophecy from God,
and there is no one there to interpret, keep it to yourself.**

In 1 Corinthians 14:28, Paul said,

> 28 But if there be no interpreter, let him keep silence in the church; and let him speak to himself, and to God.

The Holy Spirit, through the Apostle Paul, told them, "If you get a word from God, and there's not someone there that can interpret it, keep it to yourself." You say, "I can't keep it to myself. I have a word for this person." Why don't you just pray that word for them?

If you think that God is showing you a word about a person, just pray for them, whether it's good or bad. God is trying to show you something about them. Pray for them; you don't have to go to them. You don't have to run to them. However, if it's really good, then you will want to run to them, and tell them some great prophecy and say, "Oh, God is going to use you. God's going to give you this. He's calling you to this."

Have you ever thought that you might really be responsible for causing a novice to fall into the snare of the devil by pumping them up and telling them, "You are going to be a great! You're going to have the anointing like no one else has ever had it." God had them on a path, and you are being used by the devil to snare them.

Now, should you encourage them? Yes. Should you say things that the Bible says? Yes. That's what real prophesying is anyway. It's an encouragement. It's a comfort. It's to edify and build up, not to puff up. You ought to be able to tell these people what God said about them in the Word. If they ask, "How do you know God said that about me?" you could say, "Let me show you." You ought to be able to show them in the Word.

You say, "Well, I'm going to prophesy to them." No, you're trying to get a word of knowledge, a specific thing, or maybe a word of wisdom to say, "Do it this way; go this way."

**Sometimes you just need to pray,
especially if you haven't been proven.**

I've been around the block a time or two, and I have seen some things. I have seen some great people with great potential. Even in our own ministry we've had people come along that had some great potential, but they were just so full of themselves that you never saw Christ in them. People all around them would build them up and make them think, "Oh, I ought to be out holding crusades." No, you ought to be cleaning toilets, until you die to self.

You ought to be helping other people. You ought to be going out, laying hands on the sick, and ministering to people. I'm not saying you don't do that, because if you are a Christian, you do those things. A lot of people, as soon as they start hearing words like that, they stop really helping people, because they start thinking they're somebody and that they are too good for that.

If God really speaks a word to you about where you're going and what He has for you, He's telling you that because you're on the right path. Don't change. When people tell you, "Oh, you're going to be a great this or great that," don't change. That path you're on is the right path, and it is what got God's attention so He could say, "Yes, I'll be able to use you."

That's what happened with Dowie. He should have stayed on the path he was on. It would have been better for him to stay in Chicago and fight with the politicians, the newspaper people, and the alcohol people. It would have been better for him to stay there and fight for the rest of his life, rather than moving up to Zion, becoming a little pope, and getting off into something else.

You just need to be proven.

When David went to fight Goliath, Saul said, "Take my armor and take my sword." David said, "No, that's not been proven." Saul had been in battle. He'd won. His weapons were proven, but they hadn't been proven by David. David hadn't wielded Saul's sword before, and the worst thing you can do is go into battle with a new weapon that you've never handled before. It will make you a little slower, a little more awkward, and it will cost you your life.

David said, "No, God is with me." David went out with what he was used to, even though it wasn't thought of as being the best of weapons. It was generally thought that a sword or javelin with full armor was the best. David went out with a slingshot and a rock. He even told Goliath when he got out there: "Today, God is going to deliver you into my hands, and I'm going to take your head off your shoulders." You can't take somebody's head off with a rock. David was looking at Goliath's sword. He said, "This rock is going to put you down. I'm going to take your own sword and kill you with it."

You have to know what weapons you're using. Your weapons have to be proven. You ought to try things out; test them out. Pray about something, and see if it comes to pass. If you need verification, write the thing down. Start telling God, "God, I want to prove this." Do you know how much honor God gives you when you want to prove something instead of just jumping into the middle of other people's lives? Why? That's because it shows you really care about them, and you're not trying to be somebody.

"The chief priests and Pharisees heard His parables, and they perceived that He spoke of them."

Matthew 21: 23.

> 23 And when he was come into the temple, the chief priests and the elders of the people came unto him as he was teaching, and said, By what authority doest thou these things? and who gave thee this authority?

> 24 And Jesus answered and said unto them, I also will ask you one thing, which if ye tell me, I in like wise will tell you by what authority I do these things.
>
> 25 The baptism of John, whence was it? from heaven, or of men? And they reasoned with themselves, saying, If we shall say, From heaven; he will say unto us, Why did ye not then believe him?
>
> 26 But if we shall say, Of men; we fear the people; for all hold John as a prophet.

These were the religious leaders and they feared the people, because the people held John up as a prophet.

> 27 And they answered Jesus, and said, We cannot tell...

They were lying when they said, "We cannot tell."

> 27 ...And he said unto them, Neither tell I you by what authority I do these things.
>
> 28 But what think ye? A *certain* man had two sons; and he came to the first, and said, Son, go work to day in my vineyard.
>
> 29 He answered and said, I will not: but afterward he repented, and went.
>
> 30 And he came to the second, and said likewise. And he answered and said, I *go*, sir: and went not.

31 Whether of them twain did the will of *his* father? They say unto him, The first. Jesus saith unto them, Verily I say unto you, That the publicans and the harlots go into the kingdom of God before you.

32 For John came unto you in the way of righteousness, and ye believed him not: but the publicans and the harlots believed him: and ye, when ye had seen *it*, repented not afterward, that ye might believe him.

Then Jesus said, "Hear another parable:"

33 Hear another parable: There was a certain householder, which planted a vineyard, and hedged it round about, and digged a winepress in it, and built a tower, and let it out to husbandmen, and went into a far country:

34 And when the time of the fruit drew near, he sent his servants to the husbandmen, that they might receive the fruits of it.

35 And the husbandmen took his servants, and beat one, and killed another, and stoned another.

36 Again, he sent other servants more than the first: and they did unto them likewise.

37 But last of all he sent unto them his son, saying, They will reverence my son.

> 38 But when the husbandmen saw the son, they said among themselves, This is the heir; come, let us kill him, and let us seize on his inheritance.

Isn't it amazing how people can have two different viewpoints? The father said, "This is my son. They will honor him. They will listen to him." Think about that. Obviously, this father was an optimist. Obviously, he was a person of faith. He believed in the good in people, yet when the people saw his son, they thought just the opposite. They said, "This is the heir. Let's kill him, and we won't have to deal with this anymore."

> 39 And they caught him, and cast *him* out of the vineyard, and slew *him*.
>
> 40 When the lord therefore of the vineyard cometh, what will he do unto those husbandmen?

You've got to remember that Jesus was telling this to the Pharisees, to the leaders.

> 41 They say unto him, He will miserably destroy those wicked men, and will let out *his* vineyard unto other husbandmen, which shall render him the fruits in their seasons.

Various scholars say that these passages refer to the Jews and the Gospel of the kingdom being taken from the Jews and given over to the Gentiles.

KINGDOM ADMINISTRATORS – PART 1

Your life can change based on one decision!
David's entire life changed based on one decision.

In 2 Samuel chapter 11, it tells us what David did:

> 1 And it came to pass, after the year was expired, at the time when kings go forth *to battle*, that David sent Joab, and his servants with him, and all Israel; and they destroyed the children of Ammon, and besieged Rabbah. But David tarried still at Jerusalem

Kings were supposed to go to war, but David stayed in the palace. David's army went out to war, and they were fighting.

> 2 And it came to pass in an eveningtide, that David arose from off his bed, and walked upon the roof of the king's house: and from the roof he saw a woman washing herself; and the woman *was* very beautiful to look upon.

> 3 And David sent and enquired after the woman. And *one* said, *Is* not this Bathsheba, the daughter of Eliam, the wife of Uriah the Hittite?

> 4 And David sent messengers, and took her; and she came in unto him, and he lay with her; for she was purified from her uncleanness: and she returned unto her house.

> 5 And the woman conceived, and sent and told David, and said, I *am* with child.

It said that in the evening, David went to walk on his rooftop, and he saw a woman bathing on the next rooftop, and it said that she was really beautiful. David went down and asked, "Who is that?" They said, "Well, that's Uriah's wife." He said, "Well, send for her."

The people were whispering in David's palace saying, "That's Uriah's wife. What does he want with her? Why should she come over here?" The problem was that they were whispering instead of speaking up and saying, "David, don't do this. We know where you're going with this, so don't do it."

David sent for her, and she came to him. It says that he lay with her, and she became pregnant. She sent word and said, "I'm pregnant with your child."

Here was David, a man after God's own heart. Why? It was because he knew how to repent quickly. That's really what made him after God's own heart, but he didn't do it that time.

David had refused to touch Saul when he had every opportunity to kill him. Instead he showed him honor. This showed the character he had, which is why God called him. He went out, and he killed Goliath. He had great victories in battle. They were just amazing things. God was with him. He walked with God, and he was tender before God, yet he saw Bathsheba, brought her over, and she got pregnant.

In 2 Samuel 11:6-11, it says,

6 And David sent to Joab, *saying*, Send me Uriah the Hittite. And Joab sent Uriah to David.

7 And when Uriah was come unto him, David demanded *of him* how Joab did, and how the people did, and how the war prospered.

8 And David said to Uriah, Go down to thy house, and wash thy feet. And Uriah departed out of the king's house, and there followed him a mess *of meat* from the king.

9 But Uriah slept at the door of the king's house with all the servants of his lord, and went not down to his house.

10 And when they had told David, saying, Uriah went not down unto his house, David said unto Uriah, Camest thou not from *thy* journey? why *then* didst thou not go down unto thine house?

11 And Uriah said unto David, The ark, and Israel, and Judah, abide in tents; and my lord Joab, and the servants of my lord, are encamped in the open fields; shall I then go into mine house, to eat and to drink, and to lie with my wife? *as* thou livest, and *as* thy soul liveth, I will not do this thing.

Now, here was David, the great David. He was the man who wouldn't even touch Saul when he had every opportunity. Then he said, "Send for Uriah." He told Uriah, "Come in and tell me how the battle is going." Uriah said, "Oh, it's going well."

David said, "Stay here a day or two, and then go back to the battle, because I've got a message I want you to take back to Joab, the leader of the armies." Uriah said, "Okay."

David said, "Go down to your house, wash your feet, and be with your wife." It sounded good at the time. He was trying to hide his sin, and he was hoping that Uriah would lay with Bathsheba so he wouldn't know whose child it was.

Here was this man after God's own heart. Here was this man that loved God with everything he had. He used to sit and sing psalms to God when he was nobody, and then he started down that wrong path. He became an adulterer, and then he began to become a conspirator and murderer. David had a heart, and he had character; he just had a major flaw.

Uriah went out, but he didn't go home; he slept at David's doorstep. David brought him in the next morning and asked, "How are you doing? Didn't you go home?" Uriah said, "No. How could I go home and sleep in my bed whenever my general and my armies, your servants, are sleeping in the field in battle?"

You have to know the kind of character that David had, and he saw this same character in Uriah. You know it had to break his heart, and it crushed him when he realized, "What am I doing?"

In 2 Samuel 11, starting with verse 12, it continues:

12 And David said to Uriah, Tarry here to day also, and to morrow I will let thee depart. So Uriah abode in Jerusalem that day, and the morrow.

13 And when David had called him, he did eat and drink before him; and he made him drunk: and at even he went out to lie on his bed with the servants of his lord, but went not down to his house.

14 And it came to pass in the morning, that David wrote a letter to Joab, and sent *it* by the hand of Uriah.

David told Uriah, "Well, stay another day or two," and he wrote a letter, and he gave the letter to Uriah to take back to Joab. The sad thing about that was that Uriah didn't know it, but he was carrying his own death warrant.

15 And he wrote in the letter, saying, Set ye Uriah in the forefront of the hottest battle, and retire ye from him, that he may be smitten, and die.

16 And it came to pass, when Joab observed the city, that he assigned Uriah unto a place where he knew that valiant men *were*.

17 And the men of the city went out, and fought with Joab: and there fell *some* of the people of the servants of David; and Uriah the Hittite died also.

David wrote to Joab, "When you go into the battle, put Uriah right up at the front and in the thick of the battle." Then he said, "In the heat of the battle, you withdraw, yet let Uriah die." That's exactly what happened, but he lost the whole battle because of it.

> 18 Then Joab sent and told David all the things concerning the war;
>
> 19 And charged the messenger, saying, When thou hast made an end of telling the matters of the war unto the king,
>
> 20 And if so be that the king's wrath arise, and he say unto thee, Wherefore approached ye so nigh unto the city when ye did fight? knew ye not that they would shoot from the wall?
>
> 21 …then say thou, Thy servant Uriah the Hittite is dead also.

Joab told the messenger, "When David hears how we lost this battle he's going to be upset, so after you tell him that and he's angry, then you can tell him, 'Oh, but Uriah is dead,' and that will make him happy."

> 22 So the messenger went, and came and shewed David all that Joab had sent him for.
>
> 23 And the messenger said unto David, Surely the men prevailed against us, and came out unto us into the field, and we were upon them even unto the entering of the gate.

24 And the shooters shot from off the wall upon thy servants; and some of the king's servants be dead, and thy servant Uriah the Hittite is dead also.

25 Then David said unto the messenger, Thus shalt thou say unto Joab, Let not this thing displease thee, for the sword devoureth one as well as another: make thy battle more strong against the city, and overthrow it: and encourage thou him.

Now, think about that. The only reason I am bringing this story up is for one point. I'm not bringing it up to focus on David. It's not to try to get the focus on you or to get you to repent of anything. I'm not saying that at all, please understand.

All I want to bring out of this story in 2 Samuel 11 is that the whole situation started in verse 1 when it said, "It was a time when kings went to war, and David stayed in the palace." Joab shouldn't have been leading the armies of Israel. David should have been out there in that field. He should have been leading those armies.

His problems started when he got lazy and stayed home. He started walking around, looking over his kingdom, and looked over at another man's house. It was then that he saw Bathsheba. If he'd been in the field, he would have remained a great general.

Nathan exposed David's sin by telling him a story about a rich man who stole a sheep.

The amazing thing is that David thought he got away with it, and then Nathan showed up. Nathan came walking in and told David this story about a rich man who stole this little sheep, and it was the greatest little sheep. It was the only one that the poor family owned. This rich man had all of these other sheep, but he wanted that one. You can find this in 2 Samuel 12:1-7.

After Nathan told the story, David said, "Who is that man? He will pay." I'm sure Nathan pointed a finger at David and said, "You're that man." That's the first time you see where David was just crushed. David's entire life changed based on that one decision.

Every decision you make can have the possibility of being a life-altering decision, for good or for bad. You have to realize that you can live free, but at the same time, you have to know the price that some decisions cost.

David had several things take place even after this that were pretty amazing, but this thing haunted David for the rest of his life. It caused rebellion even in his own family. It caused the death of children. It was said that the violence of the sword would never leave his house. He had a daughter who was raped, and he had a son who died. Horrible things came out of one decision. One decision!

Jesus was doing the same thing that Nathan did. He exposed all of the things that the leaders had done wrong.

Let's go back to Matthew 21.

40 When the lord therefore of the vineyard cometh, what will he do unto those husbandmen?

41 They say unto him, He will miserably destroy those wicked men, and will let out *his* vineyard unto other husbandmen, which shall render him the fruits in their seasons.

42 Jesus saith unto them, Did ye never read in the scriptures, The stone which the builders rejected, the same is become the head of the corner: this is the Lord's doing, and it is marvellous in our eyes?

Jesus was doing the same thing that Nathan did by listing all of the things that the leaders had done wrong. He was talking to them about John the Baptist. He said, "You're supposed to be teaching Israel. Have you never read the Scriptures that talk about Me? Don't you see that you're doing this very thing just like David did?"

43 Therefore say I unto you, The kingdom of God shall be taken from you, and given to a nation bringing forth the fruits thereof.

44 And whosoever shall fall on this stone shall be broken: but on whomsoever it shall fall, it will grind him to powder.

They could have chosen between two responses. They could have repented instantly, and said, "Oh no, no, no, we don't want to miss this," or they could have laughed, and said, "Who do you think You are, to say that to us? We're the leaders of Israel." It goes on,

45 And when the chief priests and Pharisees had heard his parables, they perceived that he spake of them.

46 But when they sought to lay hands on him, they feared the multitude, because they took him for a prophet.

Apparently, He upset them, and they didn't like the stories. They were going to lay hands on Him. It says, "They feared the multitude, because they took him for a prophet."

We that are in the Kingdom have rights and privileges, but we also have responsibilities.

Look at Matthew chapter 23. We're talking about Kingdom, and you've got to see the Kingdom from two sides. You've got to realize that we are in the Kingdom, and as children of the Kingdom, we have rights and privileges, but we also have responsibilities.

With these rights and privileges that we have, we have the right to be free. We have the right to be healed, and we have the right to prosper. We have these rights that are provided for us in this Kingdom, that is a better Kingdom than any kingdom anybody has ever seen, but at the same time, there's a responsibility.

Most people don't see the responsibility. They just see the rights and privileges, and they think, "I'm going to learn this Kingdom teaching. Yes, we should be kings, and we ought to have dominion. I should have new cars, and new houses, and all kinds of things." Very honestly, all those things are available in the Kingdom, as long as you don't get your eye on them and as long as you realize that they are tools to be used for the Kingdom.

Deuteronomy 8:18,

> 18 But thou shalt remember the LORD thy God: for *it is* he that giveth thee power to get wealth, that he may establish his covenant which he sware unto thy fathers, as *it is* this day.

It is God who gives you the ability to create wealth, so that He may establish His covenant upon this earth. If you have an ability to create wealth, you operate in that, and create wealth. It is not so that you can heap it up on your own lust and your own desires. It is so that you can establish the covenant.

Ephesians 4:28,

> 28 Let him that stole steal no more: but rather let him labour, working with *his* hands the thing which is good, that he may have to give to him that needeth.

Notice: it wasn't enough for him to just quit stealing, get a job, and make an honest living. The reason he was to make an honest living was so that he could have something to give to other people.

It's not about what we can gather up—it's about how we can help. Everybody talks about this wealth transfer at the end, and you might see it, but you have to realize that you can't let it change you. One of the reasons Dr. Sumrall was so prosperous is because he never let it stick to him or change him; he always remained the same.

Matthew 23:13,

> 13 But woe unto you, scribes and Pharisees, hypocrites! for ye shut up the kingdom of heaven against men: for ye neither go in *yourselves*, neither suffer ye them that are entering to go in.
>
> 14 Woe unto you, scribes and Pharisees, hypocrites! for ye devour widows' houses, and for a pretence make long prayer: therefore ye shall receive the greater damnation.

He was telling them, "You are actors. Not only do you not go in, but you don't let anybody else who's trying to enter get in."

Matthew 24:12-14,

> 12 And because iniquity shall abound, the love of many shall wax cold.
>
> 13 But he that shall endure unto the end, the same shall be saved.
>
> 14 And this gospel of the kingdom shall be preached in all the world for a witness unto all nations; and then shall the end come.

I am still talking about the Kingdom and trying to give you an overall view of the Kingdom.

When Jesus comes, He will be looking for fruit.

Matthew 25:14,

> 14 For *the kingdom of heaven is* as a man travelling into a far country, *who* called his own servants, and delivered unto them his goods.
>
> 15 And unto one he gave five talents, to another two, and to another one; to every man according to his several ability; and straightway took his journey.
>
> 16 Then he that had received the five talents went and traded with the same, and made them other five talents.
>
> 17 And likewise he that *had received* two, he also gained other two.
>
> 18 But he that had received one went and digged in the earth, and hid his lord's money.
>
> 19 After a long time the lord of those servants cometh, and reckoneth with them.
>
> 20 And so he that had received five talents came and brought other five talents, saying, Lord, thou deliveredst unto me five talents: behold, I have gained beside them five talents more.

That was a 100 percent increase.

Notice that He said, "Well done," but it was referring to producing profit for the Kingdom; it wasn't just because somebody accepted Jesus. It wasn't just because you got into the Kingdom. He didn't say, "Oh, you entered the Lingdom. That's good. That's all you need." He said, "No, you're in the Kingdom; now produce profit." When Jesus comes, He will be looking for fruit.

> 21 His lord said unto him, Well done, *thou* good and faithful servant: thou hast been faithful over a few things, I will make thee ruler over many things: enter thou into the joy of thy lord.
>
> 22 He also that had received two talents came and said, Lord, thou deliveredst unto me two talents: behold, I have gained two other talents beside them.

That would be a 100 percent profit, also.

> 23 His lord said unto him, Well done, good and faithful servant; thou hast been faithful over a few things, I will make thee ruler over many things: enter thou into the joy of thy lord.
>
> 24 Then he which had received the one talent came and said, Lord, I knew thee that thou art an hard man, reaping where thou hast not sown, and gathering where thou hast not strawed:

Do you hear the attitude of that servant? His lord gave him a talent, but he said, "Oh, you want me to do all of the work for you. You're not doing it yourself, but you want profit; I know you're a hard man." Then the servant said,

> 25 And I was afraid, and went and hid thy talent in the earth: lo, *there* thou hast *that is* thine.

In other words, "I'm giving you back exactly what you gave me. I kept it safe. I didn't make any mistakes. I didn't lose one dime."

> 26 His lord answered and said unto him, *Thou* wicked and slothful servant, thou knewest that I reap where I sowed not, and gather where I have not strawed:

Notice: he didn't lose anything; he just didn't gain anything. Just because you end up with what you started with doesn't mean that He will say, "Well done." There should be profit. There should be produce. There should be fruit. There should be progress. Amen?

> 27 Thou oughtest therefore to have put my money to the exchangers, and *then* at my coming I should have received mine own with usury.

He should have brought the original along with profit.

> 28 Take therefore the talent from him, and give *it* unto him which hath ten talents.
>
> 29 For unto every one that hath shall be given, and he shall have abundance: but from him that hath not shall be taken away even that which he hath.
>
> 30 And cast ye the unprofitable servant into outer darkness: there shall be weeping and gnashing of teeth.

That sounds really harsh just for not losing anything. This isn't something somebody made up. I'm not pulling any Scriptures out of context.

31 When the Son of man shall come in his glory, and all the holy angels with him, then shall he sit upon the throne of his glory:

32 And before him shall be gathered all nations: and he shall separate them one from another, as a shepherd divideth *his* sheep from the goats:

33 And he shall set the sheep on his right hand, but the goats on the left.

34 Then shall the King say unto them on his right hand, Come, ye blessed of my Father, inherit the kingdom prepared for you from the foundation of the world:

35 For I was an hungred, and ye gave me meat: I was thirsty, and ye gave me drink: I was a stranger, and ye took me in:

36 Naked, and ye clothed me: I was sick, and ye visited me: I was in prison, and ye came unto me.

37 Then shall the righteous answer him, saying, Lord, when saw we thee an hungred, and fed thee? or thirsty, and gave *thee* drink?

38 When saw we thee a stranger, and took *thee* in? or naked, and clothed *thee?*

39 Or when saw we thee sick, or in prison, and came unto thee?

40 And the King shall answer and say unto them, Verily I say unto you, Inasmuch as ye have done *it* unto one of the least of these my brethren, ye have done *it* unto me.

You may not have much, but whatever you have, you can share.

I have the testimony of how we went to Tulsa. Very honestly, I don't know if we've ever had as little as we had when we were there, but anybody that walked up, we fed. God blessed us; God brought more. It was miraculous.

Many times you don't see the miraculous, because you're not willing to share what you already have. You think, "I don't have enough to share." So many stories about Jesus go back to where He started with what someone had. He never said to wait until you get more, and then start.

When I started this, way before I was a pastor, I never asked for money. You all know me; I don't pull for money. I go the opposite way.

I have heard so many people say, "Well, I don't believe in tithing," or "I'll tithe whenever I make more money." No, it will still be the same amount of sacrifice, and it will still affect you, whatever it is. You have to start with what you have, and then it will grow. That's the way it works.

Look at the story of Jesus with the loaves and fishes. We're talking about a little boy's lunch; he wasn't a caterer. He didn't pull up in a lunch wagon that Jesus went over to and got a few things to feed the multitude. He took a little boy's lunch and fed the multitude. It doesn't matter what you start with.

Whatever you have, that's what you start with. That is what God has given you so far. People say, "Well, why didn't He give me more?" It is probably because you haven't made room by getting rid of what you have. It's amazing how He does that. We can talk about talents, we can talk about money, we can talk about gifts, we can talk about anything, but you have to start somewhere.

I'll be the last person to come to you personally and say, "What do you have? Can you do this? Can you do that? What are you doing? You need to do this or that, and if you don't, God's not going to bless you." I'm the last person to do that. All I do is preach the Word to you, and you decide what to do with it. However, I'll tell you this: "It's a blessing."

It's a blessed life to break that thing, and to be able to step out into areas that hold you in bondage, and to be able to break that bondage, and to be set free. There's nothing better than freedom, and the way you do that is you start; you just start.

Matthew chapter 25,

> 40 And the King shall answer and say unto them, Verily I say unto you, Inasmuch as ye have done *it* unto one of the least of these my brethren, ye have done *it* unto me.
>
> 41 Then shall he say also unto them on the left hand, Depart from me, ye cursed, into everlasting fire, prepared for the devil and his angels:

People ask, "Why would God send men to hell?" He doesn't—men send themselves. The fire He was talking about was prepared for the devil and his angels. No one has to go there. There has been an antidote put in place. There has been a provision made so that no one has to go, but people won't take it.

**Jesus said to do the simple things:
feed the hungry, clothe the naked, and visit the sick.**

> 42 For I was an hungred, and ye gave me no meat: I was thirsty, and ye gave me no drink:
>
> 43 I was a stranger, and ye took me not in: naked, and ye clothed me not: sick, and in prison, and ye visited me not.

Notice that there was nothing in there about lying, stealing, cheating, and whoremongering. There was nothing about any of that. It just mentioned the simple things. He said, "You didn't feed the hungry, you didn't clothe the naked, and you didn't visit people when they were sick. You just didn't do the things that you could do.

It wasn't that you did things that you weren't supposed to do. It was about you not doing things you were supposed to do." People try to live by the words, "Thou shall not." It's not the "thou shalt not(s)" that hang you up. It's the "thou shalt(s)," because you're not doing the "thou shalt(s)." Amen?

I've had people ask me, "Well, do I have to lay hands on the sick to go to heaven?" My answer is, "No, you get to." However, with an attitude like that, you probably are not going anyway, because all you're trying to do is get by, by the skin of your teeth. You think, "What is the least I have to do to get in?" I can guarantee that whatever standard you set, it's going to be a little bit too low. You have to kill those things in you. You can't play with them; you have to kill them.

We talk about inner healing and going through counseling for inner healing. The counselor asks, "Well, what is your problem?" They keep digging and asking questions. Then they say, "I have finally found it. There is someone that you haven't forgiven for something. Let me help you with that. Let's work that out. Now, you need to forgive, even if you're not sure who to forgive. We know you need to forgive someone, so we're going to keep digging." You're on somebody's couch, and they say you are getting psychotherapy.

I can tell you how to find out who you need to forgive, and if you want to break free of it, you don't have to spend hours having someone counsel you. It's very simple. Make a list of every person you know, and then go and buy them a gift. See who it bothers you to buy a gift for, and you will find the person that you have something against. It's that simple.

When you start to do that and you say, "I don't want to buy a gift for them." That's the one you need to buy for, and then you buy that gift. When you give it to them, smile. Don't say anything; just smile. Just go ahead and give the gift to them.

Stop and think, "I'm going to go and buy another gift for them," and see if it still bothers you. Keep buying them gifts. Buy more and more expensive gifts until it doesn't bother you anymore. You can't keep buying people gifts and still have something against them, because you have too much invested in them. You can't keep on disliking them. Where your treasure is, there your heart is, also. It is really simple.

What I have just told you has saved you hours on somebody's couch. Amen? I have saved you hours of all that psycho-babble stuff. This is the simplest way in the world to find out who you need to forgive. It's easy to fix it, and then you just forgive. Finally, you will go to God and say, "God, I don't know what it is; fix me. This is costing too much money."

All of that advice I just gave you was free; every bit of it was free. That could have cost you several hundred dollars in counseling, which proves that such counseling isn't a ministry; ministries don't charge for help.

A counselor might say, "I've got to make a living somehow." Don't charge. If you go into that, and it's a ministry, and it is a gift God has given you, or a God given calling, do it on a love offering basis. Trust God and not a paycheck. If you trust a paycheck, you're a hireling.

We have got to have Kingdom attitude, Kingdom character, and Kingdom nature in us to clothe the naked, feed the hungry, and heal the sick.

Matthew 25:43-46,

> 43 I was a stranger, and ye took me not in: naked, and ye clothed me not: sick, and in prison, and ye visited me not.
>
> 44 Then shall they also answer him, saying, Lord, when saw we thee an hungred, or athirst, or a stranger, or naked, or sick, or in prison, and did not minister unto thee?
>
> 45 Then shall he answer them, saying, Verily I say unto you, Inasmuch as ye did it not to one of the least of these, ye did it not to me.
>
> 46 And these shall go away into everlasting punishment: but the righteous into life eternal.

Now, there is a responsibility.

When Adam turned this world over to Satan, Satan became the god of this world and this world's system.

Turn to 2 Corinthians chapter 4. The Apostle Paul was writing to the Corinthians:

> 3 But if our gospel be hid, it is hid to them that are lost:
>
> 4 In whom the god of this world hath blinded the minds of them which believe not, lest the light of the glorious gospel of Christ, who is the image of God, should shine unto them.

Does anybody disagree with that verse? It's not a trick question. Is what he said right? Paul called Satan the god of this world, did he not? He was talking about the god of this world's system and the way things are, but you will notice that Paul called Satan a god.

God said, "Thou shall have no other gods before Me." You can have other gods, so obviously there are other gods. Here Satan was called a god, so there are gods.

Galatians 4:8,

> 8 Howbeit then, when ye knew not God, ye did service unto them which by nature are no gods.

Paul was saying, "You were serving gods that aren't gods." When God said, "There is only one God; there is no other god like Me," He was saying, "There is one supreme God, and there are no other gods like

Me." Then He said, "Don't have any other gods before Me," so there are other gods that you could serve.

We know that a bass boat can be a god. A car can be a god. We can make anything into a god. Even though we know that those things are not gods, they're idols in our eyes, because we put them up above God. There is that aspect of gods that simply puts an idol or something in front of God, but then there are beings that are spirit beings that can also be called gods. Satan is one of those.

We know that Satan, even though he is the god of this world's system, is not a god like God is God. When he is called a god here, the god of this world, we know it is saying that he is the chief authority, the chief person, the chief being, the chief personality; he is the top thing over something. Isn't that what it's saying about him? In other words, the god of this world, Satan, is not a god like God, but he is a god, a being, that is over a world system.

Principalities, powers, and spirit beings are not called gods, but they are also over sections of this world's system.

Principalities are also over sections of this world's system. They're not called gods in the Bible; they're called principalities. In this country, there are principalities, powers, and spirit beings that are over certain sins, certain areas, and even certain geographic areas. We would call them principalities, but there are people, in other countries especially, that would call them gods, and they worship them.

In the Greek and the Roman Pantheon of Gods, they had certain gods such as Artemis the Greek goddess and Diana the Roman goddess. There was also a goddess of fertility. They saw them as gods, but we would call them principalities. They were gods in that area, because they were principalities over that area. They fell when Satan fell, and they went with him. When Adam turned this world over to Satan, Satan became the god of this world.

Is Satan the god of this world's system? Yes. It says that he was. This was Paul writing after the cross; he was writing to Christians. I want to make sure that we don't just have a knee-jerk reaction to certain terminology. We actually look at it, and find out what's being said so that we can talk about it logically and spiritually. If we do that, we have to talk about Jesus.

The temptation of Jesus was when the devil showed Him all the kingdoms of the world and offered Him all of the power and the glory of them if Jesus would only worship him.

Luke chapter 4, starting with verse 5:

> 5 And the devil, taking him up into an high mountain, shewed unto him all the kingdoms of the world in a moment of time.
>
> 6 And the devil said unto him, All this power will I give thee, and the glory of them: for that is delivered unto me; and to whomsoever I will I give it.

"And the devil said unto Him, 'All of this power, and all of this authority, will I give thee.'" Satan showed Jesus all of these kingdoms in a moment of time and showed Him the glory of them. He said, "All of this I will give you, and the glory of them, for that is delivered unto me; and to whomsoever I will, I give it." Satan became the god of this world when Adam gave it to him.

Let's look at some things here, and just take it piece by piece. Satan said, "Look at all of these kingdoms of the world. I will give them all to You. They were given to me, and I can give them to whomever I want." When were they given to him? They were given to him at the fall of Adam. When Adam turned over the world, this world's system, and all of these kingdoms to Satan, at that moment, Satan became the god of this world.

Satan wasn't the god of this world before then; Adam was. Notice how that position can be handed off so easily. Very simply, it was handed to him. Basically, Adam just bowed his knee to another god and said, "I take you as my god." "Why?" It was because he said, "I choose to listen to you, as opposed to listening to God, Himself."

That's how easy it is to change gods; whoever you obey, whoever you serve, that's whose servant you are. That's why your single decision, like when I was talking about David, is so important. Your single decision can change your destiny.

Notice this, because it says that the devil took Jesus up into a high place, into a high mountain. He showed Him all the kingdoms of the world and said, "All of this power was given to me, and the glory of them; they were delivered to me, and to whomsoever I will, I give it."

> 7 If thou therefore wilt worship me, all shall be thine.

"If…" Notice this was the temptation of Jesus. Satan said, "If You will therefore worship me, all shall be Thine."

Jesus turned Satan down.

> 8 And Jesus answered and said unto him, Get thee behind me, Satan: for it is written, Thou shalt worship the Lord thy God, and him only shalt thou serve.

"Get thee behind Me, Satan." Those were the very same words that Jesus said to Peter.

Notice that Jesus didn't say, "I have a word. I have a vision." He didn't have to go and pray. He said, "Get thee behind Me, Satan." Why? "For it is written."

Do you realize that Jesus beat the devil with the Old Testament? He beat Satan by simply saying, "Get thee behind me, Satan: for it is written, 'Thou shalt worship the Lord thy God, and him only shalt thou serve.'"

Jesus was telling Satan to get behind Him, and He used the Old Testament Scriptures to do it. Those were the only Scriptures they had at that point. Notice: this was the temptation of Christ; it was a real temptation. In other words, Jesus knew that Satan was telling the truth. The devil can tell the truth when it is in his best interest to do so, and he was telling Jesus the truth.

Jesus knew that if He bowed His knee and worshipped Satan, then at that point, Satan could have transferred the world to Him. Jesus could have won the world without having to die.

Jesus knew that Satan was not lying when he said, "It was delivered to me and I can give it to whomsoever I want." It had to be true, because Jesus didn't call him on it. He didn't say, "That's a lie." He knew it was true and that it could happen. He knew that Satan was the god of this world. He knew that He was talking to the god of this world.

The word "earth" and the word "world" are two different things. The earth is a physical thing here. The world is the system that goes on here on the earth, the kingdoms that rise up, and all of the other things that have to do with this world.

Jesus didn't call him on it, because He knew it could have been delivered to Him. He knew that Satan was the god of this world's system. At this point, Jesus had no problem dealing with another god, but if He had bowed His knee to him, then He would have had another god before God. It would have been Adam all over again.

Satan was the god of this world, and it was delivered to him to be god of this world. That position was delivered to him from Adam who was god of this world. I know I'm emphasizing it, I know I'm repeating myself, but I want you to see this because of what we're going to look at next.

He said, "Get behind Me, Satan: for it is written, 'Thou shalt worship the Lord thy God, and Him only shalt thou serve.'"

> **Jesus said, "I am come that they might have life, and that they might have *it* more abundantly."**

John 10:10,

> 10 The thief cometh not, but for to steal, and to kill, and to destroy: I am come that they might have life, and that they might have *it* more abundantly.

Notice that Jesus gave the elements of Satan's work—the thief comes to steal, kill, and destroy. His answer and remedy for all of that was that they might have life and that they might have it more abundantly. That means that if you have life and you have it more abundantly, you won't be killed, you won't have things stolen from you, and you won't be destroyed.

Everything that is evil and wrong ends up being some form of killing, stealing, and destroying. Sickness or disease will kill you; it will destroy your life. Amen? It steals your life from you. It steals your vitality, it steals your days while you're lying in bed, and then eventually, it destroys your life. It can destroy your whole family, because it can take every dime your family has.

I know people right now that had it all. Then, because of the sickness of a spouse, or maybe one of their children, it took every dime. They lost their house, because they couldn't pay their mortgage. Their entire life was destroyed because of sickness or disease.

I want to emphasize Jesus' answer to the killing, stealing, and destroying that the enemy does. It is having life and having life more abundantly. Everything in the Kingdom has to do with life.

John chapter 10, starting in verse 23:

> 23 And Jesus walked in the temple in Solomon's porch.
>
> 24 Then came the Jews round about him, and said unto him, How long dost thou make us to doubt? If thou be the Christ, tell us plainly.

They were saying, "Are You the Christ or not? Just tell us."

> 25 Jesus answered them, I told you, and ye believed not: the works that I do in my Father's name, they bear witness of me.
>
> 26 But ye believe not, because ye are not of my sheep, as I said unto you.

Those that believe in Jesus don't just give lip service to Him; they follow Him.

> 27 My sheep hear my voice, and I know them, and they follow me:

28 And I give unto them eternal life; and they shall never perish, neither shall any *man* pluck them out of my hand.

29 My Father, which gave *them* me, is greater than all; and no *man* is able to pluck *them* out of my Father's hand.

The Jews said, "You, being a man, make yourself God."

30 I and *my* Father are one.

31 Then the Jews took up stones again to stone him.

32 Jesus answered them, Many good works have I shewed you from my Father; for which of those works do ye stone me?

33 The Jews answered him, saying, For a good work we stone thee not; but for blasphemy; and because that thou, being a man, makest thyself God.

Jesus only said, "I and my Father are one." He never said, "I am God." He didn't say that. He said, "We are one."

In John 10:33, the Jews said:

33 …. because that thou, being a man, makest thyself God.

**Jesus quoted their law, saying,
"Is it not written in your law, I said, 'Ye are gods?'"**

Jesus answered them in John 10:34.

> 34 Jesus answered them, Is it not written in your law, I said, Ye are gods?

Jesus quoted this from Psalms 82:6-7.

> 6 I have said, Ye are gods; and all of you are children of the most High.
>
> 7 But ye shall die like men, and fall like one of the princes.

Right there is where people get confused, and they go off into these other things. They take things out of context. What's the difference whether I read this or if Jesus said it? I'm not saying it; I'm just reading what Jesus said. As His representative, all I'm doing is repeating what He said.

The word "god," in many cases, is referred to as the chief top person (magistrate) over a system.

We know that the word "god" does not necessarily mean a self-sufficient one totally apart from God. We know that the word "god," simply in many cases, as we just read in Luke and in Corinthians, is referred to as the chief top person over a system.

When it said in Psalms 82:7, "I have said, 'You are gods;…but you shall die like men," it was contrasting God and men.

If you go back into the Hebrew, the Hebrew word used there for *"gods"* is the word *elohiym*. It means *gods in the ordinary sense; but specifically used for the supreme God; occasionally applied by way of deference to magistrates; and sometimes as a superlative: angels; great; judges.* This is the same word that was used for God in Genesis. It's hard to really differentiate, so you have to read it in context to find out what it really means in a particular Scripture.

We have the Greek in the New Testament, and we have the Septuagint, which is the Greek version of the Old Testament. A lot of times I'll look back at the Old Testament to see how they translated words into the Greek from Hebrew.

The Greek word used in place of *"ĕlôhıym"* in Psalms 82 is the Greek word, *"theos."* That is where we get our word for "God." Again, you have to go by the context, because there are times when that word is used in the Old Testament as *ĕlôhıym* and then in the Septuagint as *theos*.

The definition of *"theos"* is: *of uncertain affinity; a deity, especially the supreme Divinity; figuratively a magistrate.* It literally means a magistrate or the top executive official of a system or nation. We wouldn't necessarily say it would be like the President, but it could be like the Chief Justice of the Supreme Court.

Remember: we're still talking about Kingdom. Let's go back to John chapter 10.

John 10:34-38,

> 34 Jesus answered them, Is it not written in your law, I said, Ye are gods?
>
> 35 If he called them gods, unto whom the word of God came, and the scripture cannot be broken;

"If He (God) called them gods, unto whom the Word of God came, and the Scripture cannot be broken."

> 36 Say ye of him, whom the Father hath <u>sanctified</u>, and sent into the world, Thou blasphemest; because I said, I am the Son of God?

"Say ye of Him, whom the Father hath *"sanctified"* (*separated, set apart*), and sent into the world, Thou blasphemest; because I said, I am the Son of God?"

> 37 If I do not the works of my Father, believe me not.
>
> **Jesus said again, "The Father *is* in Me, and I in Him."**
>
> 38 But if I do, though ye believe not me, believe the works: that ye may know, and believe, that the Father *is* in me, and I in him.

The only reason I brought that up is because there has been so much controversy over these verses. John Lake preached on them, and if you go on the internet, you will see that people try to blast him for it. It's cowardly to blast somebody who's dead; they can't answer for themselves. However, if you go in and read what he was saying, you'll understand what he meant. He was saying, "God has put us back into the dominion that Adam had."

If I asked you, "Are we back in Adam's position of dominion?" the answer would be, "Yes." "Are we even at a greater position?" "Yes!" Satan became the god of this world, because Adam gave it to him. Adam was the god of this world before that.

We have been put into a place of dominion over this world's system.

If we are back in Adam's position of dominion, then in that sense, we are *"god"* over this world's system. We should be over this system in this kingdom now, which is the manifested Kingdom of God on this earth.

We are to do this as a collective group, not individually. It is only because Christ is in us, and we are one with Him. Think about that. Jesus said, "I am one with God. The Father and I are one," and then He said, "…and you and I are one." That makes us one with God. Amen?

That does not mean that I am this supreme and divine being. I'm not saying that by any stretch. I derive my life from my connection with Jesus. That "divine life" flows from the Father, through Jesus, and through me. I want you to get this: if I severed my connection with God, there would be no "divine life" flowing through me.

By these precious promises,
we become partakers of the "divine nature."

In 2 Peter 1:4, Peter said,

> 4 Whereby are given unto us exceeding great and precious promises: that by these ye might be partakers of the divine nature, having escaped the corruption that is in the world through lust

The more we grow to look like Jesus, the more we should be partakers of "the divine nature," and the more our nature should be divine. That is because the branch is always connected to the vine; that's the only way.

If you were to sever that connection, there would be no more divine life flowing through to you. Amen? At the same time, why would we worry about that connection being severed? Now, if we're going to accept that we are in this position, then we also have to accept the responsibility that comes with it, not just the benefits.

The reason healing is yours is
because that divine life flows through to you.

It has nothing to do with you, in and of yourself. If you don't experience the blessings of God it is because you are not allowing that divine life to flow through you, and you're not becoming a partaker of that "divine nature," which is how He brings these things to you.

God gave us Jesus, and with Jesus, He gave us everything. It all comes through Jesus. The problem in the church is that people keep trying to be somebody special.

There are two ways to use the word, apostle. You can use it in your mind meaning, "I have a particular mission God has sent me on. He has appointed me to this, and I'm on that mission," or you can wear it like a tag, walk around in a fancy suit, and expect everybody to bow down and kiss your ring.

True apostleship is being on a mission for God. It is accomplishing the mission He has purposed you for. It is finding that mission, going on that mission, and having God commission you.

You have to have the mind of Christ if you're going to be like Him.

Everyone is not an apostle or a prophet, even though we all have that DNA within us. We're all moving to look like Jesus. However, as long as you are hung up on a title or some type of specialty, then what you're saying is, "I'm one-fourth like Jesus, but the other three-fourths isn't like Jesus." Why? That's because you are hung up on a tag. You have to decide what you are going to do.

Philippians 2:5,

> 5 Let this mind be in you, which was also in Christ Jesus:
>
> 6 Who, being in the form of God, thought it not robbery to be equal with God:

7 But made himself of no reputation, and took upon him the form of a servant, and was made in the likeness of men:

It said, "Let this mind be in you that was in Christ Jesus," and right after that it said, "…who took on the form of a servant (even though being equal with God)." Equal how? He was equal in nature, in character, and in Spirit. He was in a class of "being."

We have to walk in dominion. We have to understand that. When I walk into a room, if nobody else in there is born again, I am the highest level of spiritual being in that room. I don't care if that room is full of devils, full of principalities, or anything else. When I walk in, if there are no Christians in there, I am the highest level of spiritual being there.

Now, if I walk into a room and there is a Christian there, we are equal. It doesn't matter if one is an apostle and the other is not an apostle. It doesn't matter, because ministries are simply within the Body of Christ, and they are jobs that we have to do within the Body of Christ. They don't make one person any better than anyone else.

A general is a soldier. When the battle starts, if it comes down to it, the general will grab a rifle just like the other soldiers. There's a saying in the Marine Corp, "Every Marine is a rifleman." It doesn't matter what rank is on the shoulders or on the collar, because each one is a Marine.

That's what we have to get to. You can walk around, spout the terms, and wear the tags, but when you go out on the street, nobody cares what your tag says. All they want to know is, "What can you do? Can you help me? Can you help my baby? Can you help me out of this situation?" That's all that counts. Everything else is all internal.

**Everyone who is born again
and in the Kingdom is in a position of authority.**

At some point, we're going to have to decide that everybody who's born again, and in the Kingdom, is in a position of authority, which is a position of responsibility. You don't need anything else. You don't need a word, you don't need a prophecy, you don't need a gift, or anything else to put your foot on the back of any principality anywhere. You don't need a special commission.

I went up to Canada, and I went to a hospital. It was called the "Holy Spirit Hospital;" it was a Catholic hospital. I thought, "That's an awesome name." I went in there, and they were doing some things with the person, so I had to wait out in the hall.

A lady was standing there, and she asked, "What principality do you think is over this area?" I said, "I don't know. I haven't really thought about it." She said, "Well, what do you think would be the most powerful spirit over this area?" I said, "Oh, that's easy." She said, "What?" I said, "The Holy Spirit."

She said, "Well, I don't understand." I said, "The Holy Spirit is in me. I don't know if there are any other Christians in town." I was talking to a person who claimed to be a Christian. I said, "I don't know if there are other Christians here, but if not, then when I got here, the Holy

Spirit took charge. He's bigger than any principality, any spirit, or anything else, so if He is in me that puts me over everything."

We started talking about it, and I said, "From what I've seen so far, the principality would either be the god of medicine or the god of insurance. Those are the two predominant things in the city, so it would probably be one of those."

She asked, "Can you help us to learn about this?" I said, "Well, yes. I'd be glad to teach on it." She said, "I know we can't attack this principality until God gives us a Rhema word, or until God gives us a commission to go after that thing, because you just don't jump in."

I said, "Well, I agree that you don't just jump in, especially if you don't know anything about it, but you don't need a special word. These things must be brought into submission under Jesus Christ. You don't need a special word to do that, but you do need to know what you're doing; you don't want to stir this up."

There are some other things I could share with you about principalities; some things you can watch for and see. I want what I am going to say next to be a really clear-cut thing. Sometimes when a healthy family is moving into the things of God, especially if the family is in leadership in a church, then many times the wife will become pregnant. The principality in that area will try to attach itself to that child.

It usually comes through a form of sickness or disease. There are different definitions for it, but it is something that is very serious and very strong. What I mean by that is that you would look at it in the natural and say, "That's a big deal." Many times that principality is attached, and it draws its life from that child, because its whole purpose is to get that family to back off.

One of the fastest ways to get a family to back off is to make it to where they have to pay attention to their child. When they're focusing on the child, they're not focusing on advancing the Kingdom. Principalities will do that.

The other thing is that the principality will find a place to work within that child that will mess up other things around it. No one will ever deal with the principality or pray against it, because they think that the leader can do that. That's his child, and you don't want to approach the leader and say, "Well, there's a problem."

Then the leader many times will say, "Oh, that's not a problem," depending on their viewpoint of healing. They will say, "Well, God has given us this special child to teach us something, to help us, or to give us compassion." That is basically a tradition of man. These are aspects of principalities that you need to know. We've dealt with some things like this.

I just really wanted to emphasize this and get this out there, because people ask me questions about it. We haven't really gotten a chance to talk about it much. It's not that we are divine or that we are gods, or that man can become a god. It's not that at all. It is just simply going back, finding out what words were used, what they referred to, and then logically and spiritually going through it and looking at it.

Hopefully that helped you to see that this is not about saying anybody is anything, any more than saying this is a "class of being."

> **Jesus has given you the ability to walk through this world in such a way that the enemy will not be able to touch you.**

You are a son of God. You are no different now than you were before you walked in. I didn't make you a super being. I didn't make you a god unto yourself.

The Bible says that we're in charge. It's just like saying that there is an overseer. The Bible talks about shepherds, chief shepherds, and under shepherds; it's the same thing. The word "shepherd" is always there, so there is a Chief God and there are under gods. It's just a level of being in control and having dominion over something. It's that simple, so don't let people scare you with these things.

The Bible is not to instill fear, unless you are against God. If you're against God, then you might want to fear, but if you're for God, you ought to have peace. You ought to know He has given you the ability to walk above the circumstances, to put your foot on the back of principalities and everything else, and to be able to walk through this world in such a way that the enemy will not be able to touch you. Amen?

Now that you know that, it doesn't mean the enemy is going to stop. It just means that you're going to have to get serious. You've got to become as serious as the devil is, because he's serious. He doesn't like it when people start trying to step up and take away his dominion in areas. When they do that, he has no authority. Amen.

"Father,

"I believe Your Word. Your Word is true. It's always true. It is I who must come into alignment with Your Word. Your Word does not instill fear; it instills peace. Now that I have understanding, I have greater peace. I thank You, Father, that through Jesus Christ I can do all things. One of those things I can do is put my foot on the devil. I thank God who will crush Satan under my feet shortly.

"Thank You, Father, in the name of Jesus. Amen."

KINGDOM ADMINISTRATORS – PART 2

Sermon given by Curry R. Blake

"If any man *be* in Christ, *he is* a new creature."

Turn first to Isaiah chapter 9. We'll be starting our teaching there, but to begin with, I want to share a testimony of a young lady who was diagnosed with terminal bone cancer. She was about 12 years old, and it was really hard on her. The church she was in was a good faith church that really preached faith and believed in healing, so people were believing and praying.

They said she was the one that really kept everybody's hopes up, even though people would look at her and say, "What's going on with her?" She would say, "Jesus is talking to me. He says I'm going to be okay." Yet the symptoms kept progressing, and it looked bad. She actually needed a bone marrow transplant. The parents were doing everything they could to find a donor.

They were down near Alexandria, Louisiana. This young girl was African-American, and she had strong faith in God. A lot of the people around her were praying and believing, but they were also apparently wavering, but she kept saying, "Don't worry. This is going to be okay.

This is going to work out. Jesus is talking to me." She kept saying. "Jesus is talking to me, and it's going to be okay." It was amazing!

The bone cancer kept progressing, and they looked everywhere for a bone marrow donor. They were looking all around the Alexandria, Louisiana area and then even farther out. Eventually, they found a donor, so she went through the whole surgery.

The little girl was good with that. She said, "Whatever it takes. I know that Jesus is with me, and He told me I'm going to be alright. He didn't tell me it was going to be this way, or that way; He just said that I'm going to be alright." She was just going along with it.

Shortly after the transplant, everything changed with her. I mean, amazing changes! Her body picked up the new marrow. Her eye color changed. Hair texture changed. Skin color started changing. The new marrow that was transplanted started reproducing, and her body literally changed genetically to match the donor. They said it was a rare case for it to happen exactly like that, especially for the strong results that she was getting.

Then they started talking about it at the church, and she was the main topic. She was fine; her body picked it up and started going on. She apparently wasn't going to need any more medical operations or anything. They kept watching her body change, and then it got to a certain place where it seemed to stop. It was almost like they could see a tug-of-war over which genetics her body was going to go after.

The amazing thing was that her body changed genetically. After doing all of the tests on her and seeing where she was, they said to her, "The strange thing is that your body really grabbed hold of the donor's genetics, and if you ever need any other medical procedures, like a blood transfusion, you can't go back to your family."

While I was listening to that, I was thinking, "Oh that will preach. That is exactly the situation we are in and should insist that we be in, in Christ." Here we are, and we're born with a terminal disease called sin. People will say, "Well, I'm this way, because I was born this way." We're all born a certain way, but the beauty of it is, even if you were born a certain way, you get to get born again, and you don't have to be that way. Even if that is the case, we're all born sinners, and everybody has to be born again. We're all born with a terminal disease.

You needed a donor. God the Father found one. He did a blood transfusion in you. It was one of will, so by your own choice you decided to accept that and because of that, now if you need any further help or development, you can't go back to your original family; you can only go to the family of the donor for help, for transfusion, or anything else. Amen? That is like the perfect illustration of the new birth.

Our genetics are spiritual genetics. If you are in Christ, you have become a "new creature," a "new species."

The only person you can go back to is your donor. That Donor is Jesus. Our spiritual genetics should so grab the genetics of Jesus Christ that we automatically gravitate toward Him rather than away from Him and back toward past family, or history, or what they call "determinisms." There are all kinds of determinisms. There are genetic determinisms, supposedly; there are cultural determinisms; there are social determinisms. There is also something called a psychic determinism, although it doesn't really have to do with something psychic. It means that it is of the mind determinism, which is based more on what you're raised around; it is about the ideas and thoughts that you pick up.

When we became a "new creature," we became a "new species."

In 2 Corinthians 5:17-18 the "new creature" was mentioned:

> 17 Therefore if any man *be* in Christ, *he is* a new creature: old things are passed away; behold, all things are become new.
>
> 18 And all things *are* of God, who hath reconciled us to himself by Jesus Christ, and hath given to us the ministry of reconciliation;

If you are in Christ, you have become a "new creature," a "new species." That means that the old species, what you were before you got born again, cannot help you in your progression toward becoming the fullness of the species you are now.

We're going to keep going on this for a while. Obviously, I could preach the new creation the rest of my life and still not get done with it. We have to realize how the new creation and what we've been talking about with the Kingdom, fit together.

Very honestly, I wasn't trying to stay on the Kingdom. I wasn't working on it, and I wasn't going in and looking for this. This is something that I honestly believe, from all appearances, that God has brought to the front, right now and said, "Put this in."

It seems like no matter what I read, no matter what I study, even when I'm just reading the Bible, it just keeps coming out. Then I think, "Okay, what am I going to minister on?" I talk to God and I automatically ask, "Is there anything in particular that You want me to minister on?" It's like I don't even get the words out of my mouth, and ZAP! There it is. Then I have to start to type it fast, because I'm not a typist by any stretch; I know what the home keys are, but I just don't ever get home.

I don't want to just tell you things; I want you to see it for yourself. I want you to read out of your own Bible so that there are no questions about it. Then you won't be able to say, "Well, this is his view." I'm just reading the Bible.

"The government shall be upon His (Jesus') shoulder… Of the increase of His government and peace *there shall be* no end."

Isaiah 9:6-7,

> 6 For unto us a child is born, unto us a son is given: and the government shall be upon his shoulder: and his name shall be called Wonderful, Counsellor, The mighty God, The everlasting Father, The Prince of Peace.

> 7 Of the increase of *his* government and peace *there shall be* no end, upon the throne of David, and upon his kingdom, to order it, and to establish it with judgment and with justice from henceforth even for ever. The zeal of the LORD of hosts will perform this.

There's the word "government" again.

Number one: verse 6 says, "The government shall be upon His (Jesus') shoulder, and verse 7 says, "Of the increase of His government there shall be no end."

Number two: the last of verse 7 talks about His kingdom.

We know that when Jesus showed up, He came preaching the Gospel of the kingdom of heaven and the Gospel of the Kingdom of God. You'll notice there, in Isaiah 9:6, He was called "The Prince of Peace." He's not really called Prince a lot; He is usually called King. He's also called King of kings and Lord of lords.

The word "lord" is a word that you have to see in context to know what it applies to. What I mean by that is this: the word "lord" can be used in governmental or in religious connotations. In England, they have the House of Lords, which obviously is made up of men. The word lord many times is used toward a man, but many times we also know it is used toward God.

Whether it's used toward man as far as a governmental position like a king or a ruler of a physical kingdom, or whether it's used in a spiritual connotation meaning Lord God, Lord, or Master in the sense of a spiritual master, then you have to know what's being said. However, it's the only word that causes the two to intersect.

You can say "king" but king means more of a ruler-ship from royalty or from a national viewpoint, such as a governmental king of a kingdom, whereas "lord," in the sense of being a priest, or something like that, would have more to do with the spiritual aspect; the word "lord" intersects the two.

I am just trying to lay some foundation here, so we can see this as we go on.

"As He is, so are we in this world."

Let's read 1 John 4:17:

> 17 Herein is our love made perfect, that we may have boldness in the day of judgment: because as he is, so are we in this world.

It says, "As He is, so are we in this world." Whether people like it or not, that's what it says. Amen? That's just what it says, "As He is so are we in this world."

You might say, "That's really strong; let's say maybe not 'as He is,' because now we picture Jesus as the risen Lord. He's Lord and Savior, He's King of kings, He's majesty, and He has overcome. Let's make it as religious as we can: let's say that back when He was the lowly, meek, carpenter, walking the shores of Galilee, 'As He was so are we.'"

Even if we said, "As He was," and we still picture the shores of Galilee and all of that, that's still better than the way we picture ourselves now, generally speaking. Even if we went back to that, the Bible doesn't go back to just that. The Bible says, "Not as He was, but as He is so are we." This is present tense. To emphasize that it says, "…so are we in this world." It does not say that we will be like Him in the world to come.

Religion almost always tries to put the things of God in the future or in the past. It was always "the great moves of God." It was always "the great man of God." It was always some major thing of God in the past or in the future. People say, "It's going to be great over there. It's going to be great some day. It's going to be great in the sweet by and by." Religion is never now. That's why religion has no faith. Faith is now. Religion is always past or future, but it's never present.

Faith is always present. That's an easy way to tell whether you are acting as a Christian or just being religious. If you're putting something off to the future or wishing you could be back in the old days, you are probably more religious than Christian.

I'm not saying you shouldn't want to see what it was like back then, but I wouldn't trade being back with John Lake and Smith Wigglesworth for being here now. We are reaching more people on a weekly and monthly basis than Smith Wigglesworth or John Lake ever preached to face-to-face in their lives. Think about that. How? It is through the internet, through DVDs, and CDs.

One night, my phone rang and it was about 10:30 to11:00 o'clock. I had it plugged in for charging, so it took me awhile to get to it. When I got there, it had already stopped ringing. I could tell it was an out of country number. It didn't have a name; it just had a lot of numbers, and a plus symbol in front of them. I was waiting to see if the person left a message, but they didn't. I thought, "Okay, they should call back. I hope they call back."

I put the phone down, and I remembered that I needed to run upstairs and get some books. By the time I got back, my phone had just quit ringing, again. I had just caught the light going off, and I thought, "I missed them again." I went back over there and checked, and sure enough it was the same caller, but this time he left a message.

It was hard to understand, but he was saying, "Brother Curry, my daughter," and then he gave her name and said, "She is burning up with fever. It's very dangerous. We don't know what to do. This is an emergency! Please call us!" I tried to call, but I didn't know exactly what country or code so the call couldn't be completed. I thought, "Lord, they need to call back. They need to call back. Tell them to be persistent and call again."

This time I put the phone done, sat down, and opened a book. I was sitting right next to my phone. I wasn't going anywhere; I was waiting for it to ring. In about three minutes, it rang again. I grabbed it and answered it. "Oh, Brother Curry, thank you so much for answering, we're so glad. This is the problem," and he began to tell me what was going on.

It was the weirdest thing; it was different from almost any other time I can remember praying for somebody. I got up with the phone and walked across the living room area. We have the main area where the fireplace is, and we have this big rug there. I just walked over to the middle of the rug. I was barefoot, in my pajamas, trying to get ready to write, and then go to bed.

I just walked to the middle of the rug and just plopped down on the floor. I started talking to the caller. I asked, "Is she there with you?" He said, "Yes, Brother Curry, she's right here." I said, "Alright, here's what I'm going to do. I'm going to pray."

He said, "I'll put the phone on her." I said, "Well, you can, but you don't have to. That doesn't matter. We know what we're doing here; we can do this. Alright, I'm going to pray."

It was one of the strangest prayers I think I've prayed in a long time, if ever. It was one of the simplest, easiest prayers, but there was a totally different feel from what I'd felt before. It was a certain feeling that I can't describe; there's just no way. It was as if this had already been done, and I was just praying to enforce it. I knew that it had been done, and I didn't even have to pray.

As soon as I knew that situation, I knew the way it was supposed to be, and when I prayed, I had such a love for these people. I had no idea who they were. I had never talked to them before.

Apparently they had heard of us somehow, and they were calling from Thailand or Malaysia, I'm not sure which. I didn't get to talk to them very long, because they were the ones calling and it was on their minutes and their money.

They didn't have a lot of time to talk, so as soon as I finished praying I said, "Okay. That is going to do it. Tell her that she is healed, right now. Tell her to get up and start moving around."

The person said, "Oh yes! Thank you! Thank you! Thank you very much! Goodbye," and that was it.

The next morning, I got a text. I had gotten other calls and texts, and I guess it got lost in the shuffle. It wasn't until I started going through my texts that I found it. It said, "Brother Curry, I wanted you to know that Emma's fever broke. She is completely well, and she is up playing." The text said that her temperature at one point was 39.9 Celsius, close to 104 Fahrenheit, and that's hot.

My response the night before had been one of resolve. As soon as I put the phone back on the charger, I didn't even give a second thought about it being done. I was rejoicing over the fact that she had been healed. The only thing I can credit that with is what we've been saying about the Kingdom.

You ask, "Well how does that tie in together?" I don't know, but it's one of those things where you feel like the two are connected; I just don't know how. I can see it, and you can figure it out, but at the same time it's not like something said, "This is that." It is just like you know these are connected. I will touch on that a little more.

We talked about Kingdom Administrators in the last session, and we're continuing with that in this session. This is the best way to try to get across the idea that I've been trying to share without going into a long drawn out thing. I have Scriptures, so I'll give you the Scriptures.

We have taken Jesus' place in this world.
We are to go in His name or in His stead.

Let's read 1 John 4:17 again:

> 17 Herein is our love made perfect, that we may have boldness in the day of judgment: because as he is, so are we in this world.

"As He is, so are we in this world." We've taken Jesus' place. That's why He said, "Go in My name." That meant: "Go in My stead." He was saying, "You go in My place. Speak for Me, talk for Me, and act like Me. Do what I would do, and I will back you up."

As a Christian, you are never referred to as a prince. You are referred to as kings and priests. We jump over that prince thing, to being a king. Did you ever notice that? You would think that we would have to be princes before we could become kings, but it doesn't say that. We're never really referred to as princes; we're referred to as kings.

KINGDOM ADMINISTRATORS – PART 2

Revelation 1:5-6.

> 5 And from Jesus Christ, *who is* the faithful witness, *and* the first begotten of the dead, and the prince of the kings of the earth. Unto him that loved us, and washed us from our sins in his own blood,

Jesus is "The Prince of the kings of the earth." It says, "Unto Him that loved us, and washed us from our sins in His own blood."

"To Him (Jesus) *be* glory and dominion forever and ever."

> 6 And hath made us kings and priests unto God and his Father; to him *be* glory and dominion for ever and ever. Amen.

Notice verse 5 said, "And from Jesus Christ, who is the faithful witness, and the first begotten of the dead, and the Prince of the kings of the earth." Verse 6 was still talking about Jesus: "And hath made us kings and priests unto God and His Father; to Him be glory and dominion." Notice who He was saying has dominion: "Jesus has dominion forever and ever."

**Jesus has made us kings and priests
and we shall reign on the earth.**

Revelation 5: 9-10,

> 9 And they sung a new song, saying, Thou art worthy to take the book, and to open the seals thereof: for thou wast slain, and hast

redeemed us to God by thy blood out of every kindred, and tongue, and people, and nation;

Notice: "…every kindred, and tongue, and people, and nation."

> 10 And hast made us unto our God kings and priests: and we shall reign on the earth.

"And hast (past tense), made us unto our God kings and priests." That's twice in just a few verses where we're called kings and priests. Look at what it says: "…and we shall reign on the earth." Do you see where it says we're going to reign? It doesn't say anything about reigning in heaven. It says that we will reign here on the earth.

In the preceding sessions we talked about the kingdom parables. In one of those kingdom parables in Luke chapter 19, it said that the kingdom of heaven is like a man, a householder. The householder called all of his servants, and he gave to them all of his goods. Then he went on a long journey and eventually came back. He made a reckoning with them to see what they had done with what he had given them.

Those who have received abundance of grace and of the gift of righteousness shall reign as kings on this earth.

Romans 5:17 tells us that there is more about reigning in this life.

> 17 For if by one man's offence death reigned by one; much more they which receive abundance of grace and of the gift of righteousness shall reign in life by one, Jesus Christ.)

KINGDOM ADMINISTRATORS – PART 2

Over and over again you will see Scriptures that say we are to reign in this life. It means reigning here, now. "As He is so are we in this life," now. It's amazing because this is two-fold.

First of all, we are here, and we are exercising faith. The kingdom of heaven is here; it is at hand; there's no doubt about that.

At the same time, there is a consummation where all enemies will be put under Jesus' feet, and then He will reign.

It says that we will reign with Him, and it says that we're going to reign right here on earth. Basically, what you're going to be then is determined by how you exercise faith in the Word of God, now. It will determine how He says you can reign.

When the householder in Luke chapter 19 came back, the servants came to Him. He said to them, "You have been faithful over a little, and I'll put you lord over much."

Luke 19:16-19,

> 16 Then came the first, saying, Lord, thy pound hath gained ten pounds.
>
> 17 And he said unto him, Well, thou good servant: because thou hast been faithful in a very little, have thou authority over ten cities.

> 18 And the second came, saying, Lord, thy pound hath gained five pounds.
>
> 19 And he said likewise to him, Be thou also over five cities.

He was saying that when He comes, He will reward you according to your deeds, according to your works, and if you're faithful over what He's put you over now, then He will increase that when He comes back.

In the last session we referred to John 10:34,

> 34 Jesus answered them, Is it not written in your law, I said, Ye are gods?

This verse just scares people. If you look at it logically, it makes sense as long as you don't get weird with it.

I want to read through this, and I want you to look at these words. The words that we are using in this session are words like prince, king, lord, and government, and we've talked a lot about Kingdom.

> **The princes of this world would not have killed the Lord of glory (Jesus) had they known that it would be the downfall of this world's system.**

Let's look at 1 Corinthians chapter 2. Hopefully, as we read some of these things, certain words will pop out at you, and you will say, "Okay. Now I see that." If you've been around me very long, you've heard me preach this chapter many, many times. It's in the DHT, and it's in the New Man. It's in almost everything we preach.

In 1 Corinthians 2:6-8,

> 6 Howbeit we speak wisdom among them that are perfect: yet not the wisdom of this world, nor of the princes of this world, that come to nought:

The Apostle Paul was talking about some princes that are in this world, "…that come to nought," or come to nothing.

> 7 But we speak the wisdom of God in a mystery, *even* the hidden *wisdom*, which God ordained before the world unto our glory:
>
> 8 Which none of the princes of this world knew: for had they known *it*, they would not have crucified the Lord of glory.

This tells us something about these princes, because it says here that this was wisdom they didn't have, and if they had known these things, then they would not have crucified Jesus. Apparently these princes are of this world, and it's talking more about this world's system.

They would not have killed the Lord of Glory, because that was the downfall of this world's system. They had a vested interest in keeping this world's system going the way it was. If they had known, then they wouldn't have done anything to Jesus, because that messed up their future in this world's system.

Jesus was talking to non-born again, natural men, and He called them gods.

John 10:34,

> 34 Jesus answered them, Is it not written in your law, I said, Ye are gods?

I mentioned John 10:34, and I repeated what Jesus, Himself, said, "I said, 'Ye are gods.'" Jesus said that. I didn't say that. I would not have had the guts to say that, but Jesus said it, so I'm just reading what He said.

Jesus was quoting from Psalm 82:6-7:

> 6 I have said, Ye *are* gods; and all of you *are* children of the most High.
>
> 7 But ye shall die like men, and fall like one of the princes.

Notice: "I have said, 'You are gods…but you shall die like men.'"

Let's remember who He was talking to. If He had been talking to us, that would have been impressive, but He wasn't even talking to born again people. He was talking to non-born again, natural men, and He called them gods.

The Pharisees accused Jesus of making Himself out to be God. They came to Him to stone Him. He said, "What are you going to stone Me for?" They said, "Well, not for a good work, but because You being a man make Yourself out to be God."

John 10:35,

> 35 If he called them gods, unto whom the word of God came, and the scripture cannot be broken;

Jesus was saying to them, "How can you say that when the Scriptures say, 'I said you are gods to whom the Scripture was written, and the Scripture can't be broken.'" In other words, "Here, in your own Scripture, it calls you gods, and now your going to stone Me because I say I'm the Son of God?"

Again now, if you're religious, this will scare you, because there's a line drawn that religion draws. They don't want man to go across it, because once man crosses that line, they find out it wasn't God that drew that line; it was religion that drew it.

The Hebrew word *'ĕlôhıym* means *the highest official in a given area*. God, *Ĕlôhıym*, holds the highest office in His realm.

I explained in session 5 how the term "gods" was used in John 10:34 by Jesus, Himself. When I read where Jesus said, "I said, 'Ye are gods,'" it was a term used to describe the chief (top person) over a system, or a judge. Then if you'll remember, I went into the Hebrew and into the Greek in both places out of Psalm 82 and out of John 10:34 and showed how that word is used many times for a magistrate. In the Psalm, it is the Hebrew word, *'ĕlôhıym*, which is exactly the same word used for God in Genesis.

Ps 82:1,

> 82 God standeth in the congregation of the mighty; he judgeth among the gods.

"God (*Ĕlôhıym*) standeth in the congregation of the mighty; he judgeth among the gods (*'ĕlôhıym)*."

Genesis 1:26-27,

> 26 And God said, Let us make man in our image, after our likeness: and let them have dominion over the fish of the sea, and over the fowl of the air, and over the cattle, and over all the earth, and over every creeping thing that creepeth upon the earth.
>
> 27 So God created man in his *own* image, in the image of God created he him; male and female created he them.

"*God (Ĕlôhıym),* said, 'Let Us (plural), make man in Our own image, and let them (man) have dominion.'"

I showed how all of that terminology was used, and how many times that word was used in other places when it refered to magistrates, judges, or rulers. It even refered to kings over nations. It was translated into so many different words that that you can't say it means only one thing.

All of those things, which have been given different words, have one similar characteristic, in every case. If you were going to boil all of these down, the word for "*god*," *'ĕlôhıym*, is the word for *magistrate*, the word for *king*, and the word for *ruler*. If you were to give them all one definition, the one definition would simply be "*the highest official in a given area.*"

Wouldn't that be a common definition that you could use for every magistrate or chief justice of the court? A Supreme Court Justice would hold the highest office in his realm. God, obviously, holds the highest office in His realm. I think another term used is *potentate* which means *the highest official in a room*.

When Jesus said, "I said you are gods," He was saying to them, "You are the highest official in your area."

When Jesus said, "I said you are gods," He wasn't saying, "You're divine, and I'm going to enter you all into a new age. You're all going to sit around, hum, and become gods." He wasn't saying that. All He was saying was, "I said you are the highest official in your area, yet you're still going to die just like a man, like every other man." That's all He was trying to say.

Most religious people listening on the internet, or listening by CD or DVD, will never hear that part, because they have already turned it off. They are so afraid; that's what religion does.

As I took each one of these things and studied it, each one exploded inside of me. I got DHT answers; then I went into the New Man, and things started coming out about that. It is still coming out as I look at this. If you take all three of these and put them together, it's like I'm walking this thin line. It seems like every other minute I step over to the other side, and I see all of this.

I'm not talking about anything weird, or wispy, or like I am seeing visions. I'm telling you about just being there where it is all coming out. Then I step back over here, and say, "Man, this is awesome! I'll be right back," and I step back over there. I come back over here, and say, "Oh yeah! You've got to get into this. I'd love to tell you about it. Hang on; I'll be right back." I just want to stay over there all the time.

**We have to be able to present this message
in a way that people can understand it.**

As I was studying this out, I kept saying, "God, I want to make sure that we're right." That's always the first thing; I always want to make sure that what we're saying is exactly right.

The second thing is that sometimes it doesn't matter how right you are if nobody is listening. We have to be able to present this in a way that people can understand it, although, sometimes this concept scares them. Honestly, this is big.

Like I said, "It's not making us divine, in and of ourselves, but we are connected to Him." That's the key. It is amazing, and that is why we have to realize what He was talking about. This is why I said that when you study this out, the common definition should be the highest official in a given area, because He was talking to people who were not born again. He was talking to man. In Psalm 82, He was talking to God about man, if you want to get technical about it.

In John 10:34, Jesus was talking to men about what God said. If you had been there and they were fixing to stone you for making yourself out to be the Son of God (or as they saw you to be making yourself out to be God), that would not be the verse you would want to bring up.

You would want to stay away from anything that made it sound like you were saying, "Yes, you're right. I am God." He didn't do that. In so many words, He told them, "The Bible says you are gods, and I say I'm the Son of God. The Bible says you're gods, so if you're going to stone Me, stone yourself first." Think about that.

Let's trace this back. Remember, Jesus was quoting Psalm 82:6 which was an Old Testament verse that was written and applied to non-born again men.

Psalm 8 starting in verse 1,

> 1 O LORD our Lord, how excellent *is* thy name in all the earth! Who hast set thy glory above the heavens.
>
> 2 Out of the mouth of babes and sucklings hast thou ordained strength because of thine enemies, that thou mightiest still the enemy and the avenger.

Notice: "…that thou mightiest still the enemy and the avenger." If you just read that part, you would never again worry about some curse that you're told God is putting on you. It says that if you praise God and let praise come out of your mouth, that praise will still the enemy and the avenger!

It is not just your enemy, but the ones that have a right to avenge something against you, so even if you commented the wrong way, you can still praise God and it will stop you from reaping what you have sown. See how strong that is?

Just from that one thing, you begin to praise Him and worship Him for who He is, and when you do that, He will show mercy. This praise will still the enemy and the avenger, and God will protect you.

> 3 When I consider thy heavens, the work of thy fingers, the moon and the stars, which thou hast ordained;

"You have set them in their place. You have ordained that they be set there."

"What is man, that You are mindful of him? and the Son of man, that You visit Him?"

> 4 What is man, that thou art mindful of him? and the son of man, that thou visitest him?

Notice he didn't say, "man," the second time. He said, "the Son of man." First of all, in Psalm 82, verses 6 and 7, it was talking about man, starting with Adam, but here it was talking about the Son of man, and it said, "When You visit Him." We know when He (the Son of man) visited, because that was when Jesus came.

Look at what it said: "What is man?" Obviously, this refers to what God created man for. In other words, "Why would you do that to something like a man? You've got angels who are mighty in power; you've got these beings, and these principalities." When you read the Book of Revelation or you read Ezekiel, or Daniel, there are all kinds of, as we say in Texas, "critters," out there. They speak of four headed beasts, and they have things with eyes all the way around.

God put His favor on man, because we were made in His own image.

There are some powerful beings out there, and they're all worshiping God; they are all with God, yet it says, "What is man, that thou art mindful of him?" For some reason, God liked man. Out of all the most powerful creatures in the universe, God took what was, by all accounts, the weakest of all of the creatures He had ever created, and for some reason decided to put His favor on them.

God loves us because He created us in His image. He looked at us and said, "I see Me in you." It is surprising that God likes us because of the way man acts and because of what happened with Adam. We're not always the best representation, but God still loves us! Amen? He loved us so much that He sent His Son, the Son of man, to us.

I like what Jesse Duplantis says. He just stands there, smiles, and says, "You know, God just loves me. He can't help Himself. He just loves me. He likes me, and He can't help Himself." I thought, "That's exactly the way God is." Thank God, that God can't help Himself. Amen? Thank God He just likes us. Nobody knows why, but He does.

God made man a little lower than the *ĕlôhıym*.

Psalm 8:5,

> 5 For thou hast made him a little lower than the <u>angels</u>, and hast crowned him with glory and honour.

By now, you know that the word "*angels*" there is not the word for angels as we understand it. It's the Hebrew word *ĕlôhıym*. It is the same word used for God in Genesis chapter 1. It is the same word used several times, and it is almost always for God, Himself.

If, at this point, it only meant magistrate or potentate, then the question, "What is man that You made him a little lower than a judge?" wouldn't make sense. However, if you read that to say, "You made him a little lower than God, Himself," then it would take on a whole different meaning.

Actually there are several different translations that are good. One says, "Just a shade lower than God Himself." Imagine that: just a shade lower than God Himself. E.W. Kenyon said, "God made man as much like Himself as He could."

I don't care how good a copy you make of something, the next copy is not going to be as good as the original. However, it can be so close that it takes a magnifying glass to tell the difference.

Literally, the type of connotation that this makes is that God made man so close to His own image and likeness that if it was just one shade more like God, it would be God. Now, that's strong. Amen?

Let's go on and read what it says about this man. "You made him a little lower than the angels, and hast," past tense, "crowned him with glory and honor." What man was he talking about? Obviously he was talking about Adam and the way He made Adam, but then Adam fell. After Adam fell, God didn't start saying different things about man.

God still said good things about man, and God still kept talking about man like He wanted to see him, although not necessarily like he was. Why? That's because God calls those "things that be not as though they were." Amen? The last thing you want is for God to call you as He sees you or as you have been.

"You have made him (man) to have dominion."

Psalm 8:6,

> 6 Thou madest him to have dominion over the works of thy hands; thou hast put all *things* under his feet:

He says, in verse 6, "Thou (God), have made him to have *dominion* over the works of Your hands." Now, you can take any one of these Scriptures apart, study it for ten years, and just keep digging things out. Go through the Scriptures with the eye open to see this.

Honestly, it should change your life every time you read it, because it says, "You have made him to have *dominion*." The Hebrew word for "*dominion*" there is *mâshal*. It means *to have dominion, reign, rule, or have power*. You can look it up and know that's what I'm referring to. It talks about having force and *dominion*.

Another Hebrew word used for "*dominion*" is *râdâh*. That is the word used in Genesis chapter 1.

Genesis 1:26-28,

> 26 And God said, Let us make man in our image, after our likeness: and let them have dominion over the fish of the sea, and over the fowl of the air, and over the cattle, and over all the earth, and over every creeping thing that creepeth upon the earth.

> 27 So God created man in his own image, in the image of God created he him; male and female created he them.
>
> 28 And God blessed them, and God said unto them, Be fruitful, and multiply, and replenish the earth, and subdue it: and have <u>dominion</u> over the fish of the sea, and over the fowl of the air, and over every living thing that moveth upon the earth.

"Dominion" here means *to tread down; to subjugate.* You might say that *it brings into order.* You have to look up these different words that are used to know which is which.

All things made by God were to be put "under his (man's) feet."

Psalms 8:6 says, "You caused him" or made him, "to have dominion over the works of Your hands; You have put all things under his (man's) feet." He was talking about man, and all things God made were to be put "under his feet."

Where have you heard that statement before? Isn't that the statement that was used about Jesus?

"And hath put all things under His feet…" refers to all things under Jesus' feet.

Ephesians 1:22,

> 22 And hath put all things under his feet, and gave him to be the head over all things to the church,

"And hath put all things under His feet…"

Our feet are the feet of Jesus. We are the Body of Christ.

Romans 16:20,

> 20 And the God of peace shall bruise Satan under your feet shortly. The grace of our Lord Jesus Christ *be* with you. Amen.

"And the God of peace shall bruise Satan under your feet shortly." Why? That's because your feet are the feet of Jesus. You are the Body of Christ. You are one with Him.

We could just take these Scriptures, not study anything else, and focus and mediate on these for a period of time, and you would walk like Jesus. He said, "Man is made just a little lower than God Himself, and You have crowned him with glory and honor. You have made him to have dominion, authority, power, the ability to tread down, the ability to dominate, and the ability to have dominion over the works of Your hands." What were the works of God's hands? He just said in Psalm 8, "Who has set the world above the heavens."

Psalm 8:1,

> 1 O LORD our Lord…who hast set thy glory above the heavens.

In verse 3 it spoke of the works of His fingers,

> 3 When I consider thy heavens, the work of thy fingers, the moon and the stars, which thou hast ordained;

Then in the first part of verse 6 it said, "You've made man to have dominion over the works of Your hands."

> 6 Thou madest him to have dominion over the works of thy hands;

Then in the second part of verse 6, he said, "You put all things under his feet," under man's feet.

> 6 …thou hast put all *things* under his feet:

Verses 7 and 8 go on to tell what is to be put under his feet.

> 7 All sheep and oxen, yea, and the beasts of the field;

> 8 The fowl of the air, and the fish of the sea, *and whatsoever* passeth through the paths of the seas.

Now, what was he doing? He was paraphrasing Genesis 1:26-28. He was just paraphrasing and saying the exact same thing: "God made man to have that dominion."

Then in verse 9 it says,

> 9 O LORD our Lord, how excellent *is* thy name in all the earth!

You may have to go back over this, and study it out. I hope that you do because you need to start developing this in you, and as you do it will open up to you.

In the first part of Genesis, it says that God made Adam in His image.

Genesis 1:26,

> 26 And God said, Let us make man in our image, after our likeness…

He said, "Let us make man in Our image, after Our likeness." Both of these have to be there, because He made and He created. He created man in His image, and He made him after His likeness.

> 27 So God <u>created</u> man in his own image, in the image of God <u>created</u> he him; male and female created he them.

The word for *"created"* there is the Hebrew word *bârâ* which means *to make out of nothing*. First of all, God created Adam. We know that everything that was made was made by God, but in John it says specifically that anything that was made was made by Jesus.

John 1:10,

> 10 He was in the world, and the world was made by him, and the world knew him not.

It says that anything that was made was made by Him, so Jesus made everything. Jesus made Adam. He said, "Let us make man in our image." The only image we have of God is Jesus, because it says He is the expressed image of God. Adam had to look just like Jesus, at least in the physical body.

He made man in His own image and after His own likeness. The image was made after the Spirit, but the likeness was made after the physical appearance. God created the spirit of man out of nothing, according to the Word, but He made his body out of the dust of the earth.

God gave man dominion over the earth.

Genesis 1:26,

> 26 …let them have <u>dominion</u> over the fish of the sea, and over the fowl of the air, and over the cattle, and <u>over all the earth</u>, and over every creeping thing that creepeth upon the earth.

It says, "…let them (man) have *dominion.*" Man was to exercise *"dominion" as sovereignty, as a potentate, or as a ruler.* Isn't that the same definition we gave before for God?

Later on, in 2 Corinthians, we see where it says that Satan is the god of this world. He became the god of this world when Adam passed the world over to him. For that to happen, Adam had to be "god of this world" at that time, and he passed it on.

BEHOLD THE KINGDOM

God never said that man was to have dominion over one another.

As I started looking at this, bits and pieces started coming together. I have said for years that when God gave a list of all of the things that Adam was going to have dominion over, He never mentioned man. He always mentioned earth. He mentioned animals, fish, birds, and all kinds of creeping things, but He never said that man was meant to have dominion over man, yet we're called kings and priests.

He talked about being a royal, kingly priesthood, mixing kings and priests. He called them a holy nation. He said we are to have dominion over the earth, over everything that crawls, flies, swims, or creeps, but He never said to have dominion over man. He intended for man to be the top creation, the top ruler, the god of this world, if you want to call him that. He created man for that. He expected man to have dominion, yet never to have dominion over one another.

Adam was the first Adam. Jesus was the last Adam.

There are two kinds of men on the earth. There are the children of the devil and the children of God. The first man was earthly; the second man was spiritual.

In 1 Corinthians chapter 15 it says,

> 46 Howbeit that was not first which is spiritual, but that which is natural; and afterward that which is spiritual.

> 47 The first man is of the earth, earthy: the second man is the Lord from heaven.

Go back to verse 45,

> 45 And so it is written, The first man Adam was made a living soul; the last Adam was made a quickening spirit.

Adam was the first Adam. Jesus was the last Adam.

Jesus was the second man, but He was not the second Adam. He was the last Adam. Do you see it?

**Adam was the first man, but he was not the original;
he was the first copy.**

The question that came up when I started looking at this was: who made Adam? The answer is: Jesus. God put Jesus in the Godhead. The Father, Son, and Holy Spirit agreed, "Let us make man after Our image, after Our likeness."

The Godhead had to send Jesus, because He was the One that had an image; He could make Himself into the same likeness. Whenever He made Adam into that likeness, He made a copy of Himself. Adam might have been the first man, but he was not the original. He was the first copy. He was the first print.

Take a paper that you want to save. You would call it the master, which is the first or the original. If it is the original, the master, then you would want to take care of it. You would make copies of it and put it away because you would want to protect the master.

The beauty of it is, if you go to the printer and make a copy, that copy will be the first print. You could take the master and you could look at the master and the printed copy side-by-side, and with the naked eye, you couldn't tell the difference. You would have to know something about it and look much closer at it to be able to see a difference.

If you were to spill water on it, it would probably run; it would mess it up and there would be a visible difference. You wouldn't be able to use that anymore because of the damage. You couldn't make copies from that one. You would have to go back to your file and get the master in order to make a new first print.

We have our masters of our CDs and DVDs. If something happened to a master, we would be in trouble. We have recordings on those going back to 2000, and cassette tapes that we gathered over a period of time before that. We had to transfer the cassette tapes over onto CD. We have one master of each of our CDs or DVDs and if anything happened to any one of those, we wouldn't be able to make copies from the original. When you lose a master, it hurts.

When you've given your life to something, and you think, "We got that. We captured it," and then something happens, it's rough, and it affects you. You think, "We've got to take better care of them."

Well, we have a Master. Adam was the first print and Jesus was the original. Adam fell, so he was damaged, but God didn't panic, because He had the Master. Jesus came back in.

All this time we've been making copies from the damaged first print, so we have a world full of copies. Through the generations the copies are getting worse and worse. Isn't it amazing that it lines up with Newton's theory that things run down and don't get better? However, when Jesus came He said, "We're not going to use that first print anymore. We're going to use the Master now."

He went through the same thing Adam did, but He didn't get messed up, and because of that, now every reproduction in Jesus is a perfect digital copy. I hope you get the idea there. It's no longer mimeographed where it's going through the process, but now its digital; now it's a perfect imprint over and over. That's who you are.

**We should look so much like Jesus that
the devil can't tell that we're not Him.**

Why do you think the devil comes to tempt you? There are two examples of the devil tempting people. One was in the Garden when he said, "Hath God truly said?"

Then, when the devil appeared to Jesus, he came to try to tempt Him. He didn't say, "Has God really said?" like he did in the garden. He said, "If You are the Son of God…" Do you see the difference? That's how he tempts you when he comes to you. What he'll say first is, "Has

God really said that you're different?" However, the way he tempts you is by asking, "Are you a son of God, or are you a child of God?" Then you say what Jesus said.

When tempted, you have to answer the same way that Jesus answered every time: "It is written."

Jesus said: "It is written." You have to respond to him the same way that Jesus responded to him. It's the only way to win, and it's the only way he knows that he's dealing with Jesus and not somebody else. If you answer a different way, he knows he's dealing with somebody else.

When the devil asks, "Are you truly a different person?" you have to say, "It is written; I am a new creation in Christ Jesus. Old things are passed away, behold all things have become new, and all things are of God, who has reconciled me unto Him." You have to respond that way.

The devil will turn around, and say, "If you are a son of God, do this." He will try to get you to do something out of one of these three: the lust of the flesh, the lust of the eyes, or the pride of life. Isn't that what he did with Jesus? After he asked Jesus if He was the Son of God, he said, "I hear Your belly rumbling. You've been fasting for forty days. I know You're hungry. You need some bread. Look at that rock. Wouldn't that make a perfect loaf of bread? You can do that; just turn it into bread. That's all You have to do to prove you are the Son of God."

Jesus said, "No, I'm not going to do that, because if I did, I would be doing it in response to you. I would be obeying you." The one you obey is the one you become the servant of. He said, "I'm not going to do that." He said, "It is written: 'Man does not live by bread alone, but by every word that proceeds out of the mouth of God.'" Do you see how all of that ties together?

The power of words: "You will have what you say if you believe it."

When Jesus said, "You can speak to a fig tree, and it will obey you, or you can speak to a mountain, and it will obey you," He was saying, "You will have what you say if you believe it." He was talking to fallen man. He didn't say, "Well, when you're born again you can do this." He didn't say that. He was talking to fallen man and He said, "You will have what you say if you believe it."

You have people that hear that the economy is going to go down, and it is going to be tough to get jobs, and they start repeating it. They say, "Don't buy anything. Hang on to your money." Then they don't buy, and they start storing up. Those are corresponding actions, and what happens is that the world goes that direction. All of that happens because someone said that it was supposed to be that way. They said, "Indicators seem to point us to the idea that that's the way it's going to be."

The bad part is that you have born again Christians, powered by the Holy Spirit, whose words should be so much more powerful, and they are saying the same thing the world says.

Satan comes to these people of the world. I'm not saying he comes in a form, but however he does it, he works through them.

"Faith comes by hearing, and hearing by the Word of God."

If faith comes by hearing, and hearing by the Word of God, then doubt comes by hearing, and hearing by the word of man, or the word of the devil; you can say it either way.

When I started looking at that, I started saying, "When we look at those things and when we hear that as news, it should not be, 'Oh, we better stop buying,' or 'Oh, we better stock up.'" We should not respond the way the world responds. We ought to take those things that are said, and say, "Thank you for that information, and right now, in the name of Jesus, I say it will be this way." In fact, we should say the exact opposite of what the world says.

If they say that there is going to be a shortage of anything, I say, "Crops are going to grow better than they've ever grown before." When they say, "There is going to be a shortage of oranges in Florida," I laugh at that, because I speak to orange trees, and say, "Orange trees, you will produce better than you've ever produced before, because I say so and for no other reason than the fact that I am man, and I can speak and the earth and everything on it has to obey me."

I didn't say anything that only a Christian can say. I said something that man can say. You have some people doing that, but the bad part is they're doing it illegally. They are going at it through New Age, and they do that exact same thing.

It's amazing to me that some of the first people that did some of the experiments on the power of words on things were New Age people. They started talking; they would say good things over this, and they would say bad things over that, and then they would look to see the difference. Words actually affected those things. These were non-born again people, New Age type people, and it worked. Why? That's because they are man, fallen man. You will find out that God never retracted what He said about man. He never retracted that dominion that He gave or that ability to speak.

I started looking at that, and I started thinking, "We need to start taking those indicators as promptings to pray or to speak, instead of listening to the news and saying, 'Well, I've got to figure whether to get out of the stock market.'" No, you listen to it and decide, "Here's what we're going to say about it." Amen?

Start acting as the highest official over your area of influence.

That's Kingdom living. When you start acting as the highest official over your area of influence, and you start speaking over your city, He will see that you've been faithful over one city, and He'll make you master over five. Do you see this? It does not seem as far fetched as it used to, does it? If not, then that means you're getting it.

To sum these up: Adam gave ruler-ship to Satan. Satan then offered the temptation of ruler-ship to Jesus.

We know the temptation was real, or Jesus would have called Satan on it. It was presented as a temptation that Jesus overcame. Jesus responded to it like He did every other temptation.

Satan knew that if Jesus had agreed to it, then He would have gone under. He would have gained the world, but He would have lost His position; He would have been under Satan. It would actually have pushed Satan up a notch, rather than putting Jesus where He wanted to be. There's nothing to say that it wasn't a real opportunity for Him to gain all the kingdoms of the world. If it had not been a real offer, then it wouldn't have been a real temptation.

God said, "Let them (man) have dominion."

Genesis 1:26-28,

> 26 And God said, Let us make man in our image, after our likeness: and let them have dominion over the fish of the sea, and over the fowl of the air, and over the cattle, and over all the earth, and over every creeping thing that creepeth upon the earth.

Notice: man is singular, but them is plural. He was saying, "Let them," basically man, and everyone that comes out of man, "have *dominion*." *"Dominion"* in this verse is from the Hebrew word *râdâh*. It means *to tread down, subjugate, or trample under.*

"Let them have *dominion* over the fish of the sea, and over the fowl of the air, and over the cattle, and over all the earth." Do you hear that? Let them have *dominion* over all the earth, not just cattle, fish, and birds. "Let them have *dominion* over all the earth, and over every creeping thing that creeps upon the earth."

> 27 So God created man in his *own* image, in the image of God created he him; male and female created he them.
>
> 28 And God blessed them, and God said unto them, Be fruitful, and multiply, and replenish the earth, and subdue it: and have <u>dominion</u> over the fish of the sea, and over the fowl of the air, and over every living thing that moveth upon the earth.

Notice: it was repeated here for emphasis.

Jesus' disciples asked, "What kind of man is this, that even the winds and the sea obey Him?"

Matthew 8:24,

> 24 And, behold, there arose a great tempest in the sea, insomuch that the ship was covered with the waves: but he was asleep.
>
> 25 And his disciples came to *him*, and awoke him, saying, Lord, save us: we perish.

> 26 And he saith unto them, Why are ye fearful, O ye of little faith? Then he arose, and rebuked the winds and the sea; and there was a great calm.

"And He saith unto them, Why are you fearful, O ye of little faith?" I'm sure they were thinking, "Hello, look around; waves are coming over the boat. You told us to go to the other side, we're out in the middle now, and we're going to sink. Now is the time to be afraid."

He was thinking just the opposite. "That's right; I told you to go to the other side. Now there are waves coming, so you ought to get up in front of the boat and speak to it. I did not tell you to come to the middle of the sea and drown. I told you to go to the other side."

He said, "Why are you fearful, O ye of little faith? Then He arose and rebuked the winds and the sea; and there was a great calm." We know He talked to fig trees. We know He talked about talking to mountains. We know He talked to wind and sea. We know He talked to demons. We know He talked to fever. We know He talked to sickness, disease, and numerous other things.

> 27 But the men marvelled, saying, What manner of man is this, that even the winds and the sea obey him!

"What kind of man is this, that even the winds and the sea obey Him!" I'll tell you what kind of Man that was; He was the original One. He was the original Man that Adam was copied from.

KINGDOM ADMINISTRATORS – PART 2

I used to teach Bible Doctrine in the Assemblies of God church I was in. It was where I had the Sudafed anointing experience. In the book I was teaching from, I actually left out a part. I did not teach it, because I did not agree with it.

It talked about the deity of Christ, which I absolutely agree with and believe, but I did not agree with all of their reasoning of what proved Him to be divine. It mentioned the part about His miraculous virgin birth. It went back to Scripture and said, "He would be called a mighty God."

Then it said, "What proved Him to be divine were His miracles and His healings." When I read that I thought, "I can't go with that, because Elijah did miracles. Elijah wasn't God, so miracles can't prove you're God."

Jesus didn't do miracles to prove He was God. You can't use miracles to prove Jesus is God, because the minute you do that, then you have to bring in every other person that's ever worked a miracle and say they were God, too. At that point, you enter the realm of Mormonism.

I could not go along with that, so I left that part out when I taught. I did not teach that miracles or healings proved Jesus was divine. I used all of the other things that were good, such as His death, burial, and resurrection; all of that was good.

I had a problem with the part about how the 12 healed, and Judas was a devil. That should prove my point, right there. The 70 healed. There was another man casting out devils in Jesus' name. We don't even know his name, but we know he wasn't of God.

They asked, "What manner of man is this?" Well, He was the original man. He was the One after Whom everyone else was supposed to be patterned. However, over time, the copy got so weak, so bad, and so messed up that you couldn't even look at the copies and say that they came from the original.

Do you realize that Peter should have been able to look at Jesus and say, "There is something familiar about you." Why? If you traced every person, each one would go back to Noah, and then from Noah back to Adam.

They said, "Even the winds and the sea obey Him!" We know that fig trees obeyed Him, and sickness, disease, and demons obeyed Him.

We are to love one another and defer to one another.

We were never meant to have dominion over one another. Jesus Himself said, "It will not be among you like it is among the Gentiles, that you lord over one another." We are not to have dominion over one another. We are to love one another. We are to love God and love our fellowman, which means to do unto them as we would want done unto us.

Have you ever noticed that everybody just accepted Jesus as the Master? He told them, "Come, follow Me." He didn't say, "Come, follow Me, or else." He just put out the call. He said, "Come."

At some point, He did tell them, "I'm the door. The only way to get to the Father is by Me." He didn't force that; He just stated the facts. He didn't lord over anybody, and yet He was the Lord. All He lorded over was sickness, disease, wind, rain, demons, fish, and things on this earth.

Do you remember how He got the tax money? He commanded that fish fill their nets. He had the right to do that, because He told them they would have dominion over the fish of the sea. Everything He did, He did as the last Adam. Everything He did, He did as man.

The *kenosis* of Christ was where He emptied Himself of all that made Him God.

Philippians 2:5-8,

> 5 Let this mind be in you, which was also in Christ Jesus:
>
> 6 Who, being in the form of God, thought it not robbery to be equal with God:

Remember: Jesus was equal in nature, in character, and in Spirit to God. He was in a class of "being."

> 7 But <u>made himself of no reputation</u>, and took upon him the form of a servant, and was made in the likeness of men:

8 And being found in fashion as a man, he humbled himself, and became obedient unto death, even the death of the cross.

When it said, *"But made Himself of no reputation,"* the Greek word *ekenoosen was* used, which comes from the word *kenoō*. It means *to make empty, make (of none effect, of no reputation, void).*

The NASB version says, "Who, although He existed in the form of God, did not regard equality with God a thing to be grasped, but emptied Himself, taking the form of a bond-servant, and being made in the likeness of men. And being found in appearance as a man, He humbled Himself by becoming obedient to the point of death, even death on a cross."

That's what is called the *"kenosis"* of Christ, where *He emptied Himself of all that made Him God*, in the sense that He emptied Himself of any attributes of God and simply acted as a man in right union with God.

Jesus acted like the prophets did, but He stood out so drastically from everybody else, because He was the original that everybody else was supposed to be imitating. Paul said, "Follow me as I follow Christ." Imitate Christ. That's our whole purpose.

As I said before, we ought to be copies, or as we would say today, "clones." They didn't have that terminology in 1611, but we would use the word clones. That's who we are.

The Kingdom we entered into when we got born again allows us to walk, not just where Adam walked, but even better than that. We don't have to look back to our ancestors or to anyone in our past.

We are a new species of being that never existed before on this earth, in that sense. Because of that, we are able to do these things in His Name. We are bone of His bone and flesh of His flesh. We've already had the bone marrow transplant that we talked about earlier.

This is why we have to walk in love. We're not to have dominion over one another; we are all part of one another.

The first Adam became a living soul, but the last Adam was a life giving Spirit.

There are only references to two of "man" on this earth. They are the first Adam and the last Adam.

Let's read 1 Corinthians chapter 15:45-47 again:

> 45 And so it is written, The first man Adam was made a living soul; the last Adam was made a quickening spirit.
>
> 46 Howbeit that was not first which is spiritual, but that which is natural; and afterward that which is spiritual.
>
> 47 The first man is of the earth, earthy: the second man is the Lord from heaven.

It says that if we are made in the image of the first man, which was earthly or natural, we will be earthly but if we are made in the image of the second Man, the last Adam, then we will be spiritual. It says that the first Adam became a living soul, but the last Adam was a life giving Spirit.

If you go and study it out, you will find that you are made after the image of the last Adam, the second man. You are made in the image of the Original. You are an identical clone, if you want to use that term.

Because of that, we take on the image of the heavenly, the spiritual, and we walk under the conditions of this kingdom. That's all Jesus was doing. Everything He did, He did as a person living in this new kingdom.

In the new kingdom, when you speak, things come to pass for you.

This new kingdom is exactly the opposite of the old kingdom. This new kingdom is voice activated. You speak, and things happen. You speak and it comes to pass for you, because you have the right to speak and believe in your heart, and when you speak the Word of God, what you're speaking comes from the Word of God. It doesn't have to be a quote, but it's the Word of God even if you paraphrase it. Angels hearken to the voice of God's Word, and they accomplish it.

KINGDOM ADMINISTRATORS – PART 2

Believe on Him, cease from your works, and start doing His works.

I asked before what you would do if someone came to you and said that they would back you in anything you wanted to do. What would be your dream? What would you say that you want to do with your life?

How do you see yourself in five or ten years? What do you want to be doing? What if you never had to worry about money again? What would be the first thing to pop into your mind? Would it be in line with the will of God? I'm not saying that it is some special will that you've got to go out and find. If it lines up with the Bible and if it lines up with loving God and loving your fellowman as yourself, and if it lines up with doing to others what you'd have done to you, then it is God's will.

God has already said, "I don't want you to ever have to worry about food, where you're going to sleep, or what you're going to wear. I don't want you to think about any of that. I want you to focus, and I want you to be absolutely dedicated to this dream. You don't have to worry about anything else."

People say, "Well, I have to work eight hours a day to make ends meet. If I want to make enough money to start my own business, I have to work an extra four hours of overtime a day just to put money back."

God's answer to that would be: "That's just like the Gentiles. You're just like a pagan. You're religious. You'll serve Me on Sunday, but

Monday through Friday, you don't talk to Me because you are busy building your own kingdom."

God doesn't want you to worry about what you're going to eat or what you're going to wear. He wants to take care of you. He is your heavenly Father, and He wants you to be about your Father's business."

If that dream that popped up in your head when I mentioned that before is in line with the will of God, go after it! God will back you, and you won't have to worry. Most people spend so much time worrying about making a living that they never live a life. That is the reason for the world system. It is to keep you looking at eating, dressing, and being taken care of so that you don't have time to be the blessing to the world that God wants you to be.

There's not a person that God cannot use to do amazing things through. Not one. You say, "Well, you don't know me. How can you say that?" That's because I know me, and if He can use me, He can use you." Amen? He's done some amazing things through me, so I know He can do amazing things through you.

He can do that, because He is God. He's that big. I don't care how much of a mess-up you are, He is big enough to overrule that and do great things through you. Amen? That's really what I want you to realize: you have a heavenly Father. You don't have to focus on what to eat, what you're going to wear, or where you're going to sleep.

Focus on the fact that if you're born again, you are the righteousness of God, in Christ.

Matthew 6:33,

> 33 But seek ye first the kingdom of God, and his righteousness; and all these things shall be added unto you.

If you have that righteousness, that means you sought it, and you have sought the Kingdom, and you found it. That means that if you seek Him, all these things are going to be added to you, but as long as you keep providing for yourself, He'll let you do it.

What we're going to do here in the next six months to a year is going to be phenomenal. People are going to look at us and say, "How did that happen?" That's because we're going to put the Kingdom first, and we will do it through the Kingdom. We're going to do what's important; we're going to focus on that.

You have to think Kingdom. What kingdom are you in? Are you in the Kingdom of His dear Son? You say that you're born again, so I assume you're in that Kingdom.

We're in this world, but we're not of this world. We are born of heaven.

We've got American troops around the world in different places. They are in Afghanistan, but they're not of Afghanistan. If they're in Afghanistan, they're there because we sent them there. Now, please,

I'm not getting into the right and wrong of all of that; I'm just using it as an example. We sent them there.

If you talked to a soldier, they would tell you that the most important thing to them would be things sent from home. They can't get those things there. Even if they could get them, they would still want them from home, because they remind them of home. It's their way of connecting. They love to get cookies. They love to get things in the mail from home.

The amazing thing about going to a foreign country is that the minute you walk onto the grounds of an American embassy, you are on American soil.

Haiti is the most poverty stricken nation in the western hemisphere. If you walked to the American Embassy, immediately after getting off the airplane in Port-au-Prince, you would walk past people starving. You would walk past bad housing. You would walk past people who were sick, dying, poor, and begging. It's a horrible state to live in with horrible conditions.

After reaching the American Embassy, you could go into the kitchen. Their pantry would be so full of food, that they could lock the gates and live there for one year. I'm not talking about crackers and cheese to spread on your crackers; I'm talking about food. They fly food in from Florida. Whatever the ambassador wants, they fly in, because the ambassador is not limited to the resources of the country he is placed in.

KINGDOM ADMINISTRATORS – PART 2

The resources of the place where you are do not limit you. What you're limited to are the resources from where you're from. I am not of this world. I was not born of this world. I am born of heaven. I'm not limited to the resources of this world. I'm only limited to the resources of the world I'm from; I allow only those to get to me.

If I were an ambassador to a foreign country, I could starve in the American Embassy if I did not let them bring food into me. I could sit right inside those locked gates with all of the pretty gardens and all of the flower arrangements, and I could starve.

I have that passport and that passport says, "Property of the Untied States." That passport means that a person from another country can't deal with me without going through the consulate. They would have to deal with me according to the International Standards.

Colossians 1:13,

> 13 Who hath delivered us from the power of darkness, and hath translated us into the kingdom of his dear Son:

"We were delivered out of the power and authority of darkness, and translated into the Kingdom of His dear Son." What does that mean? I'm in a new Kingdom. I've got a new passport. The authority of darkness does not have the right to talk to me.

The devil (the authority of darkness) may come up and say, "Hey, you're here on the earth, and as long as you're here you have to get sick, you have to be poor, and you have to have all of these troubles." I say, "No, no, no. That's not me. Look at my passport; I'm born of heaven. Heaven will bring resources to me."

There can be trouble all around me, yet it will not come close to me, because I'm from another Kingdom.

Psalm 91:7,

> 7 A thousand shall fall at thy side, and ten thousand at thy right hand; *but* it shall not come nigh thee.

Why will it not come close to me? That's because the authority of darkness has no right. It shall not come near me, because I'm from another Kingdom.

I have a desire to go to Haiti. I want to go there, put my foot on the ground, and be able to look at that ground and say, "You will listen and obey me." Why? That's because I'm born of the original Man. I am not born from the first print; he was messed up.

I'm born of the original Man and because of that, I have dominion over the earth and the earth will obey me. I can say, "You will prosper, and you will grow," and it will grow produce four times bigger than normal. Why? That's because we need four times the amount of food. We don't have four times the amount of space, so it just has to grow four times as big.

We have to think Kingdom. Jesus thought differently than man, the first Adam. He thought according to Kingdom principles. He even asked them, "Should I pay taxes?" Then He said, "I'm trying to emphasize to you that this isn't my Kingdom. I'm not of this worldly kingdom, I'm of that other Kingdom, but to keep from getting in trouble, we'll go ahead and pay taxes; I don't have a problem with that. 'Fish, I need some tax money!'" Fish just swam over there, and they were waiting for Peter to come over and go fishing. Then they paid taxes. He didn't worry about it. He didn't have to get it by the sweat of His brow. Amen?

Delve into this and think about these things. Go over them. Get the CD and go over it again and again. Get it in you; start realizing how to live in this Kingdom, how to talk and how to walk. In this Kingdom, you don't talk about what you've got; you talk about what you want. You call those things "which are not as though they were." Anybody can talk about what they have. Anybody can call those things that are as though they are. We're not doing that. We're of another Kingdom, we talk differently. We call those things "which are not as though they were."

People will ask, "Oh, what do you think about that economy?" Just say, "I know, isn't it great?" They won't know what to think. You just talk that way, and they'll either be drawn to you, or they'll walk away. Amen?

I want you to get this message, so study it out. I'm going to keep going on it until you get it. When you get it, I will be able to tell, because you will show that you have it.

"Heavenly Father,

"We thank You. Your Word is true. I believe Your Word. Let it be unto me according to Your Word. I thank You, Heavenly Father, that Your Kingdom come, let Your will be done in my life and in the lives of those around me. I thank You now that the eyes of my understanding are enlightened, and I walk not according to this world, but according to Your Kingdom and according to Your dominion. Live through me in the name of Jesus. Amen."

ALL THAT JESUS BEGAN BOTH TO DO AND TEACH

Sermon given by Curry R. Blake

**Every person in the Kingdom will be a king
and a priest and shall reign on the earth.**

In our session called "Kingdom Administrators," Part 1, we covered the Scriptures that said, "Ye are gods."

John 10:34,

> 34 Jesus answered them, Is it not written in your law, I said, Ye are gods?

Jesus was quoting there from Psalm 82.

Psalm 82:6-7,

> 6 I have said, Ye *are* gods; and all of you *are* children of the most High.
>
> 7 But ye shall die like men, and fall like one of the princes.

Notice that it said, "I have said ye are gods…" Then it said, "…but you shall die as men." Obviously, there's always some controversy over that, but if you just study it out there's nothing really controversial about it.

Then we did "Kingdom Administrators," Part 2. We talked a little more about that, but we also brought in the fact that God essentially put us here on this earth to administrate His Kingdom as His "under ruler." Turn with me in your Bibles to Exodus chapter 19. I want to give you a couple of Scriptures. We're just going to go from the front of the Book to the back of the Book. I will show you that this was God's plan all along.

Exodus 19:5-6,

> 5 Now therefore, if ye will obey my voice indeed, and keep my covenant, then ye shall be a peculiar treasure unto me above all people: for all the earth *is* mine:

Notice the word "peculiar" in verse 5.

> 6 And ye shall be unto me a kingdom of priests, and an holy nation. These *are* the words which thou shalt speak unto the children of Israel.

Notice: "a kingdom of priests" in verse 6. Those two don't usually go together. Usually it is referred to as an order of priests, but not usually as a kingdom of priests. Essentially, He was saying that every person in the kingdom will be a king and a priest. We see that in Revelation 5, also.

Revelation 5:9-10,

> 9 And they sung a new song, saying, Thou art worthy to take the book, and to open the seals thereof: for thou wast slain, and hast redeemed us to God by thy blood out of every kindred, and tongue, and people, and nation;
>
> 10 And hast made us unto our God kings and priests: and we shall reign on the earth.

Notice: "And hast," past tense, "made us unto our God kings and priests."

We are to reign in life and not reign after death.

Romans 5:17,

> 17 For if by one man's offence death reigned by one; much more they which receive abundance of grace and of the gift of righteousness shall reign in life by one, Jesus Christ.

In other words, "If we have received the abundance of grace and of the gift of righteousness, we shall reign in life by one, Jesus Christ." It is reigning in life, and not reigning after death. It's not over there on the other side; it's over here. Amen?

I want you to get the over-all picture, so we're going to go to Matthew chapter 4, then we're going to go to Mark chapter 1, then we're going to look at Acts chapter 1.

This teaching, "All that Jesus began both to do and teach," is from Acts 1:1.

> 1 The former treatise have I made, O Theophilus, of all that Jesus began both to do and teach,

Luke was writing to Theophilus, who was obviously a lover of God, because that's what Theophilus means. Luke made sure that everything he wrote and everything that had already been written in the Gospel of Luke had been proven. He had investigated, he had researched it, and he had made sure that everything he had written was absolutely accurate.

Then Luke wrote what we call the Book of the Acts of the Apostles, which probably should have been called the Acts of the Holy Ghost. I think the main star there was the Holy Ghost, so it was more along the Acts of the Holy Ghost more than the Acts of the Apostles. There were a lot of other people in there doing some things other than just the Apostles.

"Jesus did and taught," so every believer should do and teach.

He didn't just do, and He didn't just teach. He did, and He taught. Every believer should do and teach. Every believer should be sharing with someone, more than just in a witnessing aspect. Every believer should be making a disciple of someone.

You say, "Well, I don't know that much." Believe it or not, there are people who know less than you do. They ought to be easy to find, so just find somebody that knows less then you do and teach them. Bring them up to speed, and then somebody will teach you a little more, and then this whole thing will just grow. That's the way it's supposed to work.

Now, so that we get the whole picture, we are starting at the very beginning of Jesus' ministry. Jesus had been baptized by John in the Jordan River. He had gone into the wilderness, He had been tempted, He had overcome temptation, and He had won the victory in temptation. Then it says, "He returned in the power of the Spirit." As soon as He got back on the scene, then John the Baptizer was almost immediately arrested and then beheaded. After John was arrested, Jesus started preaching.

What Jesus started doing, He continued doing.
He didn't do something one time.

John had already been preaching, "Repent for the kingdom of heaven is at hand." Then Jesus picked it up immediately and said exactly the same thing. We read this in Matthew chapter 4, starting in verse 17. I want to emphasize certain words. The key to our ministry really has been the fact that we actually pay attention to exactly what was written, and we emphasize words that most people just run past.

Matthew 4:17,

> 17 From that time Jesus began to preach, and to say, Repent: for the kingdom of heaven is at hand.

Notice the phrase "from that time." What does that mean? How would we say that today? We would say, "From then on." He didn't say, "And at this time Jesus preached this." If he had, then we would say, "Well, that was one time that He preached that," but he didn't say that. He said, "From that time," so basically he was saying, "From the very beginning of Jesus' ministry."

We know how He started, but we also know that whatever He started with, He continued all the way through. That's the whole point of this teaching.

Jesus was sent to preach the Kingdom of God.

I talk to Christians and non-Christians, and they all seem to have the idea that Jesus just went around and gave a little word here and there, preached the Sermon on the Mount, healed some people round about, and it was all disconnected—but it wasn't. He was sent with a purpose. Jesus was sent to preach the Kingdom of God, and He invited people to partake of that Kingdom. Everything He taught was about that Kingdom. Every word and every action was a demonstration of the Kingdom.

Once you start putting this whole thing in perspective, all of a sudden it will be like, "Okay, so He was just showing us how the Kingdom is supposed to be operating. He was showing us how people who live in the Kingdom live." We're going to look at that a little more.

Matthew chapter 4, verse 17 said, "From that time Jesus began to preach, and to say…" What He said was what He preached, and He began to say, "Repent for the kingdom of heaven is at hand." That meant that it was available, it was here, and it could be entered into.

Something really stood out to me when I was doing research on this. I found that the word kingdom was mentioned over 100 times from Matthew through John.

Even John said that everything that Jesus did wasn't mentioned, but we know that everything He did and said was included in the phrase, "The kingdom of heaven is at hand." I want you to get that locked in.

Jesus preached the Good News that God's Government could be entered into and exercised upon the earth.

Mark 1:14-15,

> 14 Now after that John was put in prison, Jesus came into Galilee, preaching the gospel of the kingdom of God,

What was the Gospel? It was "The Good News." Jesus wasn't preaching a sermon so much as He was preaching "The Good News." He was *"evangelizing."* To *evangelize* means *to bring forth Good News.* He was preaching "The Good News of the Kingdom;" the reign, the superiority, the supremacy, and the rules of the "Government of God." He was preaching the Good News that God's Government could be entered into and exercised upon the earth.

15 And saying, The time is fulfilled, and the kingdom of God is at hand: repent ye, and believe the gospel.

As He was preaching the Kingdom, this is what He was saying, "The time is fulfilled, and the Kingdom of God is at hand: repent ye, and believe the Good News of the Gospel."

**Notice: Jesus was preaching the Gospel,
but He was not preaching His death, burial, and resurrection.**

I always have to emphasize that Jesus was not preaching His death, burial, and resurrection. Usually, when we talk about the Gospel, we talk about His death, burial, and resurrection. That is not what He was preaching. If anything, He hid it. For the most part, He hid it in parables, and He even hid it for some time from His own disciples.

Eventually, He started to bring it out. When He did bring it out, they didn't get it. He had to keep repeating it, and they still didn't get it. They didn't get it even when He died. He had to show back up to them, and even then, when He found them they were all hiding with the door locked. It was as if He had walked through a wall. In Luke 24, verses 30-37, it showed that Jesus stood in their midst, and they supposed that they had seen a spirit.

In Isaiah chapter 55, verse 11 it tells how God's Word goes forth and doesn't return void. It accomplishes what He sent it for. His Word is like rain that comes down and makes the earth produce fruit.

Jesus said that the Kingdom starts as the smallest of all seeds, but once it's planted, it grows into a tree that all the fowls of the air can live in.

God continues to work in people's lives like a slow rain that they can't get away from, and it's always moving forward. That's the way His Kingdom is: that Kingdom starts small and then it grows. Jesus said that the Kingdom, even though it starts as the smallest of all seeds, once it's planted, it grows into a tree that all the fowls of the air can live in. In other words, it grows into this huge thing.

That's exactly what has happened with this teaching. As we moved into it, we started to see that it takes care of every part of life; it's involved in every part of life. We talk about divine healing, a topic which includes the Kingdom. We talk about the new man, which came about by what was accomplished by Jesus dying on the cross and through His resurrection. However, the new man has to function in the Kingdom, so there has to be a Kingdom for the new man to function in.

The Kingdom frees you from everyday life. Decide to tell God, "Let it be unto me according to Your Word."

People didn't function in the Kingdom of God before Jesus. There were little bursts of power, but they didn't walk in it. Jesus showed us how to walk every day in the Kingdom and how to walk free.

The thing about the Kingdom is that it frees you from everyday life. Once you understand the Kingdom, it frees you from having to think in terms of what you are going to eat, what you are going to wear, or if the bills are going to get paid. If you still have to worry about those things, I can honestly tell you that you don't understand the Kingdom yet.

In the Kingdom, you are a king and a priest unto God who is your Father, a Father who wants to take care of you. He will take care of you. It's not like the Old Covenant in this Kingdom. It's not like when people were under the law where they had to perform perfectly.

This Kingdom is already at hand. The way you activate it is simply by reading the Word and deciding, "Oh, that's true." Then you just say, "Let it be unto me according to Your Word." That's all I want you to do. I just want you to decide, "Father, let it be unto me according to Your Word." Then, as you read the Word, you find out what that is, and you just start letting that be. You will say, "Okay, that's supposed to be."

You cannot go by what has been in the past. I don't care if you've struggled emotionally, with sin, with finances, with healing, or in some other area. I'm telling you today that you just simply decide to tell God, "Let it be unto me according to Your Word." Believing will flip a switch, because this Kingdom is voice activated. Amen?

The Word in your mouth is a seed. You plant the seed, you water the seed, you believe and then you say. It works. That's the element of everything about the Kingdom, of everything about the Gospel, and of everything in Christianity. We believe, and say: "Because we have believed, therefore we speak." That's what it comes down to.

What you say has to line up with the Word of God.

No matter what is going on in your life, at some point, you have to just simply change what you say.

In 2 Corinthians 10:5 the Word says that we have to bring every thought into captivity to the obedience of Christ.

> 5 Casting down imaginations, and every high thing that exalteth itself against the knowledge of God, and bringing into captivity every thought to the obedience of Christ;

We are ambassadors of the Kingdom of God, and as ambassadors we do not have the right to our personal opinion. An ambassador can only say what the kingdom he represents or the nation he represents says. We do not have the right to our own opinion.

If somebody came to me and asked, "What do you think about homosexuality?" I would say, "I don't." "Well, what is your position on it?" "I can't give you my position, but I will tell you the position of the Kingdom that I represent. It's an abomination." That's not me saying that; I'm just representing the Kingdom. The good thing is they can be changed. There can be a change. "Well, I was born this way." "Well, guess what? I was born a sinner, too, and I had to get born again." Isn't that simple? Amen.

It doesn't matter how you were born. What counts is how you were born again. You were born again according to the incorruptible seed of the Word of God. Now you are recreated in true holiness and righteousness after Jesus Christ and after God, Himself.

Let's look at Acts chapter 1:1 again. This is the verse where we actually got the title for this sermon. Luke was writing.

Acts 1:1,

> 1 The former treatise have I made, O Theophilus, of all that Jesus began both to do and teach,

Notice: it never says He stopped. "Jesus began both to do and teach." He started something that He passed on, but He began both to do and teach.

Jesus arose from the dead and showed up at the apostles' gathering. For the next 40 days, He explained the Kingdom of God.

Acts 1:2-3,

> 2 Until the day in which he was taken up, after that he through the Holy Ghost had given commandments unto the apostles whom he had chosen:
>
> 3 To whom also he shewed himself alive after his passion by many infallible proofs, being seen of them forty days, and speaking of the things pertaining to the kingdom of God:

After Jesus had been dead for three days, and then resurrected, He was seen by them for 40 days. He just talked to them about the Kingdom of God and shared with them.

Notice: it didn't say He answered questions. You would think, "Now, this man, Jesus, rose from the dead, and He was there for 40 days. That's a long time. There was plenty of time to ask questions after the initial shock wore off."

It doesn't say what all they did, but it says He spoke to them. It said that later He explained to them all things of the law and the prophets and of how He, Christ, had to suffer. He told them all about Himself, but it also says that He spoke to them about the Kingdom of God.

Think about that. For 40 days He explained the Kingdom. That would explain why they acted the way they did right after the Day of Pentecost.

Paul was chained to a Roman guard, and he was talking like he was the boss. I'm sure the guard was thinking, "Here I am guarding you, and you are talking like you are the boss. I'm your guard to make sure you don't get away."

Paul was thinking, "I'm sure glad I have you as my bodyguard, so I don't just get swamped by people." It was just a whole different mindset.

As Paul was writing letters, the guard was probably thinking, "Well, I am not going to have this job much longer, because he's going to go before Caesar. They're going to be cutting his head off, so this is going to end quickly."

Paul was writing, "Yes, I know the Church needs me. I really want to go on, but right now, I think the Church needs me too much. I'll probably stay around awhile. I don't think I'm going to die yet. I'll just stay here and do my job."

It shows different perspectives. Paul was talking like he was in control over whether he was going to die or not. Well, he was in control. You can be around the Kingdom of God and not see it. It can be all around you and people can be experiencing it, yet you just stand there and say, "Well, what's the big deal?"

For 40 days Jesus went into detail on the Kingdom of God. I've only taught on it six or seven times in this series, and a couple of years ago I taught on the Kingdom parables and different things, but I didn't teach on it for 40 days. They were literally staying in, sitting there. Sending out for food and that kind of thing would take a couple of hours here and there, but for 40 days He continually spoke of the things pertaining to the Kingdom of God.

Go back to when Jesus first started.

Matthew 4:17,

> 17 From that time Jesus began to preach, and to say, Repent: for the kingdom of heaven is at hand.

I'm running through several places, but I just want you to get an overall view of what was going on. Jesus had started preaching and John was dead. You may be thinking, "Okay, where's the Kingdom in that?" It's all throughout these Scriptures, but again, if you don't understand it, you won't see it.

Luke 4:16,

> 16 And he came to Nazareth, where he had been brought up: and, as his custom was, he went into the synagogue on the sabbath day, and stood up for to read.

Notice that it was talking about the Son of God.

Colossians 2:3,

> 3 In whom are hid all the treasures of wisdom and knowledge.

Jesus was really smart, and He still went to church. He didn't go expecting to learn anything. He probably thought, "I've got to sit through another one, and they're going to tell it the wrong way. I was there when it happened, and I know what happened," but He still went. You wonder why He said, "How long do I have to suffer you?" We say "put up with" and He said "suffer." It means the same thing.

Notice it said in Luke 4:16, "He stood up for to read."

Luke 4:17,

> 17 And there was delivered unto him the book of the prophet Esaias. And when he had opened the book, he found the place where it was written,

Do you realize it would have taken a little while to find that place? Isaiah was on a scroll and you had to roll that thing out and go all the way through to what we call chapter 61. There weren't any chapter numbers there, so it wasn't like He could just turn and see numbers. He had to actually read it.

It would have taken a little bit of time to pull through the scrolls. It wasn't where they just tossed it down and went through it. Before they took it, they had to wash their hands, and do certain rituals.

We know that the place he was quoting from was in Isaiah.

Isaiah 61:1,

> 61 The Spirit of the Lord God is upon me; because the Lord hath anointed me to preach good tidings unto the meek; he hath sent me to bind up the brokenhearted, to proclaim liberty to the captives, and the opening of the prison to them that are bound;

Luke 4:18,

> 18 The Spirit of the Lord is upon me, because he hath anointed me to preach the gospel to the poor; he hath sent me to heal the

> brokenhearted, to preach deliverance to the captives, and recovering of sight to the blind, to set at liberty them that are bruised,

Jesus was preaching "The Good News" to the poor. What Good News? It was the Good News of the Kingdom. Remember that He wasn't preaching the good news of His death, burial, and resurrection. He was preaching the Good News that God's Kingdom was finally here.

Remember Exodus 19:6 we just read? He said, "If you will obey Me and keep My statutes and walk in My covenant, then you will be a kingdom of priests." He was saying, "There is a Kingdom coming," and that's what they wanted, but they wanted it physically.

When Jesus was asked about when the Kingdom would come, He told them that it was not going to come with observation.

They asked, "How will it come? What's it going to look like? How will we know?"

Luke 17:20-21,

> 20 And when he was demanded of the Pharisees, when the kingdom of God should come, he answered them and said, The kingdom of God cometh not with observation:

BEHOLD THE KINGDOM

The Kingdom of God is of the Spirit.

> 21 Neither shall they say, Lo here! or, lo there! for, behold, the kingdom of God is within you.

It's like when the Holy Spirit comes, or when the wind rustles the leaves. You see the results of it, but you don't see the wind. It's not going to march in and take over. It's going to be of the Spirit; it's going to be in the heart. It's going to change things. You will be able to see the results of it, but it's not a Kingdom like you would think.

Jesus said, "You're going to be a Kingdom of priests. You're going to be a Kingdom for Me, and you are going to worship Me, and My presence is going to be everywhere."

He said, "The Spirit of the Lord is upon Me, because God hath anointed Me to preach the gospel to the poor. He has sent Me to heal the brokenhearted, to preach deliverance to the captives, and recovering of sight to the blind, to set at liberty them that are bruised."

Luke 4:19-20,

> 19 To preach the acceptable year of the Lord.
>
> 20 And he closed the book, and he gave *it* again to the minister, and sat down. And the eyes of all them that were in the synagogue were fastened on him.

As soon as He said, "To preach the acceptable year of the Lord," is when He finished it, right then.

Jesus wasn't preaching vengeance.
He was preaching the Good News of the Kingdom.

He didn't go on, because the very next part of that same verse in Isaiah 61:2 said to preach the "vengeance of our God."

Isaiah 61:2,

> 2 To proclaim the acceptable year of the LORD, and the day of vengeance of our God; to comfort all that mourn;

He was preaching the Good News of the Kingdom, and He was telling them that God's reign was there. It wasn't time for the vengeance, at that point. He wasn't preaching the vengeance, because it was set off to a future date. The only people who would get the vengeance were the ones who didn't accept the Good News. Here He was saying, "I'm here to tell you good things, the Good News of this Kingdom."

You ask, "Well, where's the Kingdom in that?" That's easy. The Kingdom is preaching the Gospel, the Good News of the Kingdom to the poor.

Matthew 5:3,

> 3 Blessed are the poor in spirit: for theirs is the kingdom of heaven.

"Blessed are the poor in spirit." Why? "For theirs is the kingdom of heaven." If He was going to preach the Gospel, the Good News, to the poor, He had to preach the Gospel of the kingdom of heaven to the poor to tell them, "You have a heavenly Father."

You don't have to worry about paying your bills in the sense that you think, "Are we going to make it or not going to make it? Are we going to starve? What's going to happen to us? Am I going to go into debt, or what am I going to sell so that I can stay out of debt?" Back then if they got in debt, they would go into servitude. They would sell themselves into servitude for a set amount of years.

Jesus was saying, "Poor, you've got a heavenly Father. He wants to take care of you. Trust Him, and He will take care of you." When you seek first the Kingdom of God and His right standing, then all of these things will be added to you. You're not going to have to chase them, but you can't outrun them. That's a better promise than they had under the Old Covenant.

Jesus read down to the part where it said, "Preach the acceptable year of the Lord." Then, in the first part of verse 20 of Luke chapter 4, it said, "And He closed the book, and He gave *it* again to the minister, and sat down."

The second part of verse 20 said, "And the eyes of all them that were in the synagogue were fastened on Him." Why? That's because they weren't used to hearing somebody preach that. They knew that it related to a specific time, and that time was when the Kingdom of God was at hand.

Luke 4:21-29,

> 21 And he began to say unto them, This day is this scripture fulfilled in your ears.

"No prophet is accepted in his own country."

Notice: He had already sat down, and everybody was looking at Him. You can picture Him sitting down and everybody just staring. It was quiet, and He looked at them and said, "This day is this Scripture fulfilled in your ears (in your hearing)."

Notice: they were all looking at Him:

> 22 And all bare him witness, and wondered at the gracious words which proceeded out of his mouth. And they said, Is not this Joseph's son?
>
> 23 And he said unto them, Ye will surely say unto me this proverb, Physician, heal thyself: whatsoever we have heard done in Capernaum, do also here in thy country.
>
> 24 And he said, Verily I say unto you, No prophet is accepted in his own country.

> 25 But I tell you of a truth, many widows were in Israel in the days of Elias, when the heaven was shut up three years and six months, when great famine was throughout all the land;

Notice that He was going back to their history.

> 26 But unto none of them was Elias sent, save unto Sarepta, *a city* of Sidon, unto a woman *that was* a widow.

In other words, Elias was sent to somebody that wasn't even a part of the covenant at that point. All of the land of Israel was undergoing a drought and a famine, and here, God was sending him to a Gentile.

> 27 And many lepers were in Israel in the time of Eliseus the prophet; and none of them was cleansed, saving Naaman the Syrian.

What was He doing? He was hitting at their nationality. He was saying, "You think that just because you're of Israel, you've got it made, and yet God overlooked you and sent His prophets to people who were outside the covenant. Just because you think you're in the covenant, don't think you have a handle on it or that nothing matters now, because you're in it."

All of those in the synagogue were filled with wrath.

> 28 And all they in the synagogue, when they heard these things, were filled with wrath,

Notice: in six verses, it went from, "All bare him witness, and wondered at the gracious words which proceeded out of his mouth," to "And when they heard these things, all were filled with wrath." I'm telling you that it doesn't take but a second for the crowd to turn on you. It's amazing how fast that can happen.

After they were filled with wrath, it says that they thrust Jesus out of the city. They meant to kill Him.

29 And rose up, and thrust him out of the city, and led him unto the brow of the hill whereon their city was built, that they might cast him down headlong.

They were going to throw Him headfirst off the cliff. If you read this whole story, it says at one point that He actually went with them. He got right to the edge and then it says that He turned around and walked through their midst.

I'm actually convinced that He didn't have to go with them. He could have broken away from them. He had the power. It says that they were leading Him. I'm sure they were jostling Him around and pushing Him. Somebody probably had Him by the arm saying, "Let's throw Him over, this blasphemer, this person who thinks He is something."

I'm sure that while He was walking with them, He was calm the whole time, and He was peaceful. He knew He wasn't going to die like that because He knew Psalm 22. It said that He was going to be pierced, so He knew that it wasn't going to happen by being thrown off a cliff.

All the time they were leading Him out, I am sure He was saying, "Do you really think you're going to do this? Do you really want to do this? Don't you see that this shows your heart?" He went right with them to the edge. That was just like Abraham raising that knife.

He was giving them a chance to repent. They had from the time they were in the synagogue until they got to the edge of the cliff. He gave them enough rope to hang themselves. He proved their hearts. He got them right to the edge and when they got there, He just turned around and walked away. It makes you wonder what they were thinking when He just turned and walked off.

Jesus preached out of Isaiah 61.
We know it was about the Kingdom.

What He preached was out of Isaiah 61, so go there with me. We know it was the Kingdom, so let's go back and read this, starting with verse 1,

Isaiah 61:1-9,

> 1 The Spirit of the Lord GOD *is* upon me; because the LORD hath anointed me to preach good tidings unto the meek; he hath sent me to bind up the brokenhearted, to proclaim liberty to the captives, and the opening of the prison to *them that are* bound;
>
> 2 To proclaim the acceptable year of the LORD, and the day of vengeance of our God; to comfort all that mourn;

> 3 To appoint unto them that mourn in Zion, to give unto them beauty for ashes, the oil of joy for mourning, the garment of praise for the spirit of heaviness; that they might be called trees of righteousness, the planting of the LORD, that he might be glorified.
>
> 4 And they shall build the old wastes, they shall raise up the former desolations, and they shall repair the waste cities, the desolations of many generations.

They didn't realize that if they had just accepted Him, this is what would come. This was what was going to be available. It was what He was trying to bring in.

> 5 And strangers shall stand and feed your flocks, and the sons of the alien *shall be* your plowmen and your vinedressers.
>
> 6 But ye shall be named the Priests of the LORD: *men* shall call you the Ministers of our God: ye shall eat the riches of the Gentiles, and in their glory shall ye boast yourselves.
>
> 7 For your shame *ye shall have* double; and *for* confusion they shall rejoice in their portion: therefore in their land they shall possess the double: everlasting joy shall be unto them.

"For your shame *ye shall have* double." In other words, "You're not going to have shame and what shame has cost you anymore; I'm going to give double back to you."

> 8 For I the LORD love judgment, I hate robbery for burnt offering; and I will direct their work in truth, and I will make an everlasting covenant with them.

That's the reason Jesus turned over the tables in the temple. They were robbing the people just so they could buy animals for the offering.

> 9 And their seed shall be known among the Gentiles, and their offspring among the people: all that see them shall acknowledge them, that they *are* the seed *which* the LORD hath blessed.

Notice this next part: "…that they are the seed which the LORD hath blessed." Now, doesn't that sound like what we read in Galatians?

Galatians 3:16,

> 16 Now to Abraham and his seed were the promises made. He saith not, And to seeds, as of many; but as of one, And to thy seed, which is Christ.

"He saith not, And to seeds, as of many; but as of one, And to thy seed, which is Christ," and you are in Him.

The things that Jesus began both to do and teach:

Matthew 4:17,

> 17 From that time Jesus began to preach, and to say, Repent: for the kingdom of heaven is at hand.

If you go to Matthew chapter 4 and look at verses 18 through 22, it talks about calling the 12 disciples. Again, I want to remind you that we are talking about what Jesus began both to do and teach.

Matthew 4:23,

> 23 And Jesus went about all Galilee, teaching in their synagogues, and preaching the gospel of the kingdom, and healing all manner of sickness and all manner of disease among the people.

Where did He go? He went about all Galilee. Doing what? "Teaching in their synagogues." And what? "And preaching." The what? "The Gospel." The Good News of what? "The Kingdom." He went through all of Galilee, teaching in their synagogues (plural). He went through all of Galilee and to every city. He went to every synagogue He came across. He taught, and He preached that the kingdom of heaven was at hand.

Imagine walking in and saying "I'm really glad to be here today. I'm here to announce that what you've been waiting for is here. I am He." He probably had them up to the point where He told them that He was the One. They probably thought, "Oh, okay. We've got something happening."

You've got to remember that it had been 400 years since there had been a prophet. When John the Baptist came up, people asked, "Is he a prophet?" "We think he's a prophet." "He could be a prophet, but we're not sure, because he never gets very specific."

They were wondering: "Is this a new time? Is there a new move going? Is God bringing something in? What's going on?" Then, all of a sudden, He said, "Well, everything you've been waiting for is here, and it's all in Me." At that point He probably lost them. They probably thought, "Well, who do You think You are?"

That's what every religious person thinks about a person who walks in right standing with God and knows who they are. They always think, "Who do you think you are? Do you think God just loves you, especially?" "No. He loves you too; you just won't take it." Most of the time, that's the way things happen.

You can't preach the Kingdom without demonstrating it.

Jesus taught in their synagogues, preaching the Gospel, the Good News of the Kingdom, and healing all manner of sickness and all manner of disease among the people. He healed the sick, raised the dead, and cast out devils. He did all of that.

Matthew 4:24,

> 24 And his fame went throughout all Syria: and they brought unto him all sick people that were taken with divers diseases and torments, and those which were possessed with devils, and those which were lunatic, and those that had the palsy; and he healed them.

"And His fame went throughout all Syria, and they brought unto Him all sick people." All means there were none left sick. Wherever He went, when He left, nobody was sick there anymore. It looked like heaven; it looked exactly like the Kingdom. That's the way it's supposed to look when the Kingdom is in force in an area. There should be no sickness or disease. Amen?

The Kingdom is God's reign and rule. It's His Government over your life. It's you doing things the way God wants them done.

It said here in verse 24, "They brought unto Him all sick people that were taken with divers diseases and torments, and those which were possessed with devils, and those which were lunatic, and those that had the palsy." What did He do? He healed them. He healed all of those who were sick, all of those who had diseases and torments, those who were possessed with devils, those who were lunatic, and those who had palsy. He healed them all. That means everybody. Jesus healed all of the sick and all of the demon possessed—everybody was set free.

Jesus didn't change.
He taught, He preached, and He demonstrated.

Let's look at Matthew chapter 5 to see what Jesus began both to do and teach. I'm really trying to emphasize that He never did anything different. He didn't change. He just preached, "The kingdom of heaven is at hand." He preached the Good News of the Kingdom of God, and that's all He preached for His entire ministry. He just went about preaching the Kingdom and teaching about it.

Everything He taught was taught from the Kingdom perspective. Jesus taught, He preached, and then He demonstrated. That's what He began to both do and teach.

> **If you are poor in spirit, I've got Good News for you:
> the kingdom of heaven is yours.**

Matthew 5:1-3,

> 1 And seeing the multitudes, he went up into a mountain: and when he was set, his disciples came unto him:
>
> 2 And he opened his mouth, and taught them, saying,
>
> 3 Blessed *are* the poor in spirit: for theirs is the kingdom of heaven.

Jesus was saying, "If you are poor in spirit, I've got Good News for you; the kingdom of heaven is yours." You will see this all the way through.

Matthew 5:10,

> 10 Blessed *are* they which are persecuted for righteousness' sake: for theirs is the kingdom of heaven.

He kept saying things about the Kingdom over and over again. If you're being put down because you're living right, that's okay. Don't worry about what they say; the Kingdom is yours. People might be talking about you and saying things about you because you're living right. They may even be calling you names like Pharisee, legalist, or something else. Whatever they're calling you, don't worry about it. The Kingdom is going to take care of you.

**When you seek God's Kingdom, His rule, and
His Government first, you are in right standing with Him.**

The ones that are doing that to you are begging God to show up. They're the ones who are begging God to pay their bills and constantly asking God for something. God said, "You're not of those people." You're the people God takes care of. Why? You expect Him to do that, because that's the Kingdom. You're seeking God's Kingdom, His rule, and His Government first, and when you seek His Government and His way of doing things, you are in right standing with Him. In Matthew chapter 6, He talks about that.

You need to realize that the Kingdom is available, now.

Matthew 6:33,

> 33 But seek ye first the kingdom of God, and his righteousness; and all these things shall be added unto you.

In America, especially here in Texas, we have a big immigration situation. People are always talking about it. It's a major political, hot topic. When you look into immigration, you have legal immigrants and you have illegal immigrants.

Legal immigrants can take part in the benefits of a country. Illegal immigrants technically can't, but there are some things they can get. If they go to a hospital, they can get help.

I would not turn help away from anyone that's hurting in any way. Pain and hunger don't know national boundaries. In saying that, even if an illegal immigrant comes over and tries to get into the system, they are trying to become legal immigrants so that they can take part in the benefits of being a legal citizen.

Then you have illegal immigrants that come over and they hide because they're afraid they're going to get deported, so they really can't participate in the benefits of the nation that we have.

Too many times we have people in the Kingdom of God who don't realize the benefits that we have in the Kingdom and what we can partake of. They do not learn how to access the benefits of that Kingdom. Why? That's because they keep thinking, "Oh, it all comes after we die. It's all over there." As long as you put it over there, then you can't get it here. You need to realize that the Kingdom is available now.

There will be a point, I believe, when Jesus will physically, spiritually, and in fullness reign upon this earth. His enemies will be put under His feet. He will reign. There will be a full consummation of the Kingdom of God right here on earth.

Every knee shall bow.

We operate in the Kingdom now, in the Spirit, but it is not being manifested, because the vengeance of our God is not being enforced to where every knee is bowed.

Some knees are going to bow willingly. Hopefully, we have bowed our knee willingly, but there will come a point to where if you don't bow your knee willingly, your knee will be bowed for you.

It could be that angels will stand behind people when they stand before God and force them down to the ground and say, "You will kneel before this King and God. You will kneel before Him." Why? That's because every knee shall bow.

Every knee is going to bow, whether people do it willingly or unwillingly; that's in the future. Right now, you bow your knee willingly. He is saying, "You're able to come into this thing. You are willingly bowing your knee, and you can benefit from the Kingdom now, even in this world."

As an ambassador of the Kingdom of God, you are in this world, but you are not of it.

You are an ambassador of the Kingdom of God. You are not from here; you are from heaven.

I don't know how this message comes across to you, but to me the fact that we are ambassadors encapsulates things and really drives it home.

One of the things I want you to realize—if you get this message—is that you are not born of this world. You are born from heaven. You're in this world, but you're not of this world.

I gave you an example of this before when I talked about Haiti. Haiti is the poorest nation in the western hemisphere. There are people living on the streets, starving, and dying. It is really bad there, especially since the earthquake and all that has happened.

There is an American Embassy there, and if you went in there and you walked into their kitchen and into their pantry, you would see that they have food stacked up. They have seven course meals, every meal. They are taken care of in the Embassy, because an ambassador is not dependent upon the wealth or the resources of the place where they are. They are blessed by the resources of where they're from.

When you realize that you are an ambassador from the Kingdom of God, you do not have to bow under the circumstances of this world. You're in this world, but you're not of it. The kingdom of heaven has resources that are at your disposal, and you can live that way in the middle of a recession, in the middle of a depression, or in the middle of anything else. You can live that way if you don't identify with this world.

If you identify with this world, then you're going to have the resources of this world, and you will be limited by that identification. You have to decide. You limit yourself according to the place that you want to identify yourself with.

If you identify yourself with the world, you're going to suffer like everybody else. When the stocks go down or when the economy goes down, you're going to suffer right long with them, because you look at this world's system as your source and as your resource.

However, if you understand that you are born from heaven and that you are sent here as an ambassador, to represent the Kingdom of God, then you do not have to go through the same things they go through.

You should be walking in the goodness of the Kingdom and in the resources of the Kingdom. You, as an individual, should be able to take on families and people around you who are suffering, feed them, and take care of them.

We were going down to the David Hogan meeting recently. We stopped at a 7/Eleven store, and as I was getting back in the car, a man came up and asked for money for food. I reached in my pocket and pulled out what was there and handed it to him. I didn't count it first; I just handed it to him. I got back in the car, and my wife asked, "What did he want?" I said, "Well, he wanted money."

We got over to the meeting, and we sat there in the parking lot for a little while; we were talking about it. I kept going back to this guy and I thought, "It does something to a man when he has to beg." Men were never meant to beg. I've never seen a righteous forsaken or his seed begging bread. We were meant to have dominion over this earth.

Man was meant to walk in dominion; he was not meant to beg. When a man has to go to begging, it does something to his psyche; it does something to him. Begging takes away a person's dignity, because that's what the enemy wants. That's one thing I learned from Dr. Sumrall, and even from the times I sat under T.L. Osborn: "The devil has always been trying to remove man's dignity. God brings back dignity."

**Part of our job and part of our purpose
on this earth is to give dignity back to people.**

When you see pictures and movies that depict Biblical times, they are a good representation of what happened back then. When a person would come up, he would drop down and kneel at Jesus' feet and maybe cry. In the case of Mary Magdalene, she came up and knelt at Jesus' feet. You can just picture Him; He didn't stand there and say, "Yes, that's what you ought to do." He wasn't like that.

You can picture Him reaching down, touching her chin, and raising her face up. He would look her in the eye and say, "Woman, why are you doing this? Stand up. Get up on your feet." Jesus brought dignity back to man. He didn't bring pride and arrogance. He brought dignity.

Every human should have dignity and part of our goal, part of our job, and part of our purpose on this earth is to give dignity back to people. You don't look at a person who's asking for money or a handout on the corner and say, "Here you go, but why don't you get a job?" No. Give them dignity.

Encourage them and just tell them, "The Spirit of the living God wants you to know that you're not going to be this way all of your life. If you will just turn to God and listen to Him, He has so much more for you." Raise them up and bring them dignity. Don't put them down and get back in your car and think, "Wow, I'm glad that's not me." That's what the Pharisees did.

We have to realize that our purpose is to bring dignity back to them. It is not just to tell them, "You're okay." No, they're probably not okay, but we can get them okay. We can bring them into the Kingdom of God and let them know that this is not about religion. This is not about dos and don'ts.

Jesus got onto people a whole lot more for what they didn't do rather than for what they did do. If you're a Christian, you're going to make mistakes, and generally there are going to be more of what you didn't do, rather than what you did do.

God condemned Sodom and Gomorrah, because they did not take care of the poor of their city.

When God condemned Sodom and Gomorrah, it wasn't for the homosexuality. Go back and read it. It was because they didn't feed the poor and clothe the naked. It wasn't because of the sin they were doing, in the sense of debauchery. It was because they were committing the major sin of not loving God and not loving their fellowman as themselves. That's what really brought condemnation to them.

All of the other things they did just flowed, because if you do not love God and you do not love man, guess who you look at? You begin to look at yourself. You become self-centered and self-serving and all of a sudden it's all about pleasure. It's all about what you want and what you can have.

> **"Whosoever therefore shall break one of these least commandments, and shall teach men so, he shall be called the least in the kingdom of heaven."**

Matthew 5:19,

> 19 Whosoever therefore shall break one of these least commandments, and shall teach men so, he shall be called the least in the kingdom of heaven: but whosoever shall do and teach *them*, the same shall be called great in the kingdom of heaven.

This is the negative side of doing and teaching. If you are doing wrong and teaching others to do wrong, it says that you will be called "…the least in the kingdom of heaven."

Jesus was still preaching about the kingdom of heaven. We call this the "Sermon on the Mount." We say that sometimes, but we lose sight of the fact that even though it was preached on the mount, it was about the Kingdom. Jesus preached the Kingdom. He was always trying to tell people, "Live in the Kingdom."

"Look not at the things which are seen, but at the things which are not seen."

In 2 Corinthians 4:17-18, it says,

> 17 For our light affliction, which is but for a moment, worketh for us a far more exceeding and eternal weight of glory;
>
> 18 While we look not at the things which are seen, but at the things which are not seen: for the things which are seen are temporal; but the things which are not seen are eternal.

God says that if we live in the Kingdom, these things we go through, "our light affliction," will work a mightier weight of glory in us; that is only as long as we don't look at the things that we can "see" and we look at the things that are "not seen." In other words, He was saying, "I want you to see what other people don't see. I want you to see the Kingdom. I want you to see that when you're suffering the things going on here, that's going to work a better weight of glory in you. The reason is because you're not paying attention to the world and the things that are going on. You're focused on seeking the Kingdom."

He told us all the time to do this or to do that, and to stir up the fires, but He only told us to seek one thing and that was the Kingdom. Seek the Kingdom. Go after the Kingdom. He didn't say to seek power. He didn't say to seek an anointing. He didn't say seek a mantle. He said, "Seek the Kingdom and the righteousness of God. Seek the Kingdom of God and His right standing."

When you have right standing with God and with His Kingdom, then you can participate in the benefits of that Kingdom because the kingdom of heaven is at hand to work for you.

> **"Whosoever shall do and teach these least commandments, the same shall be called great in the kingdom of heaven."**

Matthew 5:19,

> 19 Whosoever therefore shall break one of these least commandments, and shall teach men so, he shall be called the least in the kingdom of heaven: but whosoever shall do and teach them, the same shall be called great in the kingdom of heaven.

"But whosoever shall do and teach them," not just do them and not just teach them, but whosoever shall do and teach these commandments, "the same shall be called great in the kingdom of heaven." Do you want to know how to operate in the kingdom of heaven? It's very simple. You have to teach, and you have to do.

> **His righteousness becomes your righteousness.**

Matthew 5:20,

> 20 For I say unto you, That except <u>your righteousness</u> shall exceed *the righteousness* of the scribes and Pharisees, ye shall in no case enter into the kingdom of heaven.

Here Jesus was talking about the kingdom of heaven and about your righteousness.

In Matthew 6:33 He said, "Seek first the Kingdom of God, and <u>His righteousness</u>." He was talking about the Kingdom of God and God's righteousness.

Here, in Matthew 5:20, He was talking about your righteousness, "That except <u>your</u> <u>righteousness</u> shall exceed the righteousness of the scribes and Pharisees, you shall in no case enter into the kingdom of heaven." He was preaching the kingdom of heaven.

How could your righteousness exceed that of the scribes and the Pharisees? They lived by the letter of Law. They did everything so perfect that it was wrong. Do you realize that? Yet He said, "Your righteousness can't be on the fact that you do everything just right."

Your righteousness has to be based on the fact that you know that without Him you can't do anything right. No matter what you do, even if you do it right, you're going to be doing it wrong, because you're going to do it wrong out of a wrong motive. However, once you are in Him, and once you come to Him and accept that, then at that point His righteousness becomes your righteousness.

**Everything He did, you get credit for,
and everything you do, He gets credit for.**

Once His righteousness becomes your righteousness, you realize: "I get credit for everything He did." That's the reason He wants you to do a lot now; He gets credit for it. Everything He did, you get credit for, so He wants you to let your light shine before men so that they may see your good works. Your good works will glorify your Father in heaven. Why? That is so He can get credit for it.

It's not so that you get more credit; you already have credit. You got the credit of what He did which is much better than anything you could do. Once you accept that, then everything you're doing, He gets credit for, so you should do as much as you can.

You should be thinking, "God's been so good to me. What in the world can I do to show how much I love Him and appreciate His goodness?" You can show God you love Him by loving your fellowman.

> **"He that does righteousness (he who does what is right)**
> **is righteous, even as He is righteous."**

Matthew 6:33,

> 33 But seek ye first the kingdom of God, and his righteousness; and all these things shall be added unto you.

We've been talking about this all the way through.

ALL THAT JESUS BEGAN BOTH TO DO AND TEACH

In 1 John 3:7 it says,

> 7 …he that doeth righteousness is righteous, even as he is righteous.

We are still talking about what Jesus began "both to do and teach."

Matthew 7:21,

> 21 Not every one that saith unto me, Lord, Lord, shall enter into the kingdom of heaven; but he that doeth the will of my Father which is in heaven.

He was still preaching the Kingdom. It's not as simple as saying, "Oh, okay. Yes, I want that." It's not quite that simple; you actually have to live the life.

Some people don't like this, and they want to argue about it. If they don't like it, they are going to have to argue with Jesus.

People want to quote Paul, but they don't want to quote James. They say, "Well, that's because James wrote to the twelve scattered tribes." Yes, and Paul wrote to the Colossians, and he also wrote to Ephesus. If you're going to try to say that James was only writing to the 12 scattered tribes, then you are alone with that. You either have to take it all, or leave it all. Jesus, Paul, and James all said the same thing. It was just that each had different emphasis at different times.

You have the free will to serve God.

Charles Finney was one of the greatest evangelists that the United States has ever had, and the reason wasn't that he was such a great evangelist; he was an amazing preacher. He was a lawyer that preached like a lawyer, so he convinced people of his position and got them to vote and cast a judgment in his favor. That's how he got them saved. He had the results he had because he preached, "It's not that you can't serve God; it's that you won't. You just need to make the choice to serve God." He was preaching that you have the free will to serve God.

Up until that time, everybody preached absolute predestination. Predestination says, "God picks and chooses, and if you're not picked, you can't do anything to even get God's favor." Everybody just sat there and said, "Well, if it's God's will, it will happen. If it doesn't happen, it's not God's will, and therefore I have nothing to do." Everybody got cold toward God.

Then Charles Finney came along and said, "No, it's not that at all, and you can actually have some part in it. You can actually turn toward God, and you can take the offer that He has made to you." People said, "What!? We have some part in it? We can actually get in?"

To them, it was as if he just opened the door and said, "Please come in." Prior to that, they thought the door was shut. They started rushing in, and that was called a great revival. They had a great revival, because he preached the opposite of what they'd been hearing. When he preached the opposite, people said, "Wow, this is great!" and they ran into it, and it caused a great revival.

Steve Hill is another one of the greatest evangelists America has ever had, because when he started preaching at the Pensacola Revival, America was cold toward God. He started preaching, "Repent. Turn your life around. If you repent, God will remove your sin from you and the burdens that are on your shoulder. He will set you free."

You can sit around all day long and say, "Well, it's all done. We don't have to do anything." It's just like with healing. People say, "Oh, you can't do anything to get God to use you." That is a lie. If that were true, God would be using everyone. Every time you prayed, every prayer would be answered, but the fact is that there are things you can do to make yourself more effective.

"Purge yourself to make yourself a vessel unto honor."

In 2 Timothy 2:21, it says,

> 21 If a man therefore purge himself from these, he shall be a vessel unto honour, sanctified, and meet for the master's use, and prepared unto every good work.

"Purge yourself (of certain things) to make yourself a vessel unto honor." That's not what YouTube and internet theologians say, but that's what the Bible says. The Bible says you can do things to make yourself more effective.

You cannot do one thing to make God love you, but you can do some things to actually receive that love. As a matter of fact, you have to do things to receive that love. He can make it available, but He's not going to make you take it. However, the fact that you do receive that love brings the grace of God into your life. The fact is that He made it available, and He gave you the opportunity.

You have the choice of where you set your affections.

Again, all of this goes back to what I was saying about Steve Hill. He came along and started preaching, "Repent. Turn back to God." The Bible says, "Set your affections on things above." That means you have the choice of where you set your affections. If you set your affections on things of this world, you will be cold toward God. The world generates coldness toward God, and when you set your affections on whatever you want, that's what happens.

Some say, "Well, I just don't feel like I love God that much." What are you watching? What are you listening to? It's a choice. Turn the TV off. Get your Bible out. If you've got it on CD or DVD, that's fine, too. If you have it on your computer, it will talk to you; that's good. It's amazing how much time you might actually have to pray if you just turned that TV off. You would have that much more time to spend with God.

I was raised in Pentecostalism. They used to say that you could tell when a household was captured by the devil because their house had a devil's horns sticking out of the top of the TV." That was back when televisions had antennas. What I'm telling you is that there comes a point when you need to turn the TV off.

Sometimes, I'll put something on, just to have something playing, but I will put on a DVD or a CD of preaching. Lately, I've decided to set my affections on things above and focus on the Kingdom, because there's not a lot of teaching out there on the Kingdom. There are some here and there, but almost all of it goes back to some human type of thing, rather than what God is trying to do.

A lot of times when I think, "Oh, I'm going to listen to something," there's nothing to listen to, so I just turn it off. When that happens, I spend a whole lot more time with God and talking with Him. That's when a lot of revelation comes out. I start thinking, "Yeah, okay." He will just hit me with a Scripture or some thought, and it will just come alive.

Jesus will say to some: "I never knew you: depart from Me, ye that work iniquity."

Matthew 7:22-23,

> 22 Many will say to me in that day, Lord, Lord, have we not prophesied in thy name? and in thy name have cast out devils? and in thy name done many wonderful works?

Let's just take this piece by piece. "Many will say to Me (Jesus) in that day…" What day? He was talking about the day of His vengeance, the day of the Lord. It will be the day when everyone will stand before Him at the consummation. It will be at some point in the future.

23 And then will I profess unto them, I never knew you: depart from me, ye that work iniquity.

I've been purposely in the church for three decades now, and the other two decades before that I was raised in the church whether I wanted to be there or not. In all that time, I've never seen a time where it can be more fulfilled, where people think and preach that you can live like the world, live like the devil, do anything, and still walk in the power of God, than now. People think that because God will use you it means that you're alright.

Notice that Jesus did not say, "You liar. You didn't prophesy in My name; you didn't do mighty works." He didn't say that. He said, "I never knew you: depart from Me, ye that work iniquity." With what's going on in the church, right now, that is the best Scripture that encapsulates it.

There are people who say, "The more a person sins the more grace abounds, so sin." They say that because they think that when they do it, it's not sin anymore. They think that they can do anything and it doesn't matter.

Examine yourself whether you're in the faith; prove yourself.

Even though people think that and are living in sin, people are still getting healed. You might ask, "Well how does that work?" It works because God loves the people, and He will use anybody that will let Him. People don't realize that, and just because God uses you doesn't mean you're right with God. That's the reason Paul said to examine yourselves.

In 2 Corinthians 13:5 it says,

> 5 Examine yourselves, whether ye be in the faith; prove your own selves. Know ye not your own selves, how that Jesus Christ is in you, except ye be reprobates?

That means there is a possibility that you might not be in the faith. He wrote that to the churches. Make sure that you're in the faith. Examine all these things and hold fast to what is true. Throw out the garbage but hold fast to what is true. Check these things out. If nothing mattered, Paul wouldn't have told you to examine yourself.

Colossians 1:28,

> 28 Whom we preach, warning every man, and teaching every man in all wisdom; that we may present every man perfect in Christ Jesus:

As long as God has me here, I will stand for righteousness, for living a life of gratitude toward God, which is living a life clean before God. If you're not born again, or even if you have been born again, and if you claim to be a Christian, and your life is full of sin, there is hope for you. You can decide to live for God. You can decide, right now, to get rid of that sin. He will absolutely cleanse you. It's already been paid for, but you still have to pick it up.

A person might ask, "Well, if I died, would I go to heaven?" Do you really want to set that marker there and hope you're right? Do you want to hope that that marker's where you put it?

It's so much better to live free, to live clean before God, and to live pure before God. It is not hard. You might think, "I'm bound by certain things." I'm telling you, "If God can set me free and change my life there is not a person who gets this message who is too hard for Him to change." Amen? There is not a life that is too hard, too messed up, or too far gone.

You can't know God and keep living in iniquity.

Matthew 7:22-23,

> 22 Many will say to me in that day, Lord, Lord, have we not prophesied in thy name? and in thy name have cast out devils? and in thy name done many wonderful works?
>
> 23 And then will I profess unto them, I never knew you: depart from me, ye that work iniquity.

"Many will say to me in that day, 'Lord, have we not prophesied in thy Name? and in thy Name have cast out devils? and in thy Name done many wonderful works?'"

Look at the results of iniquity and sin. "And then will I profess unto them, 'I never knew you: depart from Me, ye that work iniquity.'"

Those that work iniquity say, "Well, we're doing mighty works. We're prophesying." Jesus was saying, "You're working iniquity. All of these things are happening, but you're still living in sin." He said, "I never knew you." Why? That is because you can't know God and keep living in iniquity. You can't do it.

There's an old saying, "A praying man doesn't sin, and a sinning man doesn't pray." Why? It's because a sinning man runs from God. He is just like Adam. The more he messes up, the more he will run from God. He won't want to walk with Him and talk with Him. He will run and hide from Him.

You decide if you're going to fall or stand.

Matthew 7:24-27,

> 24 Therefore whosoever heareth these sayings of mine, and doeth them, I will liken him unto a wise man, which built his house upon a rock:
>
> 25 And the rain descended, and the floods came, and the winds blew, and beat upon that house; and it fell not: for it was founded upon a rock.
>
> 26 And every one that heareth these sayings of mine, and doeth them not, shall be likened unto a foolish man, which built his house upon the sand:

27 And the rain descended, and the floods came, and the winds blew, and beat upon that house; and it fell: and great was the fall of it.

Notice these two things: one man did the words of Jesus and the other didn't; that's the difference. It doesn't say, "Well, God ordained you to fall and you to stand." It doesn't say that at all. Jesus said, "You decide if you're going to fall or stand, based on whether you take My words and do them." He said, "If you do them, you are a wise man, and if you don't, you're a fool." Isn't that what He said? You can't get around that. Onc thing about Jesus is that He was plain spoken. You knew where He stood.

When Kim Unrau was here recently, we were riding and talking. He said, "That's one thing I like about you Curry. Nobody ever has to worry about where you stand. People know right where you stand all the time."

I said, "Yeah, if you ask me, I'll tell you. As a matter of fact, if you wait around long enough I will tell you without you asking me; I'll tell you anyway." He started laughing and said, "Yeah, that's true."

It's time to stand up for God.

I think that you do need to know where people stand. It's time to stand and say, "This is who God is! This is what He said."

In Matthew chapter 8, we're going to be reading about the centurion servant.

ALL THAT JESUS BEGAN BOTH TO DO AND TEACH

Matthew 8:10-13,

> 10 When Jesus heard *it*, he marvelled, and said to them that followed, Verily I say unto you, I have not found so great faith, no, not in Israel.

"When Jesus heard it (what the centurion said), He marveled, and said to them that followed (His disciples and those that were around), 'I haven't found this kind of faith among God's covenant people, and here you've got a Roman centurion, the oppressor of God's people, and he knows more about faith than God's own people do.'"

> 11 And I say unto you, That many shall come from the east and west, and shall sit down with Abraham, and Isaac, and Jacob, in the kingdom of heaven.

This is almost the same thing He said when He first preached in Luke chapter 4. "Many shall come from the east and west, and shall sit down with Abraham, and Isaac, and Jacob." Where will they sit? They will sit in the kingdom of heaven. What was He still preaching? He was still preaching the kingdom of heaven. Everything He did was filtered through the kingdom of heaven.

The kingdom of heaven and healing were always mentioned together. Those were things that "Jesus began both to do and teach."

> 12 But the children of the kingdom shall be cast out into outer darkness: there shall be weeping and gnashing of teeth.

> 13 And Jesus said unto the centurion, Go thy way; and as thou hast believed, *so* be it done unto thee. And his servant was healed in the selfsame hour.

Notice again, He was preaching. He was talking about the kingdom of heaven and a healing. The kingdom of heaven and healing were always together. Those were things that Jesus began "both to do and teach."

In Matthew chapter 9, we're going to bring it home to you. That's when I nail it to the point where you can't get away from it.

Matthew 9:35,

> 35 And Jesus went about <u>all</u> the cities and villages, teaching in their synagogues, and preaching the gospel of the kingdom, and healing every sickness and every disease among the people.

Did Jesus pick a few cities or villages, or did He go everywhere? He went to <u>all</u> of them. What was He doing? He was teaching in their synagogues, preaching the Gospel of the Kingdom, the rule of God, and the superiority of God. What else was He doing? He went to every city, taught in every synagogue, and healed every sickness and every disease among the people. He said that God's Kingdom would rule over <u>all</u>.

ALL THAT JESUS BEGAN BOTH TO DO AND TEACH

What Jesus began "to both do and teach," He made available to <u>all</u>.

Luke 4:40,

> 40 Now when the sun was setting, <u>all</u> they that had any sick with divers diseases brought them unto him; and he laid his hands on every one of them, and healed them.

It says that He laid hands on any that were sick. He laid hands on every one of them, and healed them. Who did He heal? He healed every one He laid hands on all who were sick. He healed everybody. He didn't heal just some of them. He didn't pick and choose who got it and who didn't. He healed them all.

Luke 4:41-43,

> 41 And devils also came out of many, crying out, and saying, Thou art Christ the Son of God. And he rebuking *them* suffered them not to speak: for they knew that he was Christ.

We know He was definitely not healing or showing signs to prove who He was, or He would have let the demons speak.

> 42 And when it was day, he departed and went into a desert place: and the people sought him, and came unto him, and stayed him, that he should not depart from them.

Notice He went through the whole night. "When it was day, the people sought Him, and came unto Him, and stayed Him." In other words, they said, "Please stay. Don't go anywhere. Please do not depart from us."

> 43 And he said unto them, I must preach the kingdom of God to other cities also: for therefore am I sent.
>
> 44 And he preached in the synagogues of Galilee.

That means He was preaching the Kingdom of God there. If He said, "I've got to preach the Kingdom of God to other cities also," then what He just preached there was also the Kingdom of God. He was preaching the Kingdom of God, and He just healed everybody.

Here He told the people, "I've been preaching the Kingdom of God here, and now I've got to go to other cities to preach the Kingdom of God (the Gospel of the Kingdom), also: for therefore am I sent."

He was saying, "I was sent to preach the Kingdom of God, the Good News of God's rule, the Good News of God's Government, how He does things, and His supremacy. This is the reason for which I was sent."

You can't preach the Kingdom of God without seeking and saving those who are lost.

Jesus was sent to seek and to save those who are lost. Yes, and that comes under the auspices of preaching the Gospel of the Kingdom of God.

Jesus also came to destroy the works of the devil. Yes, that's what preaching the Gospel of the Kingdom does; it destroys the works of the devil.

Everything falls under that canopy once you realize that there is a spiritual Kingdom that you are a part of when you're born again, and because of that, you can walk differently than anybody else has ever walked except for Jesus. He's the only One who has walked in this to any real degree. I've already shown you that He is waiting for you.

We are the kingdom of kings and priests who shall reign on this earth.

It has already been prophesied, "There shall be a kingdom of priests." What kingdom do you think that is? It's us. He said, "I've made you kings; a kingdom of priests. I've made you kings and priests unto our God." When are we kings and priests? Now! Where do these kings and priests rule? In Revelation 5:10, it says, "They shall reign on the earth," not in heaven.

In 1975 there was a picture of the last helicopter leaving from the top of the American Embassy in Saigon. I was about 16. The Vietnam War was over. The picture of that helicopter was all over the news and in the newspapers. Without saying it, that picture said, "America lost Vietnam." That was because they had to evacuate the Ambassador from the American Embassy by helicopter.

If the consummation of what God is trying to do is going to end up with Him taking us out of here, it would mean that He lost. Understand me: I'm not saying He's not going to take us out of here. Think with me. Remember what Jesus said when He talked about Lazarus? He said, "This sickness shall not end in death." Did Lazarus die? Yes, but Jesus was not lying, because death is not the end. He didn't say that Lazarus wouldn't die.

Now, put that understanding with what I just said. I'm not saying that we're not getting taken out of here; I'm just saying that it is not the end, because He says we shall reign on this earth. God put man on this earth to have dominion.

If it got to a point where God said, "I have to take you out of here," He has lost. He might have to remove us so He can do something and bring us back to a much better place. I can go with that, but what I'm saying is that if the idea is just for us to go to heaven and spend the rest of eternity there, then God basically has said, "Okay, I give up the earth to Satan." That's not God. God doesn't lose. Amen?

When Jesus comes, He's going to reward every man according to his works.

He's going to have a kingdom of priests that rule on this earth. How much you're going to rule is up to what you do now, because it's going to be very simple, and if you've been faithful over one city, He'll put you over five. If you've been faithful over two cities, He'll put you over ten. This is your chance to decide what you want to do in the future.

It depends on how much faith you walk in, how much of the Kingdom of God you understand, and how much you walk in that. All Jesus was saying was, "Show Me what you can do with your area, and make it like heaven on earth. If you do that, and if you're faithful over that one, then I'll put you over these others, also."

Jesus was just saying that you are to act like it's already here. That's what faith is; it's just acting like it's already done. It's that simple. That's how we are able to live in this world now. That's how you live in the Kingdom.

I was talking with some young men at the David Hogan meeting the other day, and apparently David had mentioned a situation between the two of us years ago. It was when I was up in Canada. David came to my room, and we discussed some things; that is apparently what he talked to them about. The thing about the situation was that David wasn't in Canada. The young men came to me and said, "Tell me about this. How did that happen? What did he do?" They asked, "How do you do this?"

I had never thought about it. Having never thought about it, I had never figured out how to do it. However, as I was talking to them, it was coming out of my mouth how to do it. It was literally by revelation. At the same time I was checking it with my filter. As I was checking it with my final filter, I was saying, "Yeah, yeah."

After I told them, they said, "Oh, yeah. I got that." I'll tell you, "Walking in the Spirit doesn't have to be weird, but it is as easy as making the decision to walk there." It's that easy. The problem is that you decide what the barriers are. You have to start by removing the barriers. To a normal man, a wall would be a barrier, whereas, to Jesus it wasn't. It didn't even slow Him down. It's the same thing. That's walking in the Spirit.

You have to decide what your barriers are. What can you not do? If you can name something you can't do, that's your barrier of belief. You have to decide that that barrier is not there.

Jesus sent forth his twelve disciples. He said, "As you go, preach, saying, 'The kingdom of heaven is at hand.'"

Matthew 10:5-7,

> 5 These twelve Jesus <u>sent forth</u>, and commanded them, saying, Go not into the way of the Gentiles, and into *any* city of the Samaritans enter ye not:

If you look up the Greek word for *"sent forth"* it's an offshoot of the word *apostellō*, or *apostle*. It means *to send out (properly on a mission) literally or figuratively.* He made them apostles and sent them on a particular mission, "…and commanded them." He didn't suggest; He commanded them saying, "Go not into the way of the Gentiles, and into any city of the Samaritans enter ye not."

> 6 But go rather to the lost sheep of the house of Israel.

> 7 And as ye go, preach, saying, The kingdom of heaven is at hand.

What are you supposed to preach? He didn't just say go and preach good sermons. He was saying, "Go and preach, and here's what you are to say, 'The kingdom of heaven is at hand.'" Wait a minute. Wasn't that Jesus' message? Isn't that what He was preaching? He told His disciples to preach the same thing. Don't change your message.

The biggest problem among new ministers, young ministers, is that they look for that revelation that's going to put them on the map. They're looking for that one teaching that's going to explode them. That's the one that is going to have people writing to them, and it's going to have people flocking to them. It is getting that one revelation that nobody else has ever gotten. I'm telling you that if nobody has ever gotten it, there's probably a reason.

I know that God can bring things out, but there are certain people in the world that I have been around, that are so far off, and they are so sure that they have a revelation. They think that's what's going to make them, and that's all they talk about. They think, "If I keep preaching that, eventually it's going to make me somebody, and I'm going to be in the ministry the way I'm supposed to be. I'm going to have people flocking to me." That is a dangerous thing to do. I'm not saying don't get revelation, but I'll tell you that sometimes it's best to start with other peoples' revelations.

One of the people I thank God for is Kenneth Hagin. Early on, he was part of the "Voice of Healing Movement." He lived right over here in Garland, Texas. I've got the street address of where he lived when he was here. I went through the old "Voice of Healing" directory and all of their addresses were listed. You can go by and see the houses they lived in; many of them are still there today. Other people live there, so don't go rubbing on the house trying to get the anointing, because you might not want the latest anointing that's been there.

Brother Hagin said that most of the guys who were in "Voice of Healing" built each of their ministries on a gift. He was right. He said, "Because of those gifts, almost every one of them ended up not staying in the group. I made a decision from the beginning that I would base my ministry on the Word of God, and that I would stick to the Word, no matter what." He had some amazing visitations, and he had some amazing revelations. He has even been called the "Father of the Word of Faith Movement." It was just his sticking to the Word that put him on the map.

If you want to get on the map, make your place. Don't go shooting for fame, fortune, or whatever else it is that people seek. Stick to the Word, because that's the only way God can promote you. You say what Jesus said, you confess Him before men, and He will confess you before His heavenly Father. You have to stay on the Word, no matter what. Don't go for a special revelation; just be a faithful minister of the Word.

Present the Gospel that Jesus preached.

Stay on the Word of God. Don't try to be somebody. The harder you try to be somebody, the longer it's going to take you to be somebody. I'm just telling you that the sooner you die to that and decide to help people, the faster you'll grow. That's the truth. If you keep trying to be somebody and keep trying to get the spotlight, you will be stifling your own growth. God wants to work through you, but He can't if you won't let Him "grow you up."

Remember, Samson had a great anointing, a great calling, but he didn't have the character to stand under it. You've got to have the character to stand under it or else that anointing (what people call the anointing), or that gift, or that calling can destroy you. Go for character, go for the truth, and go for the fruit of the Spirit of God. Go for loving God and loving people. Stay sound; stay straight. You don't have to get weird, and you don't have to be somebody.

When you are somebody, God notices you, but guess what? The devil notices you, too. If you're trying to be somebody, then you don't have the character yet to stand the heat that the devil can bring on you. You don't want that kind of attention. Stay hidden.

Colossians 3:3,

> 3 For ye are dead, and your life is hid with Christ in God.

Stay "hid in Christ." Let God promote you. Let Him put you in place. If He puts you there, nobody can do anything about it, but if you put yourself there, you won't last long.

Matthew 10:8,

> 8 Heal the sick, cleanse the lepers, raise the dead, cast out devils: freely ye have received, freely give.

Watch what He told them to do: "Heal the sick, cleanse the lepers, raise the dead, cast out devils." He was saying to them, "Just go and preach like I preach. Don't preach a different message; preach the same message. You've heard me preach it. Preach what I preached and then do what I did." He was telling them, "I want you to go and begin to do and teach." They were to go out and teach "all of the things that Jesus began both to do and teach."

Here's the good part: "Freely you have received, freely give."

You don't have to pick and choose. You don't have to figure out who, when, and how. No, just go and represent Jesus; be Jesus to the people. Just go, and teach, and do, and be free in the Kingdom of God. We are talking about what Jesus began to do and teach and what His followers did and taught. See how it's passed on down?

I'm thankful for the fact that God keeps giving me different ways to say the same thing and that you keep coming to hear it. Hopefully, when you hear it, it gets to be a part of you, and you can go out, and do it.

You can start at any time, and it will grow like everything else in the Kingdom. It all grows from a seed. It starts small and then grows. A lot of it just has to do with whether you will just keep showing up, keep doing what you've been doing, and let it grow. You don't need to get in a hurry and try to do some weird thing. If you go after visions and other things, the devil will show you that. He will give you visions, and he'll give you revelations.

Mary Baker Eddy had a revelation, and she started Christian Science, which is neither Christian nor science. Charles T. Russell, who started the Jehovah's Witnesses, had a revelation and started a cult that is taking people to a place that they don't believe even exists.

You say, "Well, I want to see a vision. I want to see an angel." The Bible says that angels are sent to you to minister to you, to minister to those who are the heirs of salvation. They work for you. You say, "Oh God, I want to see an angel," and because you asked Him, He'll do it, eventually. However, when the angel finally shows up, the angel will say, "What do you want?" You will say, "I just wanted to see you."

The angel will say, "Are you kidding me? You're more important than I am. I'm an angel; I'm a messenger of God, and you're a son! I wish I could be a son." People ask me, "Well, what makes you think that?" I think that because we're going to judge angels.

You don't judge what you're below; you judge what you're above. They wish that they could know what you know. It says that we're going to teach them the things of God. They learn from us what it's like to be in this thing called the Church, the *Ecclesia*. The *Ecclesia* is like the Senate; it's like being on the Cabinet for the president. We are to help administrate the Government of God. That's who we are.

That's the reason you have to be trained up, and this is a training center. This is not a religious place; it's a training center. It's a Kingdom training center. It teaches you how to be kings and priests. As one person said, "This is training for reigning." Amen?

Luke 9:1,

> 1 Then he called his twelve disciples together, and gave them power and authority over all devils, and to cure diseases.

Jesus called His twelve disciples together and gave them power and authority over all devils. He also gave them the ability to cure diseases.

Jesus said, "By this shall all men know that you are My disciples, if you have love one to another."

John 13:34-35

> 34 A new commandment I give unto you, That ye love one another; as I have loved you, that ye also love one another.
>
> 35 By this shall all men know that ye are my disciples, if ye have love one to another.

Do you know why you have to walk in love, especially with your brother? Jesus said, "All men will know that you are My disciples because of your love for one another." He didn't say that they will know you for your love of the world. You should love the people of the world. I'm not giving you an excuse to hate the people of the world, but you should love one another.

You know that you should love one another, and you should forgive one another. Paul was writing to the church when he said, "You bite, and you devour one another." Think about that. One Christian was biting and devouring another Christian. Every member of the Body of Christ is one cell in the Body of Christ.

Do you know what they call it when one cell in the body rebels against another cell in the body? It's called cancer. You're supposed to live in forgiveness, because if you don't, you're the one biting and devouring; you're the cancer. Do you get that? That's why you should love one another, and that's why you forgive men. If they say things against you, it will go back on them.

You don't say, "Oh, let that curse go back on them." You should pray, "No, God don't let it go back on them. God, they don't know what they're doing. God, they obviously don't know who they are. They don't know the power of the Word. God, I forgive them for what they said to me." Why? "God, I don't want them to be destroyed. I don't want them eaten up. God forgive them." That's why you live in forgiveness.

Forgiveness is not going through counseling where you say that you will forgive someone. That's not forgiveness.

If someone says anything against me, I don't get angry. I forgive quickly. Why? I don't want them to suffer for that. That's because I've been forgiven. God forgives and doesn't hold anything against me.

I'm dead to censure, critiques, or criticisms, and I'm dead to flattery. You can't be dead to one and not to the other. It's all part of the same thing. All that matters is that I say what Jesus said. All that counts is that I'm a faithful, representative of Jesus Christ. Amen?

You have to preach the Kingdom the same way Jesus preached it.

Luke 9:2,

> 9 And he sent them to <u>preach</u> the kingdom of God, and to heal the sick.

To *"preach"* means *to proclaim with gravity, solemnity and an authority so that the proclamation must be listened to and obeyed.*

He sent them to *"preach"* the Kingdom of God. He didn't say, "Go and preach good sermons." He didn't say, "Go and preach your newest revelation." He said, "Preach the Kingdom of God, preach the Government of God, and preach the rule of God."

You are to speak with authority. He spoke as One with authority, not as the scribes and Pharisees. You are to speak with that authority because you represent Him. He represents the Kingdom, and you preach the Kingdom. You've got to preach it the same way Jesus preached it.

Jesus told the disciples to heal the sick and cure diseases. The word for *"sick"* there is *astheneō,* and it means *to be feeble (in any sense), be diseased, be sick, be made weak.* In other words, you are to help anybody at whatever level of sickness or disease they have. It can be a headache, or terminal cancer, or anywhere in between; it doesn't matter. Set them free.

This is the Kingdom we're talking about. We're not talking about your power; we're not talking about how much you fast, how much you pray, or how spiritual you are. That only impresses un-dead humans. It doesn't impress Christians that are dead to sin.

He said, "You preach the Kingdom, you heal the sick; set them free." It's all Kingdom power. You set them free.

Luke 9:3-6,

> 3 And he said unto them, Take nothing for *your* journey, neither staves, nor scrip, neither bread, neither money; neither have two coats apiece.
>
> 4 And whatsoever house ye enter into, there abide, and thence depart.

> 5 And whosoever will not receive you, when ye go out of that city, shake off the very dust from your feet for a testimony against them.
>
> 6 And they departed, and went through the towns, preaching the gospel, and healing every where.

Verse 6 says, "And they departed…" Who departed? The disciples departed. "…and went through the towns." What were they doing? "Preaching the Gospel, and healing everywhere." What Gospel were they preaching? They were preaching the Gospel of the Kingdom.

Every time Jesus had a chance to talk to anyone, He talked about the Kingdom.

Luke 9:10-11,

> 10 And the apostles, when they were returned, told him all that they had done. And he took them, and went aside privately into a desert place belonging to the city called Bethsaida.

The Gospel of the Kingdom was what they taught and did. "And He took them, and went aside privately into a desert place belonging to the city called Bethsaida."

> 11 And the people, when they knew *it*, followed him: and he received them, and spake unto them of the kingdom of God, and healed them that had need of healing.

He talked to them about the Kingdom of God. Did you notice that the Kingdom of God was all the way through these verses? Every time it mentioned what He talked about, it always said He talked about the Kingdom. He didn't just preach the Sermon on the Mount. He preached the Gospel of the Kingdom.

Every time He had a chance to talk to anyone, He talked about the Kingdom. When He talked to Nicodemus, He said, "You're a teacher of Israel, and you're not far from the Kingdom. You are very close, but if you want in, you've got to get born again."

Nicodemus asked, "Well how does that happen?" Jesus said, "You're a teacher of Israel and you don't understand this?" Even to Nicodemus He was talking about the Kingdom. Everything was the Kingdom.

"They followed Him, and He spoke unto them of the Kingdom of God, and healed them that had need of healing." Why? That's because He was teaching and doing, so He healed them. Notice the people that He healed: "He healed them that had need of healing." It doesn't say, "And He healed them that gave a vow offering." No, it doesn't say that. It says, "He healed them that had need of healing," because that's how the Kingdom operates.

People in the Kingdom see people in need, go to them, and say, "What can I do for you? I see that you've been coughing, and every time you cough, I see blood on your handkerchief. What is that?" They might say, "Well, I've got tuberculosis, but what I really need is food. I'm hungry." "Okay, we can handle both of those." It's not either/or. "We can handle both of those."

Just start with what you have.

What you have is enough. Jesus fed a multitude with five loaves of bread and a few fishes that were from a little boy's lunch.

One of His disciples said, "Look at these people. Send them away; there are too many. Send them home so they can go and get something to eat before they start fainting on us. Send them home." Jesus said, "Hmm, you feed them."

All of a sudden, they were saying, "Two hundred pennyworth of bread is not sufficient." Do you realize that was a year and a half's wages? They told Jesus, "There are so many here, it would take us a year and a half's worth of wages to feed these."

Jesus said, "You feed them." They said, "We don't have that kind of money." He asked, "Well, what do you have?" Apparently the little boy was standing there with the food. One of the disciples said to the boy, "Let's see what you've got in this sack." He told Jesus, "There are five loaves and two fishes."

Jesus said, "That's enough." Notice that He never said there wasn't enough. Notice that He never said, "If we had just had three fish, I could have done a miracle." He didn't say that. He said, "What you have is enough."

ALL THAT JESUS BEGAN BOTH TO DO AND TEACH

Luke 9:16-17,

> 16 Then he took the five loaves and the two fishes, and <u>looking up to heaven</u>, he blessed them, and brake, and gave to the disciples to set before the multitude.
>
> 17 And they did eat, and were all filled: and there was taken up of fragments that remained to them twelve baskets.

It says that He looked up into heaven, and He blessed them.

When it said, "*Looking up to heaven,*" the Greek word, *anablepō*, was used. It means to *look up; by implication to recover sight, and see.* He was seeing something. He had bread and fishes in His hands, and as He was blessing them, He was looking up to heaven. He was seeing "the things that are unseen." He wasn't looking at the "seen." He was looking at the "unseen." He was seeing a multitude being fed. He was seeing them sitting down on the grass afterwards saying, "Oh, that was good."

He was looking up to heaven and saying, "Father, I thank You; bless this bread." Then He turned around, handed the loaves and fishes to the disciples, and as they passed them out, they kept multiplying. They just started with what they had.

Just start with what you have. You might say, "Well, I don't have enough power." Yes, you do—use what you've got. Give Him what you have. Look up to heaven and bless it, and say, "Father, I thank You for the talents, for the gifts, for the power, and for all of the things

You have given me. I thank You for that which You've given me, and I will use it for the Kingdom."

If you think, "I will do my best to try to die empty," you can't, because no matter what you give to Him, He pours back more. If you were to try to die empty, you would have to give it and die before He could give it back. If you see this, you are seeing the Kingdom; that's the way the Kingdom operates.

We must keep the Kingdom mentality.

In the Kingdom, nobody goes hungry. The problem is that God can't get His Church to bring the Kingdom to the hungry. When you throw a feast, don't throw it amongst people that you know and like, or those you know and don't like. Go out and throw it for the people that can't repay you.

After blessing the food, He told His disciples to feed the multitude with the five loaves and two fishes. He was doing that because the people were hungry, but He was trying to teach His disciples to look to God as their resource for help and not to look to their limited natural resources. That's Kingdom mentality.

He was teaching them by saying, "Don't look at what you've got. Look at what the people need, and when you realize what the people need, then whatever you've got has to grow to meet that need." That's Kingdom mentality.

I'm excited about this, as you might be able to tell. We've been preaching full-time like this since 2000, and every principle I have taught you, we've been practicing in the DHT. That's the reason they're not new to some of you, because we teach it.

Start with where you are. Start with what you have. Don't look at yourself; look at the needs of the people. Don't try to find their problem. You set them free. All of these principles are in the DHT.

Jesus grew in stature. As we grow to be more like Him, so should our stature grow.

When I started preaching this, I didn't see it as Kingdom principles, per se. I saw what I found to be truths that I saw in the Word of God that had to do with healing. Do you know how blessed I am, because I get to preach to you the truth, no matter what I find? I have to; I can't do anything else. I'm so thankful that in preaching for the last 13 years, I've never found anything in the Bible that disavows what I've preached before.

What I'm teaching in this series on the Kingdom just enhances what we've been preaching. We've been preaching Kingdom all along and didn't even know it. It's good not to have to come in and say, "Sorry; what I taught two years ago, scratch that. I've found something here, and what I told you then wasn't true; this is true." You will notice that I've never had to do that. Do you know what a blessing that is to not have to retract something? It shows that God had His hand in what we've been teaching for the last 13 years and that it is growing.

Jesus grew in stature and in favor with God and man. Even with His revelation, His understanding, and His being able to preach, His stature grew. As we grow to be more like Him, the same thing should be taking place in our lives. It shouldn't be just understanding in our heads, but our lives should be lining up.

Everything in our ministry is lining up. I don't even pray for things anymore. I haven't prayed for things in a long time. From time to time, things just show up. I ask our staff, "What do you need? Make a list." They'll give me a list and then I'll say, "Okay, find out what it's going to cost, and let's get it. Let's go after it." We do it and everything we need, we get. Amen?

That's Kingdom. It isn't Curry Blake Ministries. It's not even John G. Lake Ministries. It's Jesus' Kingdom, and we're just learning how to walk in that. I'm the one who is trying to lead by example. I'm trying to learn, and show the staff, and everybody who hears this message how to walk this out. Hopefully, any mistakes that are made, I will make first. I can correct them and go on without making them again. So far, it's been good.

We've been learning, and we've been seeing God do wonderful things. It has been amazing. I'm like a kid playing, and it is just the most fun thing. It's good to walk in the Kingdom, and it's not just because I'm a preacher. I'm telling you, "This will work for you." It's not just because you're a preacher, too. It's not about being a preacher; it's about being an ambassador of the Kingdom. The Kingdom should be seen in your life. Just do away with those boundaries.

The One who backs you is much richer and more able to back you than anyone else.

What would you do if somebody like Bill Gates, or Warren Buffett, or just some mega-rich person came to you and said, "I don't know why, but I just like you. I don't know why it is, but I'm telling you that I'm behind you, and whatever it is that you want to do, right now. What do you want to do?"

What would you do if you knew you couldn't fail? If you knew that you could do anything you wanted to do, where would you see yourself in five years? Where would you see yourself in ten years? Where would you see yourself, and what would you see yourself doing? If your vision is self-centered, then you haven't gotten the vision of God's Kingdom yet, but if you're thinking in terms of, "I could be in India planting Bible Schools, or I could be in Africa teaching seminars and conferences, or I could be in Haiti building orphanages," then you have the Kingdom mentality.

If you could think that way, with that person backing you, you could do anything. I'm telling you that the One who backs you is much richer, and He is much more able. The rich person might back off from you and tell you, "Oh, you can't talk like that, or I'll withhold my finances." God isn't like that. He'll correct you, but He'll keep feeding you and keep taking care of you.

Let your light shine now.

BEHOLD THE KINGDOM

Now is the time. Do things, now. Let your light shine. Don't worry. The light is not for the other side; it's for this side. There are people in great darkness that need to see a great light shine. Your light is going to pale in comparison to what's in heaven. Here in the darkness of this earth is where your light needs to shine.

Whatever you desire to do for God, whatever is in your heart, just do it; just step out.

Start with where you are and with what you have. Amen.

"Father,

"I thank You, right now, for Your Word. Your Word is truth, and we thank You, Father, that we don't have to reinvent it, and we don't have to repackage it; we just constantly refer back to it. Father, we thank You. We bless You. I thank You, right now, that the people who have sat under the voice of Your Spirit have a greater understanding of Your Kingdom, and of what Jesus did and how He passed this great opportunity on to us so that we could preach and demonstrate Your Kingdom throughout this earth.

"Father, I thank You, right now, as just part of being an ambassador of the kingdom of heaven, I have the pleasure to tell your people that their requisition for health care has been approved, and that right now, in Jesus' name, they are healed. They are healed and whole. It is done, in the name of Jesus.

"I will remind your body, right now, that it must line up with the Word of God; it must lineup now. It will function correctly, and it will do its job.

"Right now, in the name of Jesus, Father, we thank You, and we praise You for healing these people. Father, You have blessed them, and what can I do, but bless those whom You have already blessed. Father, I thank You for Your blessings throughout their lives. We bless them in Jesus' name. So Be It. Amen. Amen."

JGLM Trademarked Names

All derivatives of JGLM names are Copyrighted trademarks:

Divine Healing Technician(s)
John G. Lake Ministries
John G. Lake Healing Rooms
John G. Lake's Divine Healing Institute
Dominion Life International Apostolic Church
Dominion Bible Institute

All derivatives of these names are Copyrighted trademarks and may not be used without the express written permission of:

John G. Lake Ministries
P. O. Box 742947
Dallas, Texas 75374
www.jglm.org

Please advise JGLM if you come into contact with anyone using the following names without authorized permission:

John G. Lake Ministries
John G. Lake's Divine Healing Institute
John G. Lake Healing Rooms
Divine Healing Technicians Certified
DHT

Appendix A: Historical Information

1. The information presented in this book is for historical purposes only. References to people, organizations, professions, etc., are presented for the sole purpose of giving an accurate overall understanding of the prevailing viewpoints of particular groups, religions, denominations, and movements of the time periods referred to in the seminar.

2. Each reader is expected and required to make personal comparisons and decide for themselves which viewpoints to accept and endorse.

3. The material presented and its successful application is predicated upon the viewpoints of those during the time periods in which they lived.

4. Curry R. Blake and John G. Lake Ministries are in no way responsible or liable for the successful application of the material or for future re-presentation of the materials presented in this book.

Appendix B: Practices Concerning Medicine Or Medical Treatment

1. All information presented is not to be construed as advice or instruction in activities or practices concerning medicine or medical treatment.

2. The author of this book is not in any way a trained medical or psychological professional.

3. Any ministry services are being rendered from a position of compassion and mercy and are not to be construed as medical treatments or as substitutions for medical treatments.

4. No one can present themselves or anyone under their guardianship for ministry, without relinquishing and waiving all legal recourse that would or might be the end state of such person and/or anyone they present for ministry.

5. Anyone using this material cannot hold JGLM liable or responsible for their personal practice of ministry.

APPENDIX C: RULES FOR REPRODUCTION OF JGLM MATERIALS

1. The physical material in this book is and shall remain the property of the presenter and the JGLM organization they represent. All material in this book shall belong to the author.

2. No reproduction of the material in this book is allowed without express written permission from the author of this book.

3. Any material and/or information in this book or gained during the seminar or from audio/video material from the host organization, if presented to others at any time, shall be presented in its entirety as it is presented in this seminar, without change, adaptation, omission or addition.

4. Prior to the presentation of this material to any other persons, groups, and/or organizations, reader will contact and inform the presenting organization of personal intentions in writing. If told not to present the information, such person(s) are not to present it.

5. In the event said person is given permission to present information, they are to provide the host organization with an audio/video recording (in its entirety) of the material presented.

Appendix D: Non-Medical Advice

1. The information presented in this book is in no way intended as advice or instruction concerning the use of medicine, medical treatment, or the avoidance thereof.

2. Each person is responsible to investigate all methods of remedy they are contemplating.

3. No one has a right or responsibility to make your decision except you.

4. Any reference to medicine or medical treatment is solely for historical or informational purposes.

DOMINION BIBLE INSTITUTE

TRAINING THE NEXT GENERATION OF GOD'S GENERALS

SIGN UP TODAY!
dbiaccounts@jglm.org

John G. Lake Ministries
SAME MESSAGE. SAME POWER. SAME RESULTS.

John G. Lake Ministries
Same Message. Same Power. Same Results.

Partner With Us As We Advance God's Kingdom On Earth!

Partner Benefits Include:

- Our monthly "Laboring Together" newsletter with a ministry update directly from Brother Curry that includes detailed information about our upcoming events and activities. We compile testimonies from all over the world to encourage and strengthen your faith.

- Partner E-Newsletter includes an MP3 every month taught by Brother Curry with the option to download our monthly audio teaching.

- 30% Discount on all products during the holiday season…

- Our Promise to Protect Your Kingdom Investment.

Partners can choose to receive packets by postal mail or via email. Your faithful support allows us to help give our materials away freely to those who cannot give, such as our JGLM prison ministries, disaster relief funds and foreign missionaries. Most importantly we depend on our faithful partners as our main line of prayer support.

Email: partners@jglm.org
www.jglm.org/partners

New Man
This Changes Everything...

The Primary focus of the DHT seminar is to train believers to biblically and effectively minister healing. The purpose of the New Man seminar is to reveal to believers what was accomplished by Jesus for us through His death, burial, and resurrection. The New Man Seminar reveals what you are (in Christ) not what you will some day become. It also reveals how to begin being who you are rather than emphasizing waiting for the next "Christian Fad".

John G. Lake Ministries
SAME MESSAGE. SAME POWER. SAME RESULTS.

Get Yours Today! Call **888-293-6591** or Visit Us Online: store.jglm.org

- You are left unsatisfied by the status quo...
- You know you were meant to be a participant and not just a spectator...
- You ask "Why not?..." more than "Why?"...
- You believe that today can be better than yesterday...
- You know you were meant to walk among the Giants of the Faith, and you want the tools & training that can make it happen...
- When you hear the exploits of God's Generals, you can picture yourself doing them...

If this describes you, then you ARE JGLM... whether you know it or not.

COME.
LET'S CHANGE THE WORLD.

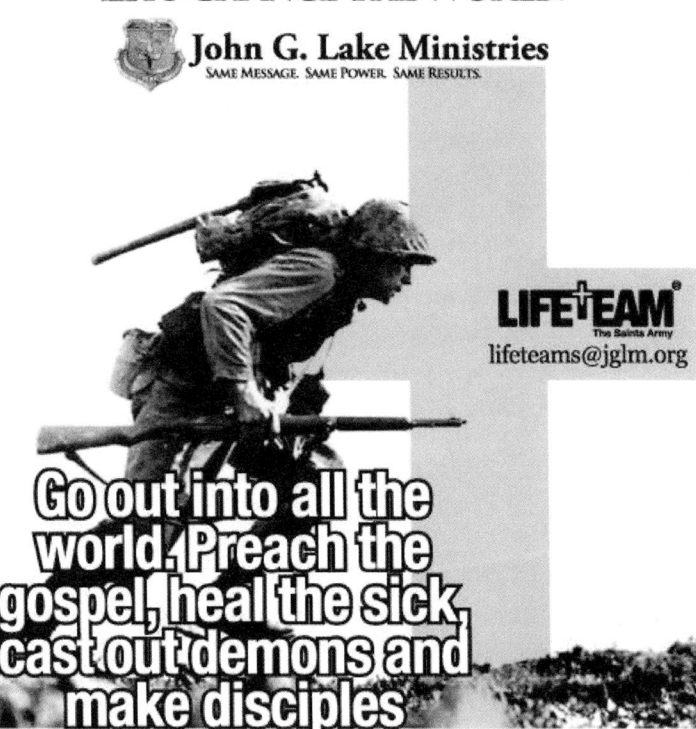

John G. Lake Ministries
SAME MESSAGE. SAME POWER. SAME RESULTS.

LIFE✝EAM
The Saints Army
lifeteams@jglm.org

Go out into all the world. Preach the gospel, heal the sick, cast out demons and make disciples

The Teaching That Birthed A Legend Is Now Raising An Army.

Get Yours Today
Call **888-293-6591**
or Visit Us Online

store.jglm.org

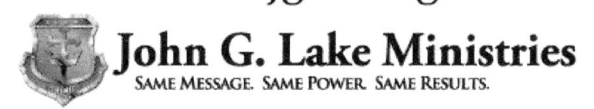

John G. Lake Ministries
SAME MESSAGE. SAME POWER. SAME RESULTS.